OCS Study MMS 2006-059

Alternative Oil Spill Occurrence Estimators for the Beaufort/Chukchi Sea OCS (Statistical Approach)

MMS Contract Number 1435 – 01 – 00 – P0 – 17141

September 5, 2006

Submitted by: TGE Consulting

Anchorage, Alaska

Authored by: Ted G. Eschenbach

William V. Harper

MMS U. S. Department of the Interior

Minerals Management Service

Alaska Outer Continental Shelf Region

Alternative Oil Spill Occurrence Estimators for the Beaufort/Chukchi Sea OCS (Statistical Approach)

September 5, 2006

Submitted by:

Dr. Ted Eschenbach, P.E.
TGE Consulting
4376 Rendezvous Circle
Anchorage, AK 99504
907-333-7817
fax: 337-2928
ted1@alaska.net

Authored by:

Dr. Ted G. Eschenbach, P.E.
Dr. William V. Harper, P.E.

This study was funded by the U.S. Department of the Interior, Minerals Management Service (MMS), Alaska Outer Continental Shelf Region, Anchorage Alaska, under Contract No. 1435 – 01 – 00 – P0 – 17141, as part of the MMS Alaska Environmental Studies Program.

The opinions, findings, conclusions, or recommendations expressed in this report or product are those of the authors and do not necessarily reflect the views of the U.S. Department of the Interior, nor does mention of trade names or commercial products constitute endorsement or recommendation for use by the Federal Government.

Abstract

This study analyzes GOM statistics for pipeline and platform oil spills, and with statistically appropriate techniques develops Poisson models for spill rates. These models are tested through analysis of exponential inter-spill intervals for several exposure variables. These exposure variables include time, oil production, pipeline mile-years, and platform-years. Weibull and lognormal models for spill volumes are developed and used to support analyses at spill thresholds of 50, 100, 500, and 1000 barrels. In each case confidence limits are calculated and reported. The stability of the results has been confirmed for different time periods.

Significant differences from past MMS publications include Poisson confidence intervals, exact binomial confidence intervals, detailed analyses for the exposure variables of pipeline mile-years and platform-years, the use of the larger spill data set of spills exceeding 50 barrels to estimate rates at higher thresholds, and the inclusion of more recent data (through 2005). A declining rate of platform spills is statistically verified, so that platform results are generally based on spills 1990 to 2005, while pipeline results are based on data from 1972 to 2005.

Spill causes are analyzed to identify spills with GOM-specific causes, such as hurricanes and fishing trawl gear. This is modeled as a binomial proportion for GOM-specific and applicable to the Arctic spills at the spill size thresholds. These results are extended to the Arctic with a method that provides a conservative confidence interval and a method that provides a minimum width confidence interval – both at each spill size threshold.

For extension from the GOM data to the Arctic using a Beaufort development scenario, spill rates per production volume are found to be unreliable as compared with spill rates per pipeline mile-year and per platform-year. There was insufficient data on the Beaufort development scenario to estimate the spill rates for ice keel gouging, but a rough approximation for strudel scour suggested that this was less significant than applicable causes, such as corrosion, human error, and operational impacts.

The estimated rates of Arctic applicable pipeline spills per pipeline mile-year and of platform spills per platform-year at spill thresholds of 50, 100, 500, and 1000 barrels are presented with minimum and conservative confidence intervals. Thus, the existing data from the GOM is extended through statistically supported techniques.

Preliminary results from a new approach to modeling pipeline spill rates based on "platform-related" spills and pipeline mile-years are presented with the conclusions and recommendations.

Table of Contents

List of Figures

List of Tables

Glossary of Acronyms

Bbbl	billion barrels
ccdf	complementary cumulative distribution function
cdf	cumulative distribution function
KMiles	thousands of miles
KPlatform	thousands of platforms
KWell	thousands of wells
LCL	lower confidence limit
Mbbl	million barrels
pdf	probability distribution function
TLAR	that looks about right
UCL	upper confidence limit

1 Introduction

This study is not a comprehensive study of all potential sources of oil spills related to development of oil fields in the Beaufort and Chukchi Seas. It does not address for example, the probability of oil spills during exploration, the possibility of oil spills during transport in TAPS, or from tanker traffic after leaving Valdez.

What this study emphasizes is the development of statistical measures with confidence intervals to describe the uncertainty in the estimate for pipeline and platform spills during production. These measures are applied both to the existing MMS data base (mostly Gulf of Mexico) and extrapolated to the Beaufort and Chukchi Seas. For statistical robustness and validity these measures are linked as closely as possible to causal relationships rather than to simple statistical correlations. This study relies on the larger context of other studies for much of the data and scenario development.

1.1 Overview of Study

There is an extensive history of MMS statistical analysis of oil spill occurrences, for example see Smith et al. (1982); Lanfear & Amstutz (1983); LaBelle & Anderson (1985); Anderson & LaBelle (1990, 1994, and 2000). For this project to add value to this extensive history, it cannot merely refine data by adding or subtracting a spill or three or by relying on a more recent subset of the data. Instead this project must evaluate whether alternative statistical approaches can improve estimated spill occurrence probabilities for Alaskan OCS areas of the Beaufort and Chukchi Seas.

Current MMS spill occurrences are expressed in terms of spills per billion barrels (Bbbl) produced. For example, the rate for US OCS pipeline spills is reported as 1.33 spills of 1000 or more bbl per Bbbl handled in Anderson & LaBelle (2000, p. 311). The data base for these statistical measures is dominated by operations in the Gulf of Mexico. Thus evaluation of possible statistical measures for Alaskan OCS areas of the Beaufort and Chukchi Seas must address two questions.

The first question is "Are alternative measures in terms of spill probabilities per platform-year and per pipeline-mile-year more appropriate for this purpose than occurrences measured in spills per billion barrels?" These measures represent an approach that is intermediate between the single production measure of number of billion barrels produced and a detailed fault-tree approach that relies on relatively detailed development scenarios.

The second question is "How to account for differences between probable Alaskan development scenarios and the historical data base?" These differences include:

1. Given the cost of operating in an Arctic environment, it is reasonable to expect that Alaskan prospects must generate higher production levels to be economically justified. Thus fewer facilities will be required for the same level of production. For the same level of production, the presence of fewer facilities means a lower contribution to the

probability of an oil spill occurrence. On the other hand, facilities with larger capacities may increase the size of spills if they do occur.

2. There are substantial differences linked to pigging and maintenance between the historic data base and expected Alaskan operating conditions. These can also be linked to general differences in the time series in the Gulf of Mexico as the U.S. regulatory and operating environment has evolved.

3. Given the difficulties in operating in the Arctic, at least initial development is likely to be at shorter average distances than in the Gulf of Mexico. This will reduce the length of required pipelines with some reduction in the probability of an oil spill occurrence. On the other hand, the Arctic has harsh environmental conditions, which may increase the probability of oil spills due to human errors in operations.

4. Finally, some of the typical causes of spills have substantially different probabilities of occurring in the Gulf of Mexico and Arctic environments. For example, fishing gear in the Gulf of Mexico has damaged valves and caused spills. On the other hand, in certain depths of water in the Arctic Ocean there can be damage from ice keels in moving pack ice.

The difficulty in answering these questions – statistically or with any other approach – is that the available data are relatively limited. It is worth noting that since the key data are based on oil spills, it is good that the number of data points is not larger – even though this makes the statistical analysis more difficult.

A third question that must be addressed is the robustness of the results as the underlying data are refined and extended by time. As the data records are examined there are significant periods with no spills – especially at larger spill thresholds, and brief periods with several spills. This is intrinsic in the stochastic nature of this problem, but for decision-makers to rely on the study's results; those results should be reasonably stable if analyzed over different periods of time.

This study addresses this specifically by analyzing spill rates over time. This identifies changes and trends in the historical series. Other results and conclusions will be analyzed at three stages. The first was represented in the reviewed preliminary analysis, where the time periods were chosen to match earlier work (Anderson & LaBelle, 2000; and Bercha, 2002). The second stage is the 1972 – 1999 analyses that contained corrections, changes, additions, or deletions identified by MMS during review. The level of consistency of the 1972 – 1999 with the third stage is discussed as needed and key results are included in an appendix to this report. The third stage includes data through 2005, which represents the bulk of the work in this report.

The balance of Chapter 1 is organized to match the balance of the report. That is Section 1.2 introduces Chapter 2 on the data, Section 1.3 introduces Chapter 3 on analyzing the existing OCS data, Section 1.4 introduces Chapter 4 on extending the results to the arctic environment of the Beaufort and Chukchi Seas, and Section 1.5 introduces Chapter 5 on recommendations and conclusions.

1.2 Overview of Data

1.2.1 Data for MMS Analyses

Previous MMS analyses have focused on spills from platforms and pipelines in OCS areas of the Gulf of Mexico (GOM) and in the Pacific. Because of the GOM's much larger operational scope, in a statistical sense these data are essentially GOM data. The published portion of the MMS analyses has focused on spills of 1000 bbl or more. These data have been carefully checked, and they are the best quality data available. The most recent publication (Anderson & LaBelle, 2000) covers 1967 to 1999.

The exposure variable in these MMS analyses has been the volume of crude oil produced, so that spill rates are reported per billion bbl (Bbbl) produced. In addition to the exposure data of volume of oil production, MMS also has made available data on the number of platforms, the number of pipeline segments, and the number of miles of pipeline miles for various product codes. Data from 1972 to 2005 has been relied on for this report.

Both the exposure and spill data supplied by MMS are described in more detail in Chapter 2.

MMS also maintains a database of "all" spills, but data on the smaller spills have received less scrutiny and checking. This larger database is statistically desirable, and it is the foundation for much of the analysis in this report. This data base includes information on location, date reported, spill volume, primary spill cause, secondary spill cause, spill volume, etc.

1.2.2 Data for Bercha Report

Bercha (2002 & 2006) relied heavily on the MMS data, but it also drew upon spill statistics from elsewhere in the world. Its analysis of the MMS data identified some discrepancies and some of these were corrected at that time, and some have been corrected since. The data on experience in other parts of the world are most applicable to the problem of extending results based on GOM data to the Arctic.

Because of the need to construct measures of statistical confidence for the results in this report, this report is analyzing the MMS data in more detail. Thus, the results in Bercha (2002 & 2006) from the MMS data are used more as a double-check than directly.

1.2.3 Data Supplied for this Report

Because this report is being completed after Anderson & LaBelle (2000) and Bercha (2002), it has been able to add data for more recent spills. Historical and recent data supplied by MMS are identified in Chapter 2. This data has been supplied with extensive discussions as to how to most reliably use and adapt it. The more recent data are being used to check the stability of the results presented here over different data sets.

1.3   Methodological Approach for GOM Spill Rate Estimation

This study was funded to estimate rates of oil spill occurrences and rates in the Beaufort and Chukchi Seas of the Arctic Ocean. Because the data set is drawn almost exclusively from the Gulf of Mexico, the authors believe the estimation methodology must first be applied in this context. If the methodology does not work with the data from which it was drawn, then extrapolating the results to the Arctic Ocean would be questionable.

1.3.1   What Oil Spill Occurrence Rate Measures Should be Considered

In estimating oil spill occurrences, one of the first choices is what is the exposure variable. In other words, how is the spill occurrence rate measured? All of the possibilities considered are spill rates which equal some number of spills per some volume or amount. Thus, to describe a spill occurrence rate without referencing a measure, it is simply referred to as a spill rate. Choices include the following:

> Spills per billion barrels of production,
> Spills per year,
> Spills per platform-year or per well-year, and
> Spills per pipeline-mile-year.

The choice must be made by balancing different concerns, and there are reasonable justifications for different choices considering the trade-offs between the concerns. These concerns include the following:

> The historical MMS measure is spills per billion barrels of production. The measure was chosen by knowledgeable professionals for good reasons, and it now has a long history of use. Because users are already familiar with the measure, it is easier for them to use in the future, and it is much easier to compare past and future uses.

> Much of the data for this problem is available on an annual basis. For example, the volume of oil production, the number of platforms, and the total number of pipeline miles were supplied as annual data. This means that it is easier to compute occurrences annually (per year), than it is to attempt to disaggregate the data into shorter periods.

> The concern over data categorization and occurrence exposure even extends to the classification of some spills. For example, a spill from a pipeline riser onto a platform is currently classified as a pipeline spill. If the exposure variables include the number of platforms and the amount of pipeline mileage, then it might be better classified as a platform spill. That is the probability of a spill from the riser is more related to the platform than to the length of the pipeline. For example, the probability of a ship crushing a riser does not change if the length of a pipeline doubles, but doubling the number of platforms would roughly double that probability.

> As much as possible, there should be a sound logic that links spills to the exposure variable. This is particularly important when the probability is changing or when the spill occurrence is being extrapolated to a different environment. The presence of this logic is reflected in a subtle, but important, change in language. The presence of a linking logic between exposure and spill probability allows the description of that exposure as a

driving variable. In other words, the description is not of just a simple statistical correlation, rather a causal linkage is suggested. In general, statistical relationships that are based on causality are much more reliable than relationships based on correlation.

As the data that can be potentially used covers as much as 40 years, one concern is changes in spills per each of the occurrence measures over time. Technology, regulatory and operating environments, volume of facilities, and the effects of corrosion have not been constant – they are changing. Thus, this study does analyze if spill rates are homogeneous or inhomogeneous over time, and how fast these rates are changing (if they are).

The choice of occurrence probability drivers involves tradeoffs among the above concerns. Moreover the desire to estimate now or in the future the probabilities of different size spills, from different causes, from platforms and pipelines, at different locations, etc. mean that other tradeoffs must also be considered.

Before discussing which spill occurrence measures are included in this analysis, and which are recommended for extrapolation to the arctic environment, the next section briefly discusses some of the spill occurrence drivers that might be useable – if there were far more data.

1.3.2   Spill Occurrence Drivers that Cannot be Considered

If the occurrence of spills is examined for contributing factors from the perspective of the system of platforms and pipelines, there are a number of factors that can be logically linked to the occurrence of spills. Data for some of these exists in some cases, but in general, the MMS database that has been made available to the study team, does not support analysis of the following potential factors. These are listed with the logical causal link that suggests that each would be "nice to know."

> Each pipeline termination or connection represents another opportunity for human error and/or an increased vulnerability to damage. Thus, the number of such points is linked to the probability of a spill. It is possible that this may be approximated by the number of platforms, wells, and/or pipeline segments.

> As each pipeline ages, it is clearly more likely to have accumulated sufficient corrosion to either be a problem for pipeline integrity or to increase the vulnerability of the pipeline to damage from other causes. Also the age of a pipeline is linked to the technology, technical understanding, and regulatory environment that were used for its design, construction, and operation. So the date each pipeline was put in service and how old it is do contribute to the probability of a spill, which can also be reduced by inspection or maintenance activities linked to the age and condition of the pipeline. Note that Bercha (2002) includes aggregate mileage placed in service in each year, but the small number of corrosion caused accidents and the lack of detailed knowledge of which pipe segments were placed in service each year, means that this cannot be linked statistically to corrosion.

The thicker the wall of a pipeline, the more likely that pipeline will survive impact damage from an anchor, ship, or fishing net. The required thickness is also connected with the operating pressure and diameter at the design stage. In turn, the diameter, operating pressure, and length of pipe between shut-off valves contribute to the size of a spill, if a spill occurs.

The depth of water over the pipeline and the depth of any cover (if any) from trenching, backfilling, or deposited sediments affect the vulnerability of the pipe to damage. That change clearly impacts the probability of a spill occurring on a segment of pipeline.

The maintenance and operating regime clearly impacts the probability of a spill. For example, if a pipeline is "piggable" and pigging is regularly conducted, then the probability of spills due to corrosion is significantly reduced. Weaknesses due to corrosion will generally be identified before they can be a threat to pipeline integrity. At the same time, spills may be caused by human error or mechanical problems when the pig is being loaded into or unloaded from the system. Similarly, the presence and use of effective leak detection systems can dramatically reduce the time required to discover a spill and the resulting size of the spill. This in turn reduces the probability of a spill of at least 500 or 1000 bbls.

While all of the above conditions influence the probability of a spill, separating out the relative impact of multiple factors requires hundreds of data points, rather than the ten to thirty-six to seventy-eight spills analyzed here. To analyze multiple factors the already small data set would have to be divided into smaller and smaller groups.

Instead, this study must focus its attention on a few of the most important factors. It is believed that the major variables of time, amount of production, number of platforms or wells, and the number of pipeline-miles represent the most that can be effectively analyzed here. In addition, correctly determining the status of all pipelines for the above data would be problematic at best.

1.3.3 Recommended Measure of Spill Probability

In order to choose between spill probability measures, it is helpful to analyze what causes of spills are based on volume of production, on time, or on the amount of physical facilities. It is also necessary to describe the data that are required about a potential development prospect in order to apply the proposed measure.

It is difficult to identify driving variables for production volume that directly increase the probability of an oil spill. However, there is no question that production volume is a proxy variable for many other variables that change the probability of an oil spill. More production means more platforms, more pipelines, more operators, etc. More importantly, if spill probability is based on volume of production, then there is no need for scenarios of development with numbers of platforms and miles of pipe. Instead this detail is replaced by the assumption that the situation where the probability measure is developed is sufficiently similar to the new situation, that the extrapolation from one to the other is valid.

As an example of a driving variable that is based on time, consider boats traveling to or from platforms and the number of fishing days in a season. The first may be linked to the schedule to move operators on/off the platform, and the latter determines for how much of the year fishing nets are a factor. Scheduled maintenance activities may also be based on time, and there is at least some level of increased probability of operator error or equipment malfunction any time operational changes are made. Time is also the driving variable behind probabilities due to hurricanes and moving pack ice. At extreme examples, there are certainly hurricane forces that are possible that would damage virtually any facility and cause a spill. Whether this is the 100-year, 500-year, or 1000-year storm is a time-based probability measure.

In order to apply a time-based probability variable to analyze a potential development prospect, it is necessary to have some measure of the expected rate of facility development and production. This will be required to compare the probabilities to the benefits for the proposed development. And it is also needed to prevent logical nonsense, such as, a time based spill probability when there are not yet any facilities in place.

It is reasonable to model exposure to dragging anchors, ice keel gouges, fishing gear from trawlers, mud slides, etc. with pipeline mileage as a driving variable. However, oil spill probabilities from pipelines are not strictly a linear function of mileage, there is a certain probability that is linked to the number of pipeline connectors, terminators, etc. However, an analysis of the causes of pipeline failures (see Bercha, 2002) suggests that most of the spills are linked to modes (corrosion, third party impact, and mud slides) that can be modeled with pipeline mileage as a driving variable.

Similarly, the number of wells or platforms will be a driving variable for the probability of a spill from a platform. The data in Anderson & LaBelle (2000) (see also Section 2.3) indicate that platform spills have historically typically been larger than pipeline spills. Thus, a complicating factor in the possible treatment of riser spills as platform spills is their different size distributions.

Another reason for using pipeline mileage and the number of platforms as driving variables is an observation from other complex systems. Basically as systems become larger and more complex, there seems to be a tendency to focus on more common or more controllable causes of system failure. Thus, operator and managerial errors of commission or inattention are more likely to miss the less common causes of system failure.

One difficulty in using the number of pipeline miles and the number of platforms as driving variables is that the calculation of spill probabilities now requires some level of scenario development for potential oil fields to determine how many platforms and how many miles of pipeline will be required. In this particular case, that requirement can be satisfied through reference to Bercha (2006).

Thus, the principal choices are the following:
    Spills per billion barrels of production,
    Spills per year, and
    Spills per platform or well-year & per pipeline-mile-year.

This study will actually use all of these methods for analyzing the OCS data, and it will test two and recommend one of these methods for calculating oil spill probabilities in the Beaufort and Chukchi Seas. One of the projection methods will be based on the volume of production. This is being chosen because it is more like past MMS practice, thus allowing a better opportunity to examine other factors in constructing estimates of oil spill probabilities. Also, it does not require the estimation of the development system. So for potential fields where development scenarios do not yet exist, some estimation of oil spill probabilities will still be possible.

The second recommended approach for extrapolation from GOM data to the arctic will be based on pipeline mileage and number of platforms. Because the requirement for a development scenario can be satisfied through Bercha (2006), it is possible to apply this and to compare the results with an extrapolation based on spill rates per production volume.

It is the professional judgment of the authors that the extrapolation based on pipeline mileage and number of platforms is better than the extrapolation based on production volume. This is detailed in Chapter 4, but a brief example is illustrative of why this recommendation is made. There are substantial differences for example in the average production volume per platform, which averaged about 130,000 bbl/year from 1972 to 2005 in the GOM and which are projected to average 8.6 Mbbl/year in the Beaufort development scenario. The factor of 66 difference means that platform spill rates/bbl of production are less reliable for extrapolation than spill rates/platform-year.

1.3.4   Spill Sizes and Data Set Size

The GOM data are extensive, and they can be analyzed in several ways. In particular, it is possible to identify spills of a variety of sizes. For example, Anderson & LaBelle (2000) identifies 16 pipeline and 13 platform spills of over 1000 barrels in the interval of 1964-1999. Bercha (2002) identifies 31 pipeline spills of over 50 barrels in the interval of 1972-1999.

Statistically models that are based on larger sets are more reliable, and the larger sample size permits tighter confidence intervals about estimated quantities. Also reporting pipeline spill probabilities for several different size spills facilitates the use of the results for a variety of purposes. Thus, this report estimates spill probabilities for pipeline and platform spills in four size ranges:

> 50 barrels or greater,
> 100 barrels or greater,
> 500 barrels or greater, and
> 1000 barrels or greater.

One of the ways that this study offers the opportunity to improve upon past MMS practice is through the use of exact confidence intervals for the spill rate parameter of the Poisson distribution. This is described in Section 3.2.2.

While the focus of this study is the probability of a pipeline or platform spill of a particular size, the spill data also support statistically derived models for the size of potential spills. This is done in Section 3.3.3 for pipelines and in 3.4.3 for platforms.

One approach for validating models is to estimate key parameters in several ways and to show that consistent results are obtained. In this case, it is possible to connect the estimated spill rates for different sizes of spills by using the spill size distribution. A more rigorous definition is presented in Chapter 3, but a hypothetical example can illustrate this. Assume that the spill rate for 50 or more barrels is 3.6 spills per year. If the spill size distribution indicates that spills of 1000 barrels or more are 1/3 as likely as the smaller spill, then the indicated rate for the larger spill is 1.2 spills per year.

This approach has the advantage of deriving the results for the larger spill sizes from the larger data set available at the smaller spill size.

1.3.5   Links between Probability Exposure Variables

As detailed in Section 2.4.6, there are very high correlations (as high as 99%) between cumulative production volume, time, and cumulative pipeline mileage for the GOM data. Thus, if a Poisson model works with one of these probability drivers, an analogous Poisson model is likely to work for the other probability drivers. This is demonstrated in Chapter 3. The high correlation between these three probability drivers is also one reason why a Poisson model can meet the standards for statistically satisfactory performance. All of the drivers are working together, instead of in different directions.

As detailed in Chapter 3, this does not mean that models based on the drivers are statistically equivalent. The length of a year is constant over time, and the annual production volumes are relatively stable. However, the amount of pipeline mileage and the number of wells and platforms are increasing at a relatively steady rate over time. Thus, the cumulative mileage and the cumulative number of pipelines (which are the probability drivers) are non-homogeneous or changing over time.

1.3.6   Poisson Distribution used in Previous MMS Models

Anderson & LaBelle (2002) nicely describes (thus not repeated here) the Poisson model for the relatively uncommon event of an oil spill. As shown in numerous statistics text, this is equivalent to modeling the time between events (in this case – oil spills) as an exponential distribution. This linkage provides another approach to modeling oil spill probabilities in this situation. Using the exponential distribution provides us a way to use a continuous model of spill dates, rather than a discrete model of number of spills per year, per interval of a billion barrels of production, or per a quantity of pipeline miles or a number of platforms.

For this study the general approach is to use the year, the production volume per year, or the total pipeline mileage (or number of spills) in each year. Thus, there is a clear identification of the year, the corresponding production volume, and the corresponding values of pipeline miles or platforms in service. This means that others can reproduce our results to try other variations or to check our results.

The previous work reported in Anderson & LaBelle (2000) has used a somewhat different approach to modeling spill probability per billion barrels than taken in this study. That approach was to construct "bins" of one billion barrels of production, and then calculate the number of spills in each bin.

The spill rate per billion barrels (Bbbl) of production developed in this study is consistent with the results of the above work. In addition, as previously noted, the approach of this study supports the construction of exact confidence intervals for the spill probability. The formulas for that approach are specified in Chapter 3. While the estimation of the point estimate for spill probability does not depend on the assumed distribution – the construction of the exact confidence intervals does. Thus, the validation of the Poisson model in Chapter 3 is an essential step.

1.3.7   Summary on GOM Spill Probability Estimation

Chapter 3 of this report entails numerous analyses including statistical distribution fitting to both inter-spill and volume data. Section 3.2 covers some initial Poisson probability distribution issues including the use of an exponential distribution goodness of fit approach to assess if a Poisson distribution is reasonable for spill rates. This issue is also examined in more detail later in Chapter 3 when other exposure variables are examined. This section also presents the mathematical formulas to compute exact Poisson confidence intervals if the Poisson assumption is justified. Exact Poisson confidence intervals are computed for pipeline spill rates and compared to those available on the MMS website.

Section 3.3 focuses on the Anderson and LaBelle (2000) pipeline spill data. This section shows that a Poisson distribution adequately fits the observed data based on time as an exposure variable (other exposure variables are considered later in Chapter 3). Additionally a Weibull distribution is found to fit the pipeline spill volumes for this $\geq$ 1000 bbl data.

Section 3.4 examines the Anderson & LaBelle (2000) platform spill data. While a Poisson distribution is found to adequately fit the 1964-1980 time interval, it is shown that the likelihood of these same Poisson data fitting subsequent years is very low. A Weibull distribution fits the platform spill data well.

Section 3.5 has analyses for pipeline spills $\geq$ 50 bbl. Evidence is presented illustrating that the use of the larger $\geq$ 50 bbl data set adds value to an understanding of OCS pipeline spills. Section 3.5.1 shows that the exponential distribution fits the inter-spill data well for exposure variables of time, production volume in Bbbl, and pipeline mile-years. Thus a Poisson distribution is justified for the corresponding pipeline spill rates. Section 3.5.2 provides the exact Poisson confidence intervals for the three different exposure variables as well as illustrating some useful comparisons related to the Poisson and exponential distributions. Weibull distributions are found to fit pipeline spill volumes for the four data sets with thresholds of $\geq$ 50 bbl, $\geq$ 100 bbl, $\geq$ 500 bbl, and $\geq$ 1000 bbl in Section 3.5.3. Section 3.5.4 examines the comparison of the four volume data sets including applications of the Weibull distribution. Conditional probabilities are introduced in this section to provide additional insights. Section 3.5.5 raises the issue of nonstationary Poisson processes in which the spill rates change over time. Alternative ways of quantifying spill rate uncertainty are explored in Section 3.5.6.

Section 3.6 examines platform spills ≥ 50 bbl. Concerns about the Poisson assumption were raised in the discussion of Table 2.5 for the Anderson & LaBelle (2000) platform spills data since 11 platform spills of ≥ 1,000 bbl occurred before 1980 and no spills from then until 1999. However for this 1971 – 2005 ≥ 50 bbl data set, the lower spill threshold includes more spills. Furthermore, the time period is split into two parts and a Poisson is found to fit both parts – with a declining spill rate. The 1990 – 2005 time period is the focus of the platform analyses.

1.4 Methodology for Extending GOM Spill Rate Estimate to Alaskan OCS

Section 4.1 introduces the structure of the problem and lists the uncertainties that make this a challenging problem. Section 4.2 introduces the Beaufort development scenario, which has been used by MMS and by Bercha (2006). In this case, it provides a concrete example to test the spill rates developed in Section 4.3 for pipelines and platforms.

The spill rate development methodology described in Section 4.3 includes methods based on using the largest possible data base and models of spill size to develop spill rates. It also includes methods driven by selecting subsets of spill data and then building a statistical model.

Section 4.4 introduces the problem of estimating spill rates for major Arctic specific pipeline hazards – ice keel gouging, strudel scour, upheaval buckling, and thaw settlement. A less quantitative discussion follows on platform hazards such as the impact of cold, dark environments or the probability of human error.

These spill rates are applied to the Beaufort development scenario, which allows for useful conclusions about the relative merit for Arctic application of spill rates per bbl of production and spill rates per pipeline mile-years and per platform-years.

1.5 Recommendations and Conclusions

Much of the final chapter is presented through three sets of "bullets" that succinctly summarize the key results, the caveats and cautions, and possible future work. Section 5.4 presents an innovative approach to modeling pipeline spill rates that should produce more accurate models.

2 Data

2.1 Introduction to Data Sets

As the authors of this study are statisticians and not oil field experts, this study has relied on previously published works and data bases supplied by MMS. The data bases relevant to the statistical estimation questions in Chapter 3 focus on oil spills, oil production, and the associated platform and pipeline facilities. In most cases the data focus on OCS operations and production in the Gulf of Mexico (GOM), however, some production data from the Pacific and Alaska OCS regions were also included.

As this study has been completed over a period of time, there has been the opportunity to update the various data sets. During the preliminary analysis of this study, data sets with an end date of 1999 were analyzed. The review by MMS of the preliminary analysis allowed the data sets to be examined in detail, and some corrections were made. For this final report, it is the current corrected version of that data that is reported and analyzed. Most analyzes have been conducted with two end dates – 1999 and 2005.

In most cases the data sets through 1999 and the more recent 2000 to 2005 data are reported separately, as there are often some specific issues to be addressed.

2.2 Pipeline Spill Size and Frequency

2.2.1 Pipeline Spill Data from MMS

The OCS or GOM data have been drawn from three sources. Table 2.1 for pipeline spills of more than 1000 barrels is drawn from Anderson & LaBelle (2000). For comparison purposes, Table 2.2 includes those points from Table 2.1 in the date range of 1972 to 1999. For the reviewed preliminary analysis of this report, data for Table 2.2 for pipeline spills of more than 50 barrels was drawn from PPLrepairs.mdb received from Cheryl Anderson in April 2001. For this final report, the data for Table 2.2 for pipeline spills of more than 50 barrels is based on the best available MMS data provided in OCSGOM50plus17April2006.xls.

Table 2.1 OCS Pipeline Spills of 1000 bbl or More (1964-1999)

Spill date	Volume
October 15, 1967	160,638
March 12, 1968	6000
February 11, 1969	7532
May 12, 1973	5000
April 17, 1974	19,833
September 11, 1974	3500
December 18, 1976	4000
December 11, 1981	5100
February 7, 1988	15,576
January 24, 1990	14,423
May 6, 1990	4569
August 31, 1992	2000
November 16, 1994	4533
January 26, 1998	1211
September 29, 1998	8212
July 23, 1999	3200

As this analysis and an earlier approach using probabilistic risk assessment (Bercha 2002) both estimate oil spill probabilities for the Beaufort and Chukchi Seas, the data used for Bercha is also included in Table 2.2. This data was established by matching spill size and cause with information in the MMS data. This is intended to support comparison of the results of the two different approaches. Where differences in the data exist, in several cases it was the joint work of MMS and the Bercha group which supported the cleaner data set on which this report is based.

Table 2.2 GOM Pipeline Spills of 50 bbl or More (1972-1999)

	A&L Volume	Spill Volumes in Bercha N = 31	Spill Volume N = 32
June 13, 1972		100	100
May 12, 1973	5,000	5,000	5,000
April 17 1974	19,833	19,833	19,833
May 21, 1974		65	65
September 11, 1974	3,500	3,500	3,500
February 29, 1976		414	414
December 18, 1976	4,000	4,000	4,000
March 29, 1977		250	250
June 5, 1977		50	50
October 18, 1977		300	300
April 8, 1978		135	135
July 17, 1978		900	900
July 15, 1979		50	50
January 29, 1980			100
August 5, 1981		80	80
December 11, 1981	5,100	5,100	5,100
January 20, 1983		80	80
February 16, 1985		323	323
November 9, 1985		50	50
February 3, 1986		119	119
December 30, 1986		210	210
February 7 1988	15,576	15,576	15,576
January 24, 1990	14,423	14,423	14,423
May 6, 1990	4,569	4,569	4,569
January 3, 1992			190
August 31, 1992	2,000	2,000	2,000
June 17, 1993		50	50
November 16, 1994	4,533	4,533	4,533
January 22, 1998		800	800
January 26, 1998	1,211	1,211	1,211
September 29, 1998	8,212	8,212	8,212
July 23, 1999	3,200	3,200	3,200

2.2.2 Pipeline Spill Data from 2000-2005

Table 2.3 summarizes spills over the most recent period. The availability of this data makes it possible to test the robustness of the methodology and the results. However, there are some caveats that are necessary with this data. First, some of the results are preliminary (especially for 2005) and they may be revised over time. As one example of this, the total for Hurricane Ivan includes a 1720 barrel spill which is in a pipeline buried under a mudslide. Recovery efforts have not yet been successful, but effort is continuing so that spill volume may be reduced. However, it was felt that the advantages of including the additional data were larger than the uncertainties introduced by potential future changes.

The second caveat is that the data for hurricanes Ivan (2004), Katrina (August 2005), and Rita (September 2005) differ from the data reported in earlier years for other hurricanes. For these spills MMS has asked for the reporting of fluids presumed lost with destroyed platforms and the linked damage to pipelines. Thus, there are more spills counted as part of each hurricane. Specifically, the Ivan total comes from 8 spills from 95 to 1720 bbl, the Katrina total comes from 6 spills, and the Rita total from 8 spills (note: one 50 bbl spill may be from either so it is counted in both the 6 and the 8 count, but as 25 bbl in each total). Undoubtedly, there were similar spills in earlier years, but the reporting focused on spills that produced a witnessed oil spill.

Table 2.3 GOM Pipeline Spills of 50 bbl or More (2000-2005)

Spill date	Volume
January 21, 2000	2240
September 15, 2004	3445
August 29, 2005	553
September 24, 2005	8162

2.2.3 Pipeline Spill Data from Bercha Report

Table 2.4 summarizes the 31 OCS pipeline spills from 1972-1999 that were relied on for the Bercha report [reproduced from Table 2.1, p. 2.2 and Table A.2.2, p. A.2.6, Bercha, 2002]. This data is included because it provides significant information about sub-categories of key variables. Fortunately, the number of spills is small enough that more statistically reliable results are obtainable if the data set is used as a whole rather than as a collection of sub-categories, such as large diameter pipe, that is longer than 5 km and in deep water.

Table 2.4 OCS Pipeline Spills Summary (1972-1999)[1, 2]

OCS Pipeline Spills By Category 1972-1999		Spill Statistics			Exposure (km-years)	Frequency (spill per 10^4 km-yr)
		Number of Spills	Average Volume (bbl)	Median Volume (bbl)		
By Pipe Diameter	< 10"	16	2,141	173	142,892	1.1197
	≥ 10"	15	4,070	1,211	111,011	1.3512
By Minimum Depth	Bad Depth Data	14				
	< 10 m	6	2,310	1,211	161,966	0.3704 [1]
	≥ 10 m	11	3,165	1,040	94,641	1.1623 [1]
By Segment Length	< 0.5 km	0	0	0	2,359	0.0000
	.5 ≤ x < 2 km	2	2,335	2,335	25,484	0.7848
	2 ≤ x < 5 km	7	820	100	35,279	1.9842
	≥ 5 km	22	3,859	850	192,270	1.1442
By Spill Size	Small	6	58	50	253,903	0.2363
	Medium	12	317	230	253,903	0.4726
	Large	10	4,133	4,267	253,903	0.3939
	Huge	3	16,611	15,576	253,903	0.1182
By Diameter, By Spill Size						
<10"	Small	4	58	50	142,892	0.2799
	Medium	7	266	135	142,892	0.4899
	Large	4	4,436	4,551	142,892	0.2799
	Huge	1	14,423	14,423	142,892	0.0700
≥ 10"	Small	2	58	58	111,011	0.1802
	Medium	5	387	312	111,011	0.4504
	Large	6	3,932	3,600	111,011	0.5405
	Huge	2	17,705	17,705	111,011	0.1802

Small	50 ≤ spill size < 100 bbl
Medium	100 ≤ spill size < 1,000 bbl
Large	1,000 ≤ spill size < 10,000 bbl
Huge	10,000 bbl ≤ spill size

[1] The frequency rates for different pipeline depths were dropped from Bercha (2006) because MMS determined the water depths in the MMS GOM database were suspect. The results in Bercha (2002) ignore the 14 spills with missing depth data. If these 14 spills are distributed proportionately between the shallower and deeper depths, then the frequency rates would be 0.6755 spills per 10^4 km-yr for the shallower category and 2.1195 spills per 10^4 km-yr for the deeper category.

[2] An early version of a data spreadsheet for Bercha (2002) was found to have 17 of 33 records (1985+) with segment, date, and general location mismatched with rest of data. This may have been corrected after transmission, and Bercha (2002)

does not use spill dates (except to separately analyze 1985+), thus the reported results should not be affected but caution should be used if this data source is used for further work.

2.2.4 Spills in State Waters

Table 2.2 does not include spills that were in state rather than federal waters. These have also been omitted from Anderson & LaBelle (2000) and from Bercha (2002). This is of some consequence for the extension of these results to the Beaufort and Chukchi Seas, as on-shore terminations of pipelines seem likely to with some frequency pass through state waters. It also seems likely that from the perspective of most stakeholders it is the occurrence of a spill that matters – not whether it is in federal or state waters. It also seems likely that distance from spill to shore will have impacts on dispersion of any spill.

There are good reasons for this omission.

1. MMS does not have quality control over, or legal access to oil industry data in state waters. Spill data are incomplete to an unknown extent. Pipeline and platform data, especially pipeline mileage data by year, depth, etc. are unavailable. Given the incomplete data, it would be misleading to include unknown fractions of the spills, pipelines, platforms, and production. It is even possible that including some recorded "state" spills could lead to a false "sense of security and completeness" for some users of the data.

2. How do you treat spills of commingled oil? If a pipeline that transports 5% OCS oil and 95% state oil, has a spill of 1000 bbl, does this count as 50 bbl OCS spill or 0.05 of a 1000 bbl OCS spill? Also, given the data problems discussed in the first point, it may even be difficult to establish the federal and state shares.

3. State waters in theory extend either 3 miles or 3 leagues (9 miles). However, offshore of Louisiana, this boundary was fixed long ago, before several additional miles of coast were eroded away. These differences exacerbate the difficulties of state-to-state comparisons and extrapolations.

From a statistical perspective the difficulty is that for some measures of spill occurrence probabilities, it seems inappropriate to remove spills in state waters. For other measures of spill occurrence, it may be appropriate to remove the "state" spills. The principle that drives the choice is that the event (the spill) and the measure should treat the "state" question the same way. The following are suggested as consistent choices:

Eliminating spills, platforms, and pipeline miles for state waters has the effect of treating the event and the variable consistently. Thus, the total of pipeline miles and of platforms must also be only in "federal" waters, if only "federal" spills are reported.

Then the estimation of the probability of spills in state waters would be addressed using data bases specific to the pipeline and platform development, hurricane exposure, distances, etc. of each state. This is obviously beyond the scope of this study.

TGE Consulting

The following are inconsistent choices:

> Eliminating spills in state waters for models using oil production or time as the occurrence measure is inconsistent. It reduces the event by removing spills in state waters from the data set. But there is no corresponding reduction in the measure of spills per billion barrels or spills per year. Thus this combination understates the true probability of an oil spill for oil that starts in "federal" pipelines but passes through "state" pipelines.

This decision must balance the above principle with the complication and potential confusion created by using different data sets for different models. Also in some cases the pipeline and platform information may not exist for a proposed development, so that only spill rates based on production or time are possible.

The application of spill rates to the Beaufort and Chukchi Seas is clearly affected by this choice. This can be illustrated by comparing the application of a spill rate per pipeline mile with a spill rate per Bbbl of production. For MMS's responsibility for OCS areas, the focus may be on spills in that "federal" area. However, for other stakeholders and especially those state residents who live on the North Slope and who depend on marine subsistence resources, the question is the probability of a spill – not whether it is in state or federal regulated areas. Thus, approach 1 is recommended over approach 2.

1. Applying a spill rate per pipeline mile can be applied to the total length of a pipeline through both federal and state areas. This does require the assumption that the probability of a spill in the two areas is not statistically different. Different water depths and different patterns of activity may imply this is a weak assumption; but, it is clearly better than no assumption at all.

2. Applying the spill rate per Bbbl of production which includes only the "federal" spills analyzed in this report would mean that there would be no consideration of spills from pipelines in state areas.

MMS applications in oil spill risk analyses for the Alaska OCS Region do include estimates of spills from existing or permitted offshore State platforms and pipelines. In the recent past, spillage estimates have derived from a combination of onshore North Slope spill statistics, TAPS experience, and extrapolation of OCS spill rate estimates.

2.3   Platform Spill Size and Frequency

2.3.1   OCS Platform Spill Data from MMS for 1964 – 1999

The OCS platform data have been drawn from two sources. Table 2.5 for spills of more than 1000 barrels is drawn from Anderson & LaBelle (2000). This table includes the 1969 Santa Barbara spill of 80,000 barrels. Table 2.6 for GOM spills of more than 50 barrels is drawn from OCSGOM50plus17April2006.xls received from MMS in April 2006. Since Table 2.6 is limited to GOM spills it does not include any Pacific spills.

A major distinction from the spills reported for pipelines is that many of these platform spills involve refined petroleum products such as diesel rather than crude oil or condensate. This will be addressed in more detail when spill causes are analyzed.

Two items from Table 2.5 are worth noting. First Anderson & LaBelle (2000) reasonably combined three spills caused by one hurricane into a single spill "event," which is done throughout this report. This can be justified as the three spills have a common cause. However, it is also necessary as the Poisson distribution assumes events do not happen simultaneously. The exponential inter-spill time is not zero. If needed the time interval is measured more finely. Similar statistical issues arise with the multiple spills reported at a common size such as 50 bbl (see also, discussion of estimated 50 & 100 values at end of this section). For estimating spill events this treatment of a hurricane as a common cause is appropriate, but it would not be for modeling the requirements for spill response equipment.

The second item is that the data in Table 2.5 from 1964 to 1999 reflect a non-homogenous data series. There are 11 spills in 17 years and then 0 spills in 19 years. Unfortunately the long-period without large spills ended in 2005 with spills associated with hurricanes Katrina and Rita.

Table 2.5 OCS Platform Spills ≥ 1000 bbl (1964-1999)

Spill date	Volume
April 8, 1964	2559
October 3, 1964	11,869[1]
July 19, 1965	1688
January 28, 1969	80,000
March 16, 1969	2500
February 10, 1970	30,000
December 1, 1970	53,000
January 9, 1973	9935
January 26, 1973	7000
November 23, 1979	1500
November 14, 1980	1456

[1]Hurricane Hilda destroyed 3 platforms with spill volumes of 5180, 5100, & 1589 bbl. The total volume is entered as a single spill.

Table 2.6 uses a 1971 start date rather than the 1972 start date used with the bulk of the platform analysis and with the pipeline data. This was done because 1972 happened to be a year with no GOM platform spills ≥ 50 barrels, while 1971 has 8 spills of this size. For consistency most analyses are done with the 1972 start date, but the inclusion of the 1971 data supports analysis of the impact of this choice.

Table 2.6 with its 77 spills illustrates one of the difficulties with these data. Some of it is estimated rather than measured so the round numbers like 50 (10 spills) or 100 barrels (5 spills) are vastly over-represented in the data base.

As discussed in Chapter 3, this requires that some values be adjusted by small amounts. With continuous probability distributions the probability is zero that two values will be the same if measured with sufficient accuracy, such as 50.00 and 50.01. Thus, statistical tests can be affected by measurement accuracy in a data set, and some tests require that values not be identical. These clusters of estimated values are adjusted so they are not identical so that the tests will work. However, these adjustments are much smaller than the variability concealed by estimating a spill of 75 to 125 barrels as 100 barrels. Thus, the statistically tested fit of the adjusted data to an assumed distribution (such as exponential inter-spill intervals) is worse than would be the fit of "measured or real" data. Thus, the statistical tests are more likely to reject the "fit" with estimated data than they would be with measured or real data.

A second complication is that the use of 50 or 100 may have a systematic bias. Those reporting spills may round-up to be safe that they are not "under-reporting" or they may round-down to minimize the seriousness of the spill. MMS review acknowledged the potential of this bias, but suggested that estimating to round numbers is more likely than systematic bias.

One consequence of the 10 spills estimated at 50 barrels is an unknown amount of over-estimation of spill rates. If there is no bias of under- or over-reporting of spill volumes, then about half of the 10 spills should be below the 50 barrel threshold; and would thus if measured not be part of the data for this study. The impact of this overestimation is limited by the unknown number of spills whose reported (estimated) volume was less than 50 bbl, but whose actual volume was over the threshold.

Table 2.6 GOM Platform Spills of ≥ 50 bbl (1971-1999) N = 77

Spill Date	Volume	Spill Date	Volume	Spill Date	Volume
1971-04-05	200	1980-01-23	286	1985-01-23	60
1971-05-15	50	1980-03-08	258	1985-02-23	50
1971-05-27	50	1980-03-11	95	1985-06-03	643
1971-05-29	135	1980-05-16	150	1985-07-30	50
1971-07-20	100	1980-06-11	80	1985-09-02	66
1971-08-13	50	1980-10-15	83	1985-09-26	58
1971-10-16	450	1980-11-14	1,456	1986-11-13	52
1971-12-09	50	1980-12-02	118	1987-03-20	60
1973-01-09	9,935	1981-02-15	58	1988-02-19	50
1973-01-26	7,000	1981-04-06	210	1988-11-07	64
1973-06-20	239	1981-08-19	50	1988-11-16	55
1973-12-08	95	1981-11-28	64	1989-02-15	400
1974-07-10	130	1982-01-19	400	1991-10-13	280
1974-09-07	75	1982-04-29	228	1992-12-26	100
1974-10-04	50	1982-08-18	214	1994-11-23	148
1974-11-27	120	1983-01-30	600	1995-01-25	600
1974-12-22	200	1983-02-01	125	1995-07-06	75
1975-03-18	166	1983-03-09	77	1995-10-03	89
1975-09-21	100	1983-03-20	320	1995-12-15	435
1976-10-19	300	1983-04-14	200	1996-09-29	105
1977-12-14	77	1983-05-09	77	1996-12-31	62
1978-05-11	104	1983-05-16	95	1997-12-16	170
1979-01-30	321	1983-08-02	119	1998-04-29	100
1979-01-31	165	1984-06-20	50	1999-01-23	105
1979-04-14	60	1984-07-08	100	1999-09-09	125
1979-11-23	1,500	1985-01-22	107		

Table 2.7 compares the Bercha (2002, 2006) spill data set with this data set for platform spills. While the individual spills were not identified with dates in Bercha (2002, 2006), the provided list of spill sizes and spill causes (Bercha 2002, Table 2.4 and Bercha 2006, Table 2.5) could be matched with the current data set. The subset of spills from Table 2.6 that are listed in the last column of Table 2.7 was formed by deleting all spills that were not crude oil or condensate (i.e. diesel and other refined petroleum products) and all spills that involved a well blowout.

Table 2.7 Comparison of Bercha (2002) and Similarly Selected Spills from Current GOM Platform Spill Data Set (1972-1999) N = 21

Spill Date	Bercha Volume	Current Volume
1973-01-09	9,935	9,935
1973-01-26	7,000	7,000
1974-07-10	130	130
1974-09-07	75	75
1974-10-04	50	50
1974-11-27	120	120
1978-05-11	104	104
1979-04-14	60	60
1980-11-14	1,456	1,456
1981-02-15	58	58
1983-02-01	125	125
1984-06-20	50	50
1985-09-02	66	66
1988-02-19	50	50
1988-11-16	55	55
1989-02-15	400	400
1991-10-13	280	280
1995-01-25	600	600
1995-07-06	75	75
1995-12-15	435	435
1997-12-16		170[1]
1998-09-17	108[2]	5

[1]Product spill was mix of condensate and yellow paraffin, and loss of control during well shut-in. Either could be why not included in Bercha platform spill data set.
[2]Incident explanation noted that 103 bbl of 108 bbl spill recovered, so could be classified based on initial or final spill volume.

2.3.2 GOM Platform Spill Data from MMS for 2000 – 2005

The 9 spills from 2000 to 2005 included in Table 2.8 are drawn from OCSGOM50plus17April2006.xls received from MMS in April 2006. Since Table 2.8 is limited to GOM spills it does not include any Pacific spills. The 2005 spills from hurricanes Katrina and Rita are based on MMS interim working documents with the information provided by Cheryl Anderson (personal communication, April 2006).

While different platforms may have been damaged on different days by the same hurricane, it is much more reasonable to treat these as single events. As detailed in the notes to Table 2.8, the most recent hurricane spills are each aggregated values that can represent multiple products and multiple platforms.

While there is no question about the severity of the hurricanes with spills included in Table 2.8, there was a significant difference in how the data were gathered as compared with earlier hurricane related spills. Those earlier spills typically were reported as a result of some spill response activity. Beginning with hurricane Lili, MMS adopted a much more aggressive strategy in identifying spills. Operators were queried about quantities of petroleum products that were never recovered as a result of the hurricanes.

For example the 6 individual Ivan spills that were aggregated into a total volume of 1053 barrels include 4 platforms that were destroyed or missing. In each case crude oil and refined petroleum products on the platform before the hurricane are included in the spill total. If a similarly aggressive data collection strategy had been started in 1972, we believe that hurricanes would have placed more spills into this data base.

Table 2.8 GOM Platform Spills ≥ 50 bbl (2000-2005) N = 9

Spill Date	Volume
2000-02-28	200
2000-08-09	60
2001-03-30	127
2002-10-03	1,588[1]
2003-05-09	264
2003-05-10	430
2004-09-15	1,053[2]
2005-08-29	2,225[3]
2005-09-24	7,371[4]

[1] Lili (3 spills of ≥ 50 bbls)
[2] Ivan (6 spills of ≥ 50 bbls)
[3] Katrina (14 spills of ≥ 50 bbls)
[4] Rita (10 spills of ≥ 50 bbls)

2.3.3 GOM Platform Spill Data Set

The 78 GOM platform spills combine the data from Table 2.6 (except for the 1971 spills) with the data from Table 2.8. A few summary statistics are shown in Table 2.9, as two key decisions were required for this data.

First, after consultation with MMS it was decided to include spills of refined petroleum products, as well as spills of crude and condensate. This was done because diesel spills were in many years the most common type of spill, and the average volumes were significant. The inclusion of the refined petroleum product spills is the major difference for platform spills between the Bercha (2002 & 2006) reports and this report. That is the main reason why Table 2.7 is a subset of Table 2.6. Second, as detailed in Chapter 3, the rate of platform spills has declined over the 1972 – 2005 time period.

Table 2.9 Summary of GOM Platform Spills ≥ 50 bbl (1972-2005) N = 78

| | Average bbls (#) | | | |
	Crude & Condensate	Refined Petroleum	Mixed	All
1972-1989	1,005 (20)	215 (36)	(0)	498 (56)
1990-2005	217 (10)	163 (08)	3,059 (4)	714 (22)
1972-2005	743 (30)	206 (44)	3,059 (4)	559 (78)

2.4 Spill Occurrence Exposure Variables

2.4.1 Potential Spill Occurrence Factors

Section 2.4 describes the data for the exposure variables, which were discussed in Section 1.3.1 and 1.3.3. These are combined with spill information for measures that include:

Spills per year,

Spills per billion barrels of production,

Spills per pipeline-mile-year, and

Spills per platform-year or per well-year.

2.4.2 Time as a Spill Occurrence Measure

For spill causes such as hurricanes, time seems to be a possibly appropriate spill occurrence measure. Each year there is a hurricane season and so each year this is a potential spill occurrence cause. This cause is logically related more strongly to the season than to the volume of oil production.

Spills per year is also the most easily understood platform spill occurrence measure, so if it can adequately model a situation it is a natural choice.

Table 2.10 Yearly GOM Pipeline and Platform Spills of 50 bbl or More (1972-2005)

year	Pipeline Spills	Platform Spills
1971		8
1972	1	0
1973	1	4
1974	3	5
1975	0	2
1976	2	1
1977	3	1
1978	2	1
1979	1	4
1980	1	8
1981	2	4
1982	0	3
1983	1	8
1984	0	2
1985	2	7
1986	2	1
1987	0	1
1988	1	3
1989	0	1
1990	2	0
1991	0	1
1992	2	1
1993	1	0
1994	1	1
1995	0	4
1996	0	2
1997	0	1
1998	3	1
1999	1	2
2000	1	2
2001	0	1
2002	0	1
2003	0	2
2004	1	1
2005	2	2

2.4.3   Volume of Oil Produced

For use when scenario information on facilities cannot yet be estimated, this is the only probability measure possible. As the measure currently used by MMS, this also facilitates comparison with past work. There is one significant difference between how this variable is treated in this study and previous work by MMS. This report relies on exact Poisson confidence intervals for reported spill rates rather than other approaches used by MMS

For analysis of production volume as a probability measure, this study takes the approach of measuring the interval between spills in units of production. Then this interval data can be tested as an exponential distribution to validate the Poisson assumption. If the Poisson function is acceptable, then the spill rate and exact Poisson confidence intervals can be estimated using the number of spills over the total exposure variable.

While this data is dominated by OCS production in the Gulf of Mexico, about 5% and 0.7% of the volume in recent years are respectively from the Pacific and Alaska regions. Table 2.11 summarizes the data extracted from "OCS Crude&Condensate Production 1954 to Estimated 2005 28April2006.xls" that was received from MMS.

Since spill statistics are for GOM spills without inclusion of Pacific spills, the most consistent choice of production volume is for the GOM. That is what was done for all analyses related to platform spills.

However, the total OCS production volume was used for the calculations of pipeline spills in Chapter 3. Key spill rate values were re-calculated using GOM production volume for extrapolations to Alaska in Chapter 4. As discussed in Section 2.4.6, these are highly correlated values so the statistical validity of Chapter 3 is not affected, although there are differences in calculated values.

Table 2.11 Oil Production Volume (1972-2005)

Year	OCS Production Volume (10^6 bbl)	GOM Production Volume (10^6 bbl)
1972	395.9	373.3
1973	384.8	366.0
1974	354.9	338.1
1975	325.3	309.8
1976	314.5	300.5
1977	295.9	283.7
1978	287.9	276.0
1979	334.2	318.2
1980	274.7	264.6
1981	282.9	263.3
1982	314.5	286.1
1983	350.8	320.2
1984	385.1	354.6
1985	380.0	350.3
1986	384.3	355.5
1987	358.6	327.5
1988	332.7	301.2
1989	323.7	290.6
1990	304.4	274.5
1991	326.3	294.7
1992	347.5	304.8
1993	359.2	308.6
1994	372.3	314.0
1995	417.4	345.0
1996	433.1	368.8
1997	466.1	411.6
1998	490.6	444.3
1999	534.4	495.3
2000	559.1	523.0
2001	591.7	558.3
2002	602.3	567.4
2003	594.8	561.1
2004	567.0	535.0
2005	488.0	459.1

2.4.4 OCS Pipeline Exposure

Table 2.12 summarizes the number of miles of pipeline and number of pipeline segments for the OCS area of the GOM and Pacific. These data were provided by MMS [OCSOilPipelines1948to2006.xls, March 2006], and they are limited to those pipelines carrying oil. While petroleum spills can occur from other products, such as condensate, these are clearly the pipelines that represent a very large share of the spill occurrence rate. While it is better to focus on these data, as detailed in Table 2.14 this table of pipeline miles is proportional (r values exceed 99%) to the total number of km (miles) of pipeline used in Bercha (2002) and the draft data initially supplied with a much broader array of product codes.

With the large correlations for different mileage measures, the results within the existing GOM dominated database would be comparable for all measures. However, when extrapolating to the Beaufort and Chukchi Seas, selection of the correct mileage data base is quite important as total reported mileage ranges from less than 8000 miles to more than 33,000 miles.

If a pipeline segment were doubled in length, the spill probability associated with it would not double. Some portion of the probability depends on the number of connections to other pipelines, risers, and valves the pipeline has. That is probably better measured using the number of segments variable in Table 2.12. However, as detailed in Table 2.16, the correlation between pipeline segments and pipeline mileage is 0.905, thus both cannot be included in a statistical model based on a small data set due to problems with multi-collinearity.

While the best data available, these values should be treated as estimates and not exact values. There are no available data on the accuracy of the estimate. However, it is likely that most errors in these data would consist of segments that are either erroneously included or excluded, and this type of error is likely to be reasonably consistent from year-to-year. Thus for estimating trends these data can be treated as being accurate enough that other uncertainties will be far more important.

Table 2.12 OCS Pipeline Mileage and Segments

Year	Number of Segments	Miles	Year	Number of Segments	Miles
1964	859	537	1985	2,095	4,063
1965	870	565	1986	2,134	4,238
1966	885	654	1987	2,173	4,345
1967	919	742	1988	2,213	4,451
1968	957	887	1989	2,250	4,562
1969	1,002	1,170	1990	2,294	4,737
1970	1,062	1,339	1991	2,345	4,836
1971	1,153	1,504	1992	2,362	4,979
1972	1,249	1,740	1993	2,395	5,030
1973	1,312	1,932	1994	2,436	5,287
1974	1,344	2,049	1995	2,462	5,536
1975	1,389	2,200	1996	2,501	6,148
1976	1,442	2,451	1997	2,531	6,433
1977	1,497	2,563	1998	2,576	6,753
1978	1,568	2,818	1999	2,578	6,996
1979	1,643	2,956	2000	2,584	7,247
1980	1,695	3,120	2001	2,594	7,466
1981	1,766	3,343	2002	2,578	7,651
1982	1,837	3,511	2003	2,463	7,842
1983	1,907	3,703	2004	2,466	8,516
1984	2,012	3,925	2005	2,388	8,369

To support comparison of the results of Bercha (2002 & 2006) with this study, Table 2.13 summarizes that data. The original data (Bercha 2002, Table A.2.1 (a), 8th column) is stated in terms of kilometers of pipeline placed in service in each year with an additional 2% added for pipelines with undated origins. This is the second column of Table 2.13. The third column of Table 2.13 is simply the cumulative values for each year. For comparison purposes with Table 2.12 the fifth column of Table 2.13 states these cumulative values in terms of miles rather than kilometers, and the last column reports comparable values from Table 2.12.

It is suggested that the differences between the last two columns are the result of the additional efforts by MMS subsequent to the Bercha work to provide better quality data on the existing GOM infrastructure.

Bercha (2002 & 2006) calculate the spill rate as the number of spills during the total time frame divided by the total exposure over the period. Thus, the total number of kilometer-years of pipelines represents the total exposure. This is calculated as the sum of the number of cumulative kilometers for each year. This exposure is shown in the last row of Table 2.13.

Table 2.13 Bercha Pipeline Exposure

Year	Pipeline (km)	Cumulative Pipeline (km)	Cumulative Pipeline Mileage	Cumulative Pipeline Mileage from Table 2.12
1972	435	435	270	1,740
1973	324	759	472	1,932
1974	214	973	605	2,049
1975	358	1,331	827	2,200
1976	526	1,857	1,154	2,451
1977	373	2,230	1,386	2,563
1978	657	2,887	1,794	2,818
1979	339	3,226	2,005	2,956
1980	343	3,569	2,218	3,120
1981	508	4,077	2,533	3,343
1982	400	4,477	2,782	3,511
1983	439	4,916	3,055	3,703
1984	469	5,385	3,346	3,925
1985	425	5,810	3,610	4,063
1986	385	6,195	3,849	4,238
1987	399	6,594	4,097	4,345
1988	610	7,204	4,476	4,451
1989	682	7,886	4,900	4,562
1990	808	8,694	5,402	4,737

1991	501	9,195	5,714	4,836
1992	394	9,589	5,958	4,979
1993	291	9,880	6,139	5,030
1994	821	10,701	6,649	5,287
1995	667	11,368	7,064	5,536
1996	1358	12,726	7,908	6,148
1997	997	13,723	8,527	6,433
1998	947	14,670	9,116	6,753
1999	667	15,337	9,530	6,996
Total Exposure		185,694	115,385	114,705

The total exposure value shown in Table 2.13, 185,694 km-years does not precisely match the value of 187,183 km-years given in Bercha (2006, Table 2.1, spill size exposure). Note the value in Bercha (2002) must be lower, as all spill rates reported in 2002 (Table 2.1) are 35.65% higher than in 2006 (Table 2.1). While the cumulative mileage reported in each year for this report differs from the Bercha reports, the total exposure is very similar and the variables are very highly correlated, which will be discussed in section 2.4.6.

2.4.5   Number of Platforms and Number of Operating Wells

Table 2.14 summarizes the number of platforms in the GOM. This data was transmitted as Fixed_Facilities_production_history.xls by MMS in April 2006. This data included sub-categorizations of platforms by type and amount of production and drilling activities. The most promising groups were all platforms, platforms with oil production, and all platforms except those with no production. For these three groups the minimum correlation was 0.975, so statistically their predictive abilities are virtually identical. During consultation with MMS, the professional judgment was that the total platform count variable was the most reliable, so that is listed in Table 2.14 and used for analysis.

Table 2.14 GOM Number of Platforms

Year	GOM # of Platforms	Year	GOM # of Platforms
1972	1623	1990	3444
1973	1691	1991	3456
1974	1749	1992	3434
1975	1798	1993	3478
1976	1869	1994	3466
1977	1956	1995	3513
1978	2075	1996	3557
1979	2179	1997	3601
1980	2296	1998	3551
1981	2411	1999	3585
1982	2562	2000	3595
1983	2735	2001	3575
1984	2854	2002	3573
1985	3009	2003	3578
1986	3052	2004	3530
1987	3159	2005	3435
1988	3307		
1989	3391		

Table 2.15 is drawn from Bercha (2002) Table A.3.1, and it presents the data that was used to judge the spill rate for platforms in Bercha (2002 & 2006). The final row shows the total of well-years (119,714) that was used in both reports as the total exposure over the 1972 – 1999 time frame.

Table 2.15 Active Oil Wells from Platforms (Bercha 2006, from Federal Offshore Statistics report, MMS, October 2000)

Year	Active Oil Wells	Year	Active Oil Wells
1972	3,744	1986	4,406
1973	3,814	1987	4,543
1974	3,686	1988	4,627
1975	3,477	1989	4,507
1976	3,555	1990	4,515
1977	3,747	1991	4,549
1978	3,648	1992	4,612
1979	2,781	1993	4,774
1980	5,375	1994	4,846
1981	4,522	1995	4,950
1982	4,734	1996	5,040

1983	4,142	1997	4,727
1984	4,138	1998	4,731
1985	4,321	1999	3,203
		Total well-years	119,714

2.4.6 Correlation Analysis

There are very high correlations between time, cumulative production volume, and cumulative pipeline mileage in the OCS data base. Table 2.16 contrasts data from several sources including:

Year	1972 – 2005
Number pipeline segments	Table 2.12
Pipeline mileage	Table 2.12
Platforms	Table 2.14
OCS Cumulative production volume	Table 2.11
GOM Cumulative production volume	Table 2.11
Bercha pipeline exposure (km-year)	Table 2.14
Bercha platform exposure (well-year)	Table 2.15

Table 2.16 Correlations between Exposure Variables

	# pipeline segments	Pipeline mileage	# Platforms	OCS Cum. prod.	GOM Cum. prod.	Bercha pipe km[1]	Bercha wells[1]
Year	0.949	0.990	0.926	0.775	0.711	0.984	0.530
# pipeline segments	1.000	0.905	0.992	0.636	0.548	0.936	0.570
Pipeline mileage		1.000	0.875	0.832	0.783	0.995	0.481
# Platforms			1.000	0.571	0.480	0.890	0.592
OCS cum. prod.				1.000	0.989	0.807	-0.005
GOM cum. prod.					1.000	0.733	-0.176
Bercha pipe km						1.000	0.468
Bercha wells							1.000

[1]The correlations with the Bercha data set are only for 1972 – 1999.

Most of these correlations are strong, and some are very nearly equal to 1.0 or a perfect correlation. This has two major implications. First, there is likely to be little or no added value to models that have more than 1 predictor variables. Second, results that are true for one exposure variable are almost certainly true for other highly correlated exposure variables.

2.5 Spill Cause Analysis

2.5.1 Introduction to Spill Cause Analysis

There are several issues that must be addressed in developing statistically valid estimates for the causes of oil spills. These are required for this effort because of the differences between the Gulf of Mexico and the Beaufort and Chukchi Seas with respect to exposure to the different causes. One frequent cause of pipeline spills in the Gulf of Mexico is "third party impacts," which are predominantly due to dragging anchors and fishing nets. Neither of these will be common in the arctic environment.

These issues can be divided into four major categories. Spills can also be differentiated between those occurring on platforms and those from pipelines. Sections 2.5.3 and 2.5.5 include results for both pipeline and platform data.
1. Identifying the primary spill cause
2. Multinomial statistical variability
3. Differences due to time and the manner of development
4. Binomial statistical variability for GOM vs. general causes.

An additional issue with respect to spill cause is the relationship between cause and size, which is analyzed in the final sub-section of this section.

2.5.2 Identifying the Primary Spill Cause

During the time span in which the Bercha reports (2002 & 2006) and this report have been conducted, MMS has made extensive efforts to improve the quality of information in its databases that summarize oil spills. This has included discussions for this analysis of which classification would be most appropriate for particular spills. As a result there are some

significant differences between the causes reported here, the earlier Bercha work, and past classifications in the MMS data bases.

2.5.2.1 Pipeline Spill Causes

In spite of this work, spill cause classification still requires the exercise of judgment as to which of several causes is the primary one. So that others can double-check or modify this work, Table 2.17 details how each GOM pipeline spill from 1972 – 2005 is classified as to cause. Table 2.17 divides the causes into two groups, which will be important for the extension of GOM spill rates to the Beaufort and Chukchi Seas. Some spills have causes that occur in the GOM but not the Arctic, such as hurricanes, damage from trawl fishing gear, and damage from the anchors of general ship traffic. In some cases it is unclear whether the anchor damage is from a workboat or third party traffic. Indicators such as distance from a platform or a greater likelihood that the damage from workboats will be noticed and reported have been used as needed. Other spills are due to causes such as corrosion and oil field operations that can occur anywhere. Table 2.18 summarizes this into categories.

Table 2.17 Primary Cause of GOM Pipeline Oil Spills

Spill Date	Spill Size	GOM Specific	Cause
1972-06-13	100		Corrosion
1973-05-12	5,000		Corrosion
1974-04-17	19,833	GOM	Anchor drag
1974-05-21	65		Operational: anchor from derrick barge
1974-09-11	3,500	GOM	Hurricane Carmen
1976-02-29	414		Corrosion: after pipeline kinked by anchor
1976-12-18	4,000	GOM	Shrimp trawl damaged valve
1977-03-29	250		Natural: mud slide
1977-06-05	50		Operational: lay barge anchor
1977-10-18	300	GOM	Anchor drag
1978-04-08	135		Mechanical/operational
1978-07-17	900		Operational: anchor drag 600' from platform
1979-07-15	50		Operational: workboat searching for rig anchor
1980-01-29	100	GOM	Trawler drag broke valve
1981-08-05	80		Corrosion: external or metal fatigue
1981-12-11	5,100		Operational: service vessel anchor
1983-01-20	80		Natural: mud slide
1985-02-16	323		Operational: pipeline dented, cracked during construction
1985-11-09	50		Operational: spud barge anchor
1986-02-03	119		Mechanical/operational: pinhole leak during abandonment
1986-12-30	210		Mechanical/operational: anchor or original construction
1988-02-07	15,576	GOM	Ship illegally dropped and dragged anchor
1990-01-24	14,423	GOM	Fishing net or anchor
1990-05-06	4,569	GOM	Trawler net drag
1992-01-03	190		Unknown
1992-08-31	2,000	GOM	Rig broke loose during Hurricane Andrew
1993-06-17	50		Operational: workboat anchor
1994-11-16	4,533	GOM	Trawl net damaged valve
1998-01-22	800	GOM	Mechanical damage: probably anchor
1998-01-26	1,211		Operational: anchor during overboard rescue
1998-09-29	8,212	GOM	Hurricane Georges
1999-07-23	3,200		Operational: jackup rig set down on pipeline
2000-01-21	2,240		Operational: anchor drag from drill rig
2004-09-15	3,445	GOM	Hurricane Ivan
2005-08-29	553	GOM	Hurricane Katrina
2005-09-24	8162	GOM	Hurricane Rita

Table 2.18 Summary of Primary Cause of GOM Pipeline Oil Spills (N = 36)

Number of Spills	GOM Specific Cause
9	Third party damage
6	Hurricanes
	Non-GOM Specific Cause
14	Operational/mechanical
4	Corrosion
2	Natural: mud slide
1	Unknown

Table 2.19 summarizes the causes of the pipeline oil spills as previously reported in the Bercha reports. The table has been simplified from the original, by reporting on the number of spills in each cause classification without breaking these categories down into their sub-categories. For the purposes of this report it does not matter whether the corrosion was internal or external or whether the third party impact was due to anchors or trawling gear. Also the more aggregated data support statistical estimates with tighter confidence intervals due to the larger percentage of items in each category.

One of the major differences between Table 2.19 and the work reported here is the definition of third party impact. For example the 3200 bbl spill listed in Table 2.19 under third party cause is from a jack-rig or spud barge. Due to the oil field related nature of the cause in the previously reported data this is classified as an operational impact. Similarly, several of the "anchor" impacts have been from work boats. Thus, the third party category in Table 2.18 contains significantly fewer spills than that category in Table 2.19.

Table 2.19 Causes of GOM Pipeline Oil Spills from Bercha (2002 Table 2.2 & 2006 Table 2.2)

Cause classification	# of spills	Spill sizes (Bbls)
Corrosion	4	80, 100, 5000, 414
Third party impact	16	19833, 65, 50, 300, 900, 323, 15576, 2000, 800, 1211, 3200, 4000, 100, 14423, 4569, 4533
Operation impact	4	50, 50, 5100, 50
Mechanical	2	135, 210
Natural hazard	4	250, 80, 8212, 3500
Unknown	1	119
Totals	31	

2.5.2.2 Platform Spill Causes

The data on platform spills is presented differently than that for pipelines for two reasons. First, in several cases it is simply not possible to identify a primary cause. As a simple example, when a spill occurs during a diesel transfer from a coupling that breaks or separates is it a mechanical failure or human error because the transfer was unattended. Second, unlike pipelines the only GOM specific cause is hurricanes. Thus, the level of detail that was needed to present the classification of pipeline spills as operational or third party is not needed here. Thus Table 2.20 identifies the spills where a hurricane was identified as the primary cause. Table 2.21 summarizes the number of spills by spill cause. A useful reference on platform spills is Sharples et al. (1989).

Table 2.20 GOM Specific Cause (Hurricanes) Platform Spills

Spill Date	Spill Size	Cause
1974-09-07	75	Carmen
1974-12-22	200	repair of Carmen damage
1985-09-02	66	Elena
2002-10-03	1,588	Lili
2004-09-15	1,053	Ivan
2005-08-29	2,225	Katrina
2005-09-24	7,371	Rita

Table 2.21 Summary of Causes of GOM Platform Spills 1971-2005 (N = 78)

Cause	Primary Cause	
7	7	GOM Specific Cause (N = 7)
		Hurricanes
		Non-GOM Specific Cause (N = 71)
65	35	Equipment failure
33	23	Human error
17	6	Sea condition
13	5	Collision
2	2	External damage

Table 2.22 summarizes the causes of the platform oil spills from Table 2.5 of Bercha (2002). As indicated in the discussion with Table 2.7, these 21 spills are the crude or condensate spills that did not involve a fire or blowout from 1972 – 1999.

Table 2.22 Causes of GOM Platform Oil Spills from Bercha (2002 Table 2.4 & 2006 Table 2.5)

Cause classification	# of spills	Spill sizes (Bbls)
Process facility release	13	130, 50, 120, 104, 60, 1456, 125, 50, 50, 55, 400, 280, 75
Storage tank release	3	9935, 7000, 435
Structural failure	1	58
Hurricane/storm	2	75, 66
Collision	2	600, 108
Totals	21	

2.5.3 Statistical Variability and Multinomial Confidence Intervals

When examining spill causes the appropriate probability distribution is the multinomial. This is a multiple category generalization of the two category binomial distribution which in a set of random events counts the number of heads or tails, the number of successes or failures, etc. Because this is a relatively straight-forward application of descriptive statistics it is included in this chapter rather than Chapter 3.

One large difference from previously published work is the inclusion of confidence intervals on the multinomial proportions (Goodman, 1965). This will help clarify realistic limits for the accuracy of these proportions and any calculations that might be based on them. Table 2.23 shows a variety of confidence intervals for a specific cause and Table 2.24 shows 95% confidence intervals for all pipeline spill causes. In both tables the estimated proportion is simply divides the number of spills for the category (shown in Table 2.18) by the total number of spills (N = 36).

Table 2.23 Confidence Intervals for Third Party GOM Pipeline Spill Proportion with Estimated Proportion of 25.0% = 9/36

Confidence Level	Lower Confidence Limit	Upper Confidence Limit
80%	11.8%	38.2%
90%	9.6%	40.4%
95%	7.7%	42.3%
99%	3.8%	46.2%

Table 2.23 shows that even at a low or 80% confidence level for a high proportion category; the upper confidence limit is about 3.5 times the lower limit. At a high or 99% confidence level the upper limit is more than 10 times the lower limit. The 6 listed causes and the relatively small number of spills are the reason why these limits are relatively broad. Table 2.23 has been included to give a sense of how much difference the choice of a confidence level makes. In keeping with typical practice, Table 2.24 reports 95% confidence intervals for all causes.

Table 2.24 95% Confidence Intervals for GOM Pipeline Spill Cause Proportions

Estimated Proportion	Lower 95% Confidence Limit	Upper 95% Confidence Limit	GOM Specific Cause
25.0%	7.7%	42.3%	Third party damage
16.7%	1.8%	31.5%	Hurricanes
			Non-GOM Specific Cause
38.9%	19.4%	58.3%	Operational/mechanical
11.1%	0%	23.7%	Corrosion
5.6%	0%	14.7%	Natural: mud slide
2.8%	0%	9.3%	Unknown

Table 2.25 applies the same statistical approaches to the 31 spills summarized in Table 2.19 from Bercha (2002 & 2006).

Table 2.25 95% Confidence Intervals for Bercha (2002 & 2006) Pipeline Spill Cause Proportions

Estimated Proportion	Lower 95% Confidence Limit	Upper 95% Confidence Limit	Cause
12.9%	0%	27.3%	Corrosion
51.6%	30.1%	73.1%	Third party impact
12.9%	0%	27.3%	Operation impact
6.5%	0%	17.0%	Mechanical
12.9%	0%	27.3%	Natural hazard
3.2%	0%	10.8%	Unknown

The data in this study for platform spill cause (Table 2.21) is used to construct Table 2.26 which reports 95% confidence intervals for all causes.

Table 2.26 95% Confidence Intervals for GOM Platform Spill Cause Proportions

Estimated Proportion	Lower 95% Confidence Limit	Upper 95% Confidence Limit	
			GOM Specific Cause (N = 7)
9.0%	1.2%	16.7%	Hurricanes
			Non-GOM Specific Cause (N = 71)
44.9%	31.4%	58.4%	Equipment failure
29.5%	17.1%	41.8%	Human error
7.7%	0.5%	14.9%	Sea condition
6.4%	0%	13.0%	Collision
2.6%	0%	6.8%	External damage

Table 2.27 applies the same statistical approaches to the 21 spills summarized in Table 2.22 from Bercha (2002 & 2006).

Table 2.27 95% Confidence Intervals for Bercha (2002 & 2006) Platform Spill Cause Proportions

Estimated Proportion	Lower 95% Confidence Limit	Upper 95% Confidence Limit	Cause
61.9%	37%	86.6%	Process facility release
14.3%	0%	32.0%	Storage tank release
4.8%	0%	15.6%	Structural failure
9.5%	0%	24.4%	Hurricane/storm
9.5%	0%	24.4%	Collision

2.5.4   Differences Due to Time and Conditions

While the focus of this study is on the extrapolation of GOM data to the arctic, there are additional differences between the data and potential developments which are outside the scope of this study. While some of these have been mentioned before, their potential impact on these estimates requires some further discussion.

The GOM database analyzed here includes about four decades of data, and the extrapolation into the arctic will extend the time frame by several more decades. Over that period of time, there have been and will be advances in technology and regulation that can reasonably be expected to reduce the probability of oil spills. However, the effect of this is clearly not uniform across the various spill causes. For example, the understanding of corrosion, and the ability to monitor and control it are steadily advancing; along with the regulatory environment to improve in this area. On the other hand, the ability of an oil pipeline to withstand the impact of a dragging anchor or the ice keel of pack ice may not be advancing at the same rate.

While this study focuses on statistically extrapolating from the experience represented in the GOM data base to the arctic environment, this initial study cannot address all issues. This study can reasonably be expected to address, and it does address larger issues such as GOM or arctic unique hazards, such as trawling gear and strudel scour. The scope of this study does not address more subtle impacts. For example, the probability of human error is linked to working conditions, such as extreme cold or darkness, which are larger issues in the arctic.

There are also the impacts due to differences in the manner of development. Such differences include the typical platform size, water depth, and distance from shore and the typical pipeline diameter, length, water depth, and depth of burial (if any). These details are better addressed through engineering studies rather than this type of statistical analysis.

As these factors are outside the scope of this study, the approach taken is to assume that the net effect of them would leave the statistically calculated oil spill risk unchanged. Obviously, this assumption is simply for the purposes of this study, as those with greater knowledge of the factors will apply that knowledge to move beyond the limitations of this study.

2.5.5   Statistical Variability and Binomial Confidence Intervals

Instead of focusing on the individual spill causes which requires the use of a multinomial distribution, this problem can be thought of as involving two binomial probability distributions. For the application to the arctic, there is the binomial proportional split between arctic and "applicable or general" causes. For the GOM spill data, there is the binomial proportional split between GOM-specific causes and "applicable or general" causes.

Thus, for pipelines the spill cause analysis is simplified to estimating the proportion of GOM pipeline spills with causes that are relevant to the Beaufort and Chukchi Seas. Table 2.28 is based on a characterization of hurricane and third party impact causes as GOM specific (at least as compared with Beaufort and Chukchi Seas spills). Table 2.28 is based on the normal approximation to the binomial, which is covered in most introductory statistics texts and courses.

Exact binomial confidence limits (Clopper and. Pearson, 1934) implemented as Excel functions (Harper, 2005) are used to compute exact binomial confidence intervals used in some of the tables below and at various parts of subsequent chapters. The lower and upper confidence bounds are given below. Unlike the approximate normal based intervals, exact binomial confidence intervals are generally not symmetric. Normal based approximations to the binomial may not be accurate for small sample sizes or proportions that are close to 0 or 1.

$$p_L^\alpha(n,B) = \frac{B}{B+(n-B+1)f_{\alpha/2,\,2(n-B+1),\,2B}}$$
$$p_U^\alpha(n,B) = 1 - p_L^\alpha(n,n-B)$$

where B is the number of successes in the n Bernoulli trials and f_{γ,n_1,n_2} is the upper γ^{th} percentile of the F distribution with n_1 and n_2 degrees of freedom.

Table 2.29 provides the exact binomial confidence intervals that may be compared to the normal approximation intervals in Table 2.28. Since the proportion (p-bar in the table) is close to 50% the normal approximation is mainly limited by the small sample size in this case. The normal approximation is in this case too optimistic with tighter confidence intervals than given with the exact Table 2.29 intervals.

Table 2.28 Binomial Characterization of the Causes of Pipeline Oil Spills (Normal Approximation)

# general causes	21
# GOM specific causes	15
total	36
p-bar	58.3%
σ_p	0.082
±conf. int.	
80%	6.9%
90%	10.5%
95%	13.5%
99%	19.1%

Table 2.29 Exact Binomial Characterization of the Causes of Pipeline Oil Spills

# general causes	21
# GOM specific causes	15
total	36
p-bar	58.3%
σ_p	0.082
Conf. Int.	
80%	(46.3%, 69.6%)
90%	(43.3%, 72.3%)
95%	(40.8%, 74.5%)
99%	(35.9%, 78.5%)

For platforms the spill cause analysis is simplified to estimating the proportion of GOM platform spills with causes that are relevant to the Beaufort and Chukchi Seas. Table 2.30 uses the normal approximation to the binomial, and it is based on a characterization of hurricane causes as GOM specific (at least as compared with Beaufort and Chukchi Seas spills). Table 2.31 reports the same results but as exact confidence intervals. Once again the normal approximation is too optimistic though the main reason in this case is the closeness of the proportion p-bar to 100%. As the proportion gets close to 0% or 100%, the normal approximation variance gets unrealistically small.

All binomial confidence intervals used in subsequent chapters are based on the exact binomial Excel functions. This results in a more defensible approach to quantifying distribution based parameter uncertainty.

Table 2.30 Binomial Characterization of the Causes of Platform Spills (Normal Approximation)

# general causes	71
# GOM specific causes	7
total	78
p-bar	91.0%
σ_p	0.032
±conf. int.	
80%	2.7%
90%	4.1%
95%	5.3%
99%	7.5%

Table 2.31 Exact Binomial Characterization of the Causes of Platform Spills

# general causes	71
# GOM specific causes	7
total	78
p-bar	91.0%
σ_p	0.032
Conf. int.	
80%	(85.4%, 94.9%)
90%	(83.8%, 95.7%)
95%	(82.4%, 96.3%)
99%	(79.4%, 97.3%)

2.6 Arctic Hazards and Extrapolating to the Arctic Environment

Because some readers of this report will be relatively unfamiliar with Arctic specific hazards, this section is written at an introductory level. While these Arctic specific hazards are a key part of defining oil spill risk in the Arctic, this study's focus has been on the extension of statistical results from the GOM to the Arctic.

While much of the research cited here dates back to the 1970s and 1980s, there have been significant recent advances in knowledge driven by the Northstar and Liberty projects. The former is in production (14.4 Mbbl from 2001 to 2005 according to OCS Crude&Condensate Production 1954 to Estimated 2005 28April2006.xls transmitted by Cheryl Anderson). Northstar involves a subsea pipeline that has some to significant exposure to each of the hazards presented here. Because Northstar is placed on a man-made gravel island (Seal Island), the recent experience is more relevant to subsea pipelines than it is to oil platforms in the Arctic. Example differences between gravel islands and platforms include size, typical ice forces, do ships dock or anchor, and the use of ice roads vs. ships and helicopters.

A good summary of Northstar can be found in Owen et al. (2001), while more specific topics are addressed in Paulin et al. (2001), Leidersdorf et al. (2001), Dickins et al. (2001), and Miller (2001).

2.6.1 Ice Keel Gouging

As noted in Palmer and Niedoroda (2005),

"gouges are found almost everywhere in the Arctic, that they occur from shore to water depths of at least 40 m, that some gouges are very deep (> 5m) and wide (> 50 m), and that gouges are contemporary and not relic. A simple calculation shows that the force that the ice must apply to cut a deep gouge is very large, often of the order of 100 MN. It is not practicable to design a pipeline to withstand such a force."

While more recent work is also cited, the definitive work on ice keel gouging is still Weeks, et al. (1983, 1984). The scale of the effort and some key observations are summarized in the following quote from the 1984 reference (p. 229):

"... between the barrier islands and the 38-m isobath the deepest gouge among 20,313 measured along 1500 km of sampling track was 3.6m. In protected lagoons, on the other hand, the deepest gouge (0.7m) was much shallower (from a sample of 41 gouges obtained from 298 km of sampling track) and a large percentage of the 1-km segments examined (92%) contained no gouges at all."

The spatial distribution for this data is from Smith Bay in the west to near Camden Bay in the east with the heaviest concentration off-shore of the current North Slope on-shore infrastructure. This is the most likely area for initial off-shore developments.

One important parameter for ice keel gouging is the number of gouges per mile or per kilometer. For the gouge density, Weeks et al. (1983, p. 20) obtained an average of 5.2 gouges/km-year (with a range from 2.4 to 7.9 over 3 years). In addition, no relationship with water depth was found (for deeper water). The shallower segments in the lagoons had fewer gouges.

From 1974 to 1990 data on 5329 gouges was gathered in the Canadian Beaufort Sea (reported in Chayes et al. (2006). This showed a decreasing rate of gouging in deeper water (from about 1.5 gouges/km in about 8 m to about 0.22 gouges/km in 30 m of water). There are a variety of explanations that could be advanced for the differences between the Weeks and Chayes results, but resolution of this is outside the scope of this study. As the Weeks data represent a larger sample in the right spatial location, this study relies on the Weeks data set.

A second important parameter for ice keel gouging is the depth of the incision. Weeks et al. used the exponential distribution to model the probability of different incision depths. The parameter, λ, which is the inverse of the average incision depth, was found to depend on water depth. Specifically, the deeper the water was, then the deeper was the average incision depth (and the smaller was the λ). The relationship between water depth, z, and λ (both measured in meters) is shown in Equation 2.1. Note this equation is shown with the data it is derived from in Weeks et al. (1983, Figure 10 & 1984, Figure 4).

$$\lambda = 9.97e^{-0.04z}$$
(2.1)

More recently between 1996 and 1999, 48 ice gouges exceeding the minimum measurement threshold of 0.1 m were detected in the Northstar pipeline corridor (Leidersdorf, et al., 2001). These were all in shallower waters (< 12 m) and the maximum incision depth was 0.4 m. "In all four years, however, measurable gouges were confined to water depths exceeding 5 m." These results are consistent with the earlier work, and these results are limited to shallow water. Thus, this study will rely on the earlier work by Weeks et al. which includes deeper gouges and deeper water depths.

The work by Weeks et al. included the development of a probabilistic model for an ice keel gouge contacting the pipeline. Thus, rather than attempting to summarize a voluminous and detailed analysis, this study will simply rely on that probabilistic model. However, one key parameter of the probabilistic model is addressed in the data included in that original work. A key question is: what is the orientation of the ice gouge relative to the pipeline? If the ice gouge is angled to the pipeline then a gouge of a given length has a smaller probability of contacting the pipeline. Thus, the original example application is done at angles of 90° and 20°. This appears to have been done for illustrative purposes, and an angle must be chosen for this study.

In shallower waters the gouge orientation has more variability. However, "because the fast ice edge generally parallels the isobaths, ice-ice interactions tend to force the nearshore ice to drift parallel to the coast even when the free-drift direction is not exactly parallel with the coast." Since the principal ice movement in deeper waters is parallel to the coast and pipelines will generally be perpendicular to the coast, the angle between the pipeline and the ice gouge is best modeled as nearly perpendicular.

Other work on ice keel gouging includes
- Croasdale et al. (2005) which focuses on failure modes for the ice in ice keel gouging,
- Croasdale et al. (2001) which focuses on design for icebergs (on the Grand Banks),
- Morrison and Marcellus (1985) comparing Alaskan & Canadian Beaufort Sea scour data and methodologies,
- Wadhams (1977) which describes ice keels in the Arctic.

2.6.2 Strudel Scour
Strudel scours represent the removal of bottom material by the drainage of fresh water on top of the ice during the spring. The most thorough study and modeling of the phenomenon was done in May 2000 to support the proposed Liberty Development Pipeline (Blanchet, Cox, Leidersdorf, and Cornell, 2000) with review by Eschenbach (2001).

Based on that study and review, the following observations are made:
1. Concerns about strudel scour are the largest directly in front of river mouths, as the rivers are the source of the water on top of the ice. During spring flows not all of the water flows under the ice. Thus, the more distant pipeline routes are from river mouths, the less of a concern there is with strudel scour.

2. The width and depth of the strudel scour depends on the water depth.

   a. While scours do occur under ice that is bottom-fast, those scours are smaller in size. While their relative significance has not been verified, there are at least two limiting factors for shallow water strudel scours. First, because the ice is bottom-fast or nearly so, it cannot be depressed by the weight of water on top of the ice to form a pool of significant depth. Second, the limited space under the ice, can limit the ability of water to flow away from the strudel scour.

   b. For the Liberty Pipeline Data Set, the majority of the strudel scours occurred in 5 to 10 feet of water. In water deeper than this, the strudel scours were shallower. Essentially, the water between the ice and the bottom is dissipating the erosive force of the water draining through the scour. A second possible effect is the "relief" provided by water draining through strudel features closer to shore. While the water depth limits may vary with the volume of water being discharged by a particular river in a particular year, further data gathering and analysis could define whether a 12', 15', or 20' water depth represents a limit to the area of concern for strudel scour. Note that in strudel scour studies linked to the Northstar development (Leidersdorf, 2001) "all of the strudel scour depths greater than 1.5 m were found to occur in water depths less than 4 m."

   c. A second limit for the water depth in which strudel scour can occur is the maximum extent of the "over-flood" limit. For example, Blanchet et al. (2000, p. 130) identifies a maximum over-flood extent of 3.3 miles off-shore with an average over 11 years of 2.59 miles (2.79 typo in final draft). This was in the area of the Sagavanirktok, Kadleroshilik, and Shaviovik Rivers. As another example measured a different way, Walker (1974) reported that overflood off of the Colville River extended only to the 3-6 m water depth in the Colville delta in three years of observations.

3. While scour occurrence statistics can be calculated, the water depth limits imply that only a limited portion of any pipeline length is truly exposed to strudel scour. A pipeline from an off-shore platform generally starts at the deepest depth it is exposed to and goes relatively directly to shore. Thus, it is much more nearly perpendicular to the shore, than parallel with it. Thus, the question for determining the concern with strudel scour, is how much of this pipeline is in for example, 5 to 12 or 15 or 20 feet of water?

More recent work by Leidersdorf, Hearon, and Swank (2006) included data that suggests pipelines with hot oil may induce strudel scours – at least in shallow waters. "Given this relatively low frequency, an unexpected finding was the occurrence of five scour depressions in close proximity to the Northstar pipeline alignment. Four of the depressions were relatively small features in water depths less than 1.5 m, suggesting that the heat radiating from the pipelines predisposes the ice to strudel formation in shallow water." While not advanced in the paper, another possible explanation is the trapping of along-shore flow of overflood waters when an ice road is built over the pipeline (see Trefrey et al., 2004, Figure 3-28b, p. 45).

Strudel scour alone does not cause a pipeline spill. Rather it represents the possibility of uncovering enough of a buried pipeline, which could lead to failure modes such as upheaval buckling, or even digging out underneath a pipeline to create a free-span. Thus, probability models must consider the density of strudel scours and the probability of scours of sufficient dimension to uncover a critical length of pipeline.

Blanchet et al. (2000, Table 3.10) calculated a density at the Liberty location of 4.0 scours/mile^2-year for 1997 data, 1.1 for 1998 data, and 2.9 for the combined data.

There are several issues that cannot be addressed in this study for these data from Blanchet et al. First, it is not known how representative these values are of other potential pipeline locations. Second, while detailed strudel scour information from other years was not available, analysis of photo imagery indicated that in 11 years of data, the 1997 and 1998 years had the smallest extent of overflooding at this location. (Overflooding extent represents how far out to sea the freshwater has flowed on top of the ice.) See also Dickins et al. (2001) for more discussion of overflooding.

To calculate the probability of uncovering a "critical length," it is also necessary to know (Liberty values used shown in parentheses) the following:
    Depth of burial (8')
    Probability distribution for width of scour (see Blanchet et al. 2000)
    Relationship between width and depth of scour (assumed 45° slope)
    Length of pipeline vulnerable to strudel scours (1.8 miles)
    Critical length of uncovered pipe (100').

In the sensitivity analysis, use of a 27° slope rather than 45° was tested, and it reduced the probabilities by an order of magnitude. Perhaps due to granular sediments in the area of the Liberty pipeline route for those data points with width and depth measurements, the calculated average slope values were much lower. These were average slopes for individual scours ranging from 1° to 27° off the Sagavanirktok River, 1° to 14° off the Kadleroshilik River, and 1° to 5° off the Shaviovik River (Blanchet et al., 2000, p. 90).

As a first order approximation within the limits of that data, it is reasonable to believe that likelihood of larger scours from years with more overflooding is balanced by the conservatism between the 45° assumed average slope, and the measured average slopes that were typically much less than 27° value used in the sensitivity analysis.

With these parameters the probability of a free span greater than 0' was calculated to be 3.8×10^{-4} and the probability of a free span $\geq 100'$ was calculated to be 5.2×10^{-5} (Blanchet et al., 2000, p. ix).

2.6.3   Upheaval Buckling
Upheaval buckling is more of an issue in the Arctic than in other locations, because the principal force is due to thermal expansion of the pipeline when filled with warmer oil as compared to its

temperature during construction – which is colder in the Arctic. However, for a spill to occur, this must result in fracture or buckling – not just result in pipe movement.

As the engineering expertise and assumptions to model this are not within the scope of this study, it is assumed that the critical length defined for the probability of a strudel scour has appropriately considered the probability of upheaval buckling. Thus, the probability of upheaval buckling is assumed to equal the probability of a strudel scour.

Assuming that the probability of upheaval buckling is equal to the probability of a problem due to strudel scour requires the assumption that design and construction of any buried pipeline has a sufficient margin of safety that upheaval buckling does not occur on its own. Note that if a pipeline is not restrained by burial in a trench, thermal expansion can be accommodated by side to side rather than vertical movements.

2.6.4 Thaw Settlement

Thaw settlement has been an issue for portions of the Trans-Alaska pipeline, where warm oil has melted permafrost and ice lenses below the pipe. This sinking of the pipe can be likened to an electric line that sags due to the weight of ice on it until the line snaps.

Erosion due to the melting of permafrost is common along the North Slope of Alaska, thus the problems with thaw settlement start on-shore, can be high at pipeline landing sites, and can extend off shore due to subsea permafrost. This subsea permafrost off the North Slope of Alaska has long been recognized as a potential problem for oil and gas infrastructure. Nearest to the shore, the ice is frozen to the bottom and permafrost can form just as it does on-shore, but as detailed in Miller (2001) salt concentrations may be high and large ice lens and ice bonding may be rare. Farther off-shore permafrost does not extend all the way to the soil/water boundary. More importantly, the further off-shore that you are the deeper into the soil are the boundaries between unfrozen soil, seasonally frozen soil, and permafrost. It is only in permafrost that you find ice lens which when they melt lead to the most extreme cases of thaw settlement.

This suggests that once a pipeline is "far" enough off-shore, then thaw settlement is not likely to be a problem. While more data and engineering analysis of heat flows is required to determine how "far" off-shore this is, there is substantial work on subsea permafrost that has been done. For example one approach to defining the problem is the mapping of permafrost depths. Work of this type for the North Slope includes Osterkamp and Harrison (1977 and 1976), Neave and Sellman (1982), Rogers et al. (1975), Sellman et al. (1989), and Barry (1989).

Paulin et al. (2001) describes how thaw settlement was an issue near-shore for the Northstar project, and the modeling and over-trenching with thaw stable backfill that was done (see also Owen and Miller, 2001).

A potential complication in some less expected locations may be the presence of relic permafrost. In the Laptic Sea of eastern Siberia, where the OCS is wider than is Alaska's, relic permafrost from when the sea levels were lower and the shelf was land has been found (Romanovsky, 2006).

As there is no statistical basis for estimating the probability of an oil spill due to thaw settlement, this study will not attempt to do so.

While it is outside the scope of this study, it is worth noting that if a clear design standard will be applied to this phenomenon, then the design standard is potentially another way to establish a spill probability. For example, suppose that the design standard is for 1 spill every 100 or every 1000 years. Such values can be converted into the probability of a spill.

3 Gulf of Mexico Spill Rate Estimation

3.1 Introduction to Analysis of Data

This chapter covers numerous statistical analyses and often involves fitting theoretical statistical distributions to the data sets described in Chapter 2. The primary focus of the distribution fitting is either on modeling the inter-spill distributions or on the volume of the spills. The inter-spill distributions lead directly to assessing if the assumption of a Poisson distribution is appropriate for the OCS and GOM data. The Poisson process assumption has been attacked in some reviews (Givens 2002 & Zeh 2002) of the Anderson & LaBelle (2000) publication. Because of the criticality of the Poisson assumption, Section 3.2 will focus on the general use of the Poisson distribution before subsequent sections assess the applicability of the Poisson for the OCS data.

After the initial Poisson section, the data from Anderson & LaBelle (2000) are analyzed for both inter-spill and volume aspects in Section 3.3. Applications of the exact Poisson confidence intervals described in Section 3.2 are applied to these data. Pipeline spills are covered in Section 3.3, and platform spills are covered in Section 3.4.

Sections 3.5 and 3.6, respectively for pipelines and platforms, introduce extensions to the work in Anderson & LaBelle (2000). One form of extension is using smaller thresholds, such as spills ≥ 50 bbls, for data selection as described in Chapter 2. Results of integrating distributions based on differing thresholds is given, as it may be more accurate to use larger data sets to predict even just those spills of at least 1000 bbl. These sections also address a key issue of different exposure variables and tests if the Poisson assumption is relevant over time, production volumes, pipeline miles, and platform numbers.

Minor adjustments in spill volumes are sometimes made to avoid duplicate values. For example if there are four spill volumes of 50 bbl, these are changed to 50 bbl, 51 bbl, 52 bbl, and 53 bbl. If many volume ties are found at say 50 bbl, these are changed to 50 bbl, 50.1 bbl, 50.2, etc. Theoretically, the probability of any two continuous values being identical is zero, and these minor adjustments avoid some technical issues such as the stacking of points on a probability plot and do not impact the relevance of the findings presented here.

3.2 Poisson Distribution

3.2.1 Poisson Concerns about Exposure Variables

The Poisson distribution is often used in counting processes in which events occur over some elapsed exposure variable. Often the exposure variable is time and the Poisson is used to estimate the likelihood of so many events over a time period of interest. For example, what is the likelihood of 15 phone calls in a ½ hour time period at a call center? Even if a Poisson is appropriate, does the mean arrival rate of phone calls change over time? If the arrival rate changes over time, such as spills becoming less likely due to better regulation and management, then the Poisson process is defined by statisticians as non-stationary.

Time is only one of many potential exposure variables. One of the beauties of the Poisson is that it is flexible over both time and space, and that it can be measured in units of produced oil, pipeline-miles, or number of platform-years.

One issue with testing the Poisson assumption is that few discrete distributions are in common practice compared to the many continuous distributions used. Additionally fewer methods exist to test discrete distribution assumptions than for continuous distributions. The approach undertaken in Chapter 3 indeed relies on a link between the Poisson and a continuous distribution.

Generally found in calculus based probability and statistics text is the relationship between the discrete Poisson distribution that can realize only values of 0, 1, 2 … for counting events and the continuous exponential distribution that can realize any observed values ≥ 0. In such texts it is shown that if and only if the inter-event times are exponentially distributed then the process generating the discrete events is a Poisson process. Thus one can test the inter-event times to see if a theoretical exponential distribution adequately fits the observed data. If so, then the assumption of a Poisson distribution for the events is justified. As discussed earlier there are generally more ways to test a goodness-of-fit question when the distribution is continuous.

In the context of the OCS data, inter-event is inter-spill for each of the potential exposure variables. For both pipeline spills and platform spills, three exposure variables are analyzed. Time is the first exposure variable and is tested in subsequent sections of Chapter 3. A second exposure variable has been production volume in Bbbl. A third exposure variable is pipeline mile-years in thousands of miles (KMiles). For platforms the third exposure variable is platform-years.

Testing the Poisson assumption via an exponential goodness-of-fit requires that the days between spills, or the production volume between spills, or the number of pipeline mile-years between spills, etc. be computed. If these inter-spill amounts are found to be adequately modeled by an exponential distribution, then using a Poisson for the spill events is justified.

Data given in Chapter 2 show the annual production volumes and annual pipeline miles. To compute the volume and pipeline mile-years between spills, the number of days in each year of the study horizon that capture the inter-spill time is computed. Assuming that the production volumes and mileage are relatively constant with any given year, the Bbbl of production and KMiles of pipeline mile-years represented by the inter-spill time period are computed. These numbers are then input to the corresponding exponential goodness-of-fit tests. If the exponential fits these inter-spill amounts, then a Poisson assumption is justified for that exposure variable.

3.2.2 Exact Poisson Confidence Intervals

Once a Poisson distribution has been justified, one can begin to estimate the spill rate. The rate is merely the mean of the Poisson distribution. Concern still must exist to see if a time varying Poisson mean (also known as a non-stationary Poisson process or a non-homogeneous Poisson process) is needed. For the time being in this section it is assumed that the assumption of a stationary non-changing mean is appropriate though this assumption is examined in Section 3.6.

Bounding the uncertainty in a parameter estimate is standard statistical practice, and it has been mentioned in several reviews. Quantification of this uncertainty is based on the level of confidence desired and the appropriate method for the parameter of interest. The parameter of interest for OCS is the estimate of the mean of the Poisson process. This is the rate at which events (spills) are estimated to occur. As discussed earlier this rate depends on the selection of an exposure variable (time, production volume, pipeline mile-years, platform-years are used in Chapter 3).

While not mandatory it is common practice to develop 95% confidence intervals. For the Poisson distribution the corresponding interval should not be developed using standard normal based confidence interval approaches. That is, one should not break an exposure variable – say the continuous variable production volume in Bbbl into individual bins from which a mean and standard deviation are computed to form a confidence interval. Exact methods for Poisson confidence intervals have been documented (in obscure places admittedly) for many years and are given below. These may easily be computed in Excel though with a caution (Buchan, 2004 on the web at http://www.nwpho.org.uk/sadb/Poisson%20CI%20in%20spreadsheets.pdf) due to an Excel function inaccuracy that does not impact the OCS application.

From Johnson and Kotz (1969, pp. 96) are the formulas in Equation 3.1 where λ (the more common Poisson mean notation) is used instead of the θ used in Johnson and Kotz. The first formula for λ_L represents an exact lower confidence interval for the mean spill rate λ while the second for λ_U is the formulation for the upper confidence interval. Taken together these form the 95% confidence interval used later in Chapter 3 where α is set to 0.05. These confidence intervals are based on the chi-square (χ^2) distribution.

$$\lambda_L = \left(\frac{\frac{1}{2}\chi^2_{2x,\frac{\alpha}{2}}}{\sum Exposure\,Variable} \right); \quad \lambda_U = \left(\frac{\frac{1}{2}\chi^2_{2(x+1),1-\frac{\alpha}{2}}}{\sum Exposure\,Variable} \right) \tag{3.1}$$

Generally in statistics increasing the sample size decreases the width of confidence intervals. In this case, the subscript x is the number of spills, and the basis for the number of degrees of freedom for the chi-square variable. Then the amount of the exposure variable is in the denominator of Equation 3.1. To check that this formula behaves as expected, assume that the number of spills and the amount of exposure are both doubled (which keeps the spill rate constant). Doubling the number of degrees of freedom more than doubles the lower χ^2 value, so the lower limit goes up and is closer to the estimated average, since the exposure doubled. In like fashion doubling the number of degrees of freedom less than doubles the upper value, so the upper limit has decreased. Thus, a larger sample at the same spill rate has a tighter or narrower confidence interval.

The resulting confidence interval will generally be tighter than the inaccurate intervals based on dividing the exposure variable into artificial subunits.

3.2.3   Comparison of MMS and Exact Poisson Confidence Intervals

Below is a comparison of the 95% confidence intervals found on the web at http://www.mms.gov/eppd/sciences/osmp/pdfs/ConfidenceIntervals2.pdf and exact Poisson confidence intervals. Both are endeavoring to create 95% confidence intervals for the pipeline spill rates between the time periods given in the below Table 3.1.

Table 3.1 95% Confidence Interval Comparison Based on Anderson & LaBelle (2000) Pipeline Data with Production Volume as the Exposure Variable

OCS Pipelines	# Spills	Volume (Bbbl)	Rate (Spills/Bbbl)	MMS Confidence Interval	Exact 95% Poisson Confidence Interval
1964-1999	16	12.00	1.333	(0.54, 2.12)	(0.76, 2.17)
1985-1999	8	5.81	1.377	(0.00, 2.77)	(0.59, 2.71)

The intervals reported on the web are based on dividing the production volume into 1 Bbbl units and then computing the confidence intervals based on N = 12 (for 1964 – 1999) assumed independent observations. With small sample statistics, this approach would also typically assume that the data are from a normal distribution. This introduces an unnecessary binning process and one that may be inaccurate for non-integer Bbbl. The associated statistical procedure may allow the possibility of negative values in the confidence intervals which are then set to zero. The exact approach with results seen in the final column of Table 3.1 is based on sound conceptual theoretical underpinnings and is also easier to compute.

3.2.4   Compound Poisson Distribution

A topic worth mentioning is the compound Poisson distribution (also called a mixture of Poisson distributions). Clark & Harper (2000, beginning pp. 113) discuss this topic from an application perspective while Johnson & Kotz (1969, beginning pp. 111) provide a more theoretical foundation.

For example, if there are multiple spill modes each represented by a Poisson, then the combined spill probability may be represented by a combination of individual Poisson distributions. The weighting function for each individual Poisson depends on the appropriate assumptions that should be based on sound engineering and/or statistical rationale. In future work, this could potentially be employed in the GOM to Arctic transition. It would have to fold in both the uncertainty in the Poisson rates and the uncertainty in the proportions (weighting functions) for the different spill modes.

3.3   Pipeline Spill Analyses Based on Spills ≥ 1000 bbl (1964 – 1999)

Section 3.3 covers pipeline spills using the data found in Anderson & LaBelle (2000). Both inter-spill and volumes are analyzed. In a similar vein Section 3.4 examines platform spills using the data from Anderson & LaBelle (2000).

3.3.1 Pipeline Inter-Spill Distribution Analysis

A variety of statistical hypothesis tests and graphical procedures were used in the analyses supporting Chapter 3; however, the presentation in this chapter will often be limited to the two graphical based procedures found to be the most understandable and informative. These figures will be supplemented by other results when felt necessary to support a given situation. We note for the non-statistician that fitting statistical distributions to data is both an art and a science. Different statistical tests may give differing results and an engineering statistician must be willing to blend these sources to find the most logical choice.

Figures 3.1 and 3.2 are based on the 16 pipeline spills of at least 1000 bbl found in Table 2 of Anderson & LaBelle (2000) (also in Table 2.1 of this report). For each spill the inter-spill time in days was computed resulting in 15 inter-spill times. As this is approximately a 31 year time interval (1967 – 1998), the mean inter-spill time is 773.6 days (a little over 2 years). This excludes an inter-spill time for the final spill of July 23, 1999 as there is no subsequent spill date.

Figure 3.1 is a probability plot for an exponential distribution. The blue lines represent 95% confidence limits on the modeled exponential distribution while the red circles represent the actual observed data. The AD (Anderson-Darling) goodness-of-fit test statistic of 0.337 is not meaningful by itself; however, the associated p-value of 0.739 clearly indicates that an exponential distribution adequately fits the data based on this test statistic. P-values ≥ 0.05 indicate that the associated goodness-of-fit test is not rejected at the 95% confidence level.

Statistical tests are aids and should not be relied on in isolation. Graphical assessments are more important and some language is needed to represent the application of professional assessment. While somewhat colloquial, this report uses the acronym of TLAR (That Looks About Right) in line with what may be approaching nearly a century of use. In Clark and Harper (2000a) the acronym is credited to Walt Giffin who introduced it to the authors in their graduate statistical work. The TLAR (That Looks About Right) is a visual assessment of how the empirical or observed data fits a given theoretical model. Data analysis should always involve visual assessments as this provides a medium easily understood by almost anyone and the human pattern recognition capability is a needed tool for identifying trends, outliers, and data requiring detailed analyses. While it does take a trained eye with necessary experience to fully assess such visual goodness-of-fit measures, it allows the selection of statistical distributions in those cases where numerical statistics are not sufficient to make a final determination. Figure 3.1 along with the Anderson-Darling results support an exponential distribution.

Figure 3.2 further supports an exponential distribution for the inter-spill times based. The smooth line represents the theoretical cumulative distribution function (cdf) for the hypothesized distribution (exponential in this case) versus the step function empirical cdf. A visual TLAR comparison finds these two lines in good agreement. Since these inter-spills times are adequately modeled by an exponential, as explained in Section 3.2.1, the assumption of a Poisson distribution over time is justified.

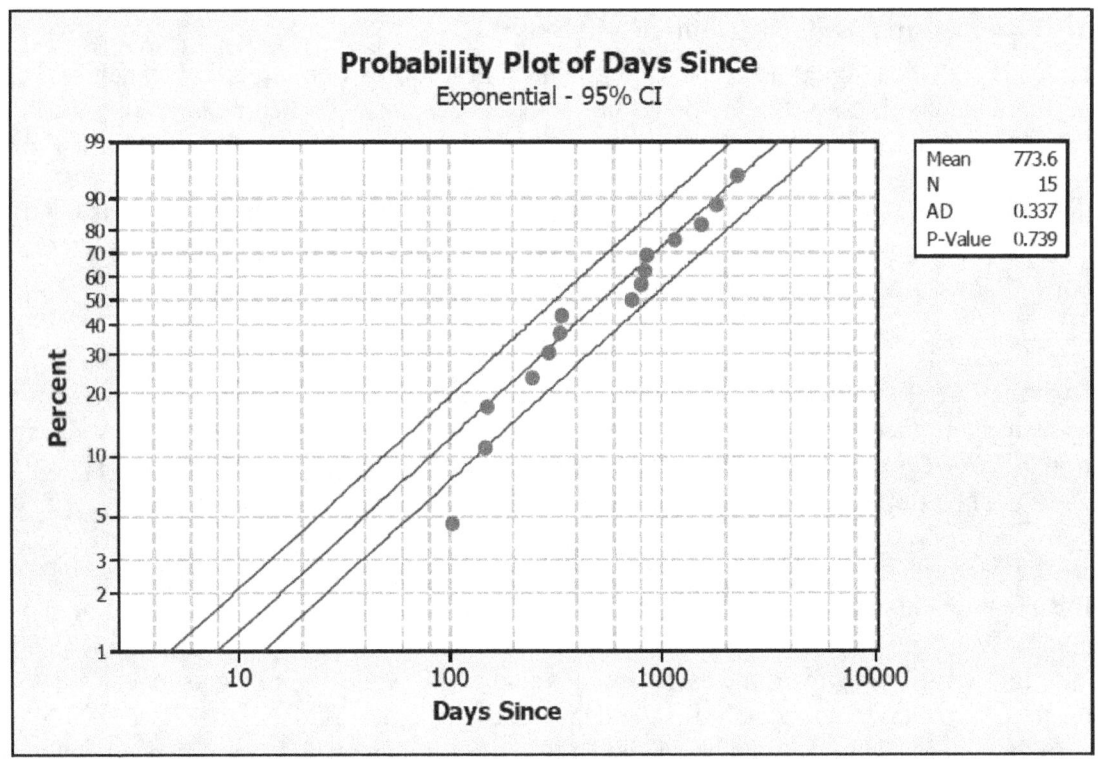

Figure 3.1 Exponential Probability Plot of Pipeline Inter-Spill Times Using Anderson & LaBelle (2000) Data

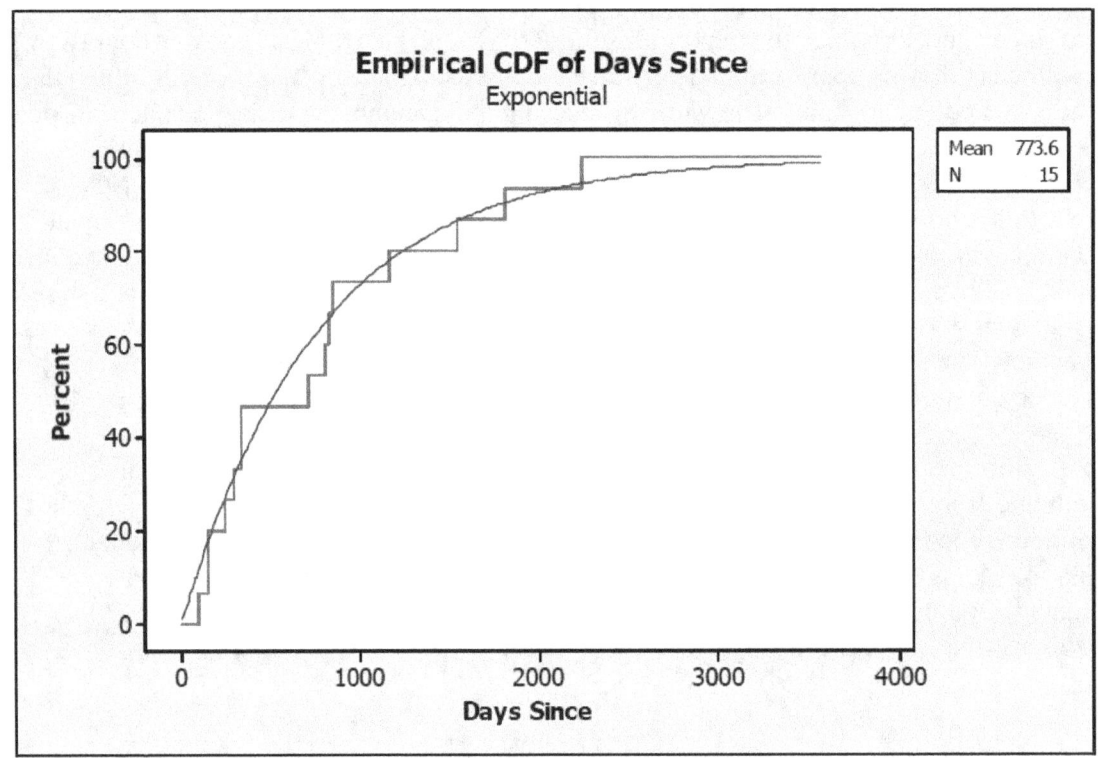

Figure 3.2 Exponential Empirical CDF Plot of Pipeline Inter-Spill Times Using Anderson & LaBelle (2000) data

3.3.2 Poisson Rate for ≥ 1000 bbl Spills

The last section examined and affirmed the validity of the Poisson assumption for larger spills when using time as the exposure variable. Table 3.2 defines the rate and confidence intervals for that data set and a later subset. The later subset 1985-1999 inter-spill times have also been found to be well fit by an exponential distribution (though the results are not shown) and thus the application of the Poisson distribution for quantification of spill rates is justified.

Table 3.2 Spill Rate per Year for ≥ 1000 bbl Spills

Time Period	# Spills	Exposure Variable	Sum Exposure Variable	Rate (Spills/year)	LCL	UCL
1964-1999	16	Integer Years	36	0.444	0.254	0.722
1985-1999	8	Integer Years	15	0.533	0.230	1.051

Intuitively, one would expect the average rate for the Poisson distribution (spills/year) to be the inverse of the average rate for the exponential inter-arrival time between spills. This is only approximately true, because the inter-arrival distribution data have 1 less data point, and it ignores the time before the first spill and after the last spill. Thus for 1964-1999 inverting the average 773.6 days between spills, and converting from days to years equals 0.472 spills/year (= 365/773.6) rather than the 0.444 spills per year shown in Table 3.2.

Because of its importance, the exact relationship between the Poisson and exponential is detailed and illustrated for three exposure variables in Section 3.5.2. This important relationship allows the better set of statistical tools for continuous distributions to be used effectively; otherwise, less precise goodness of fits goodness of fit tests for discrete distributions such as the Poisson would require binning of the data and more serious sample size concerns.

For example, Minitab 14 (the current version of this well known statistical package) does probability plots along with the Anderson-Darling goodness of fit test for numerous continuous distributions such as the exponential and Weibull distributions used often in this report. No goodness of fit for a Poisson existed in Mintab until summer 2005 in which a downloadable patch that upgrades the user to Minitab 14.2 adds a chi-square goodness of fit test for the Poisson. However chi-square goodness of fit tests requiring binning of the data, which is somewhat arbitrary, so that different users may get varying results. Additionally the chi-square goodness of fit tests requires minimum expected bin frequencies to be valid. A common standard is an expected bin count of at least 5 observations. Thus, 12 bins of one Bbbl of production would require roughly 60 spills for a quality application of the Chi square test. This is likely to be a problem for the small data sets available.

3.3.3 Pipeline Spill Volume Distribution Analysis

A brief overview of the Weibull distribution is included here. The cumulative distribution function (cdf) in all of the empirical cdf plots, such as Figure 3.2, is the probability of the random variable being ≤ some value. The cdf is represented in the statistical literature by F(x). For continuous distributions such as the exponential or Weibull, this is the integral of the f(x) that represents the probability density function (pdf). The random variable x in F(x) is whatever variable is being modeled such as spill volumes. For example F(5000) = P(x ≤ 5000) or probability that a spill volume would be less than or equal to 5000 bbl. For the Weibull distribution F(x) is given below where v, α, β represent the threshold (or Thresh on the plots), scale, and shape parameters given in the Minitab probability and empirical cdf Weibull plots.

$$F(x) = 1 - \exp\left[-\left(\frac{x-v}{\alpha} \right)^{\beta} \right], for\ x \geq v;\ 0\ otherwise.$$

where exp *implies e raised to a power.*

The complementary cumulative distribution function (ccdf) is 1 – F(x). For example P(x > 5000 bbl) = 1 – F(5000), and it is the probability that a given spill will exceed 5,000 bbl. Since each Weibull Minitab plot gives us values for Thresh, Scale, and Shape or v, α, β it is relatively easy to compute either F(x) or 1 – F(x).

The analysis reported here supports the Weibull distribution (parameters for shape, location, and threshold given in figures) as an adequate model for the sixteen pipeline spill volumes in Anderson & LaBelle (2000). This fit of a Weibull distribution is not as good as subsequent Weibull fits for volumes in other sections of this chapter primarily due to the inclusion of the 1967 spill volume of 160,638 bbl that is not in the time period covered in other sections. The Weibull is the best fit based on the Input Analyzer's Squared Error criterion (Kelton, Sadowski, and Sturrock, 2004, chapter 4), is not rejected by the Input Analyzer's Kolmogorov-Smirnov goodness-of-fit test (p-value > 0.15), and looks reasonable visually in the probability plot below in Figure 3.3 as well as the empirical cdf plot in Figure 3.4. It does not pass the Anderson-Darling test as seen in Figure 3.3; however, the other evidence leads to the overall acceptance of the Weibull distribution.

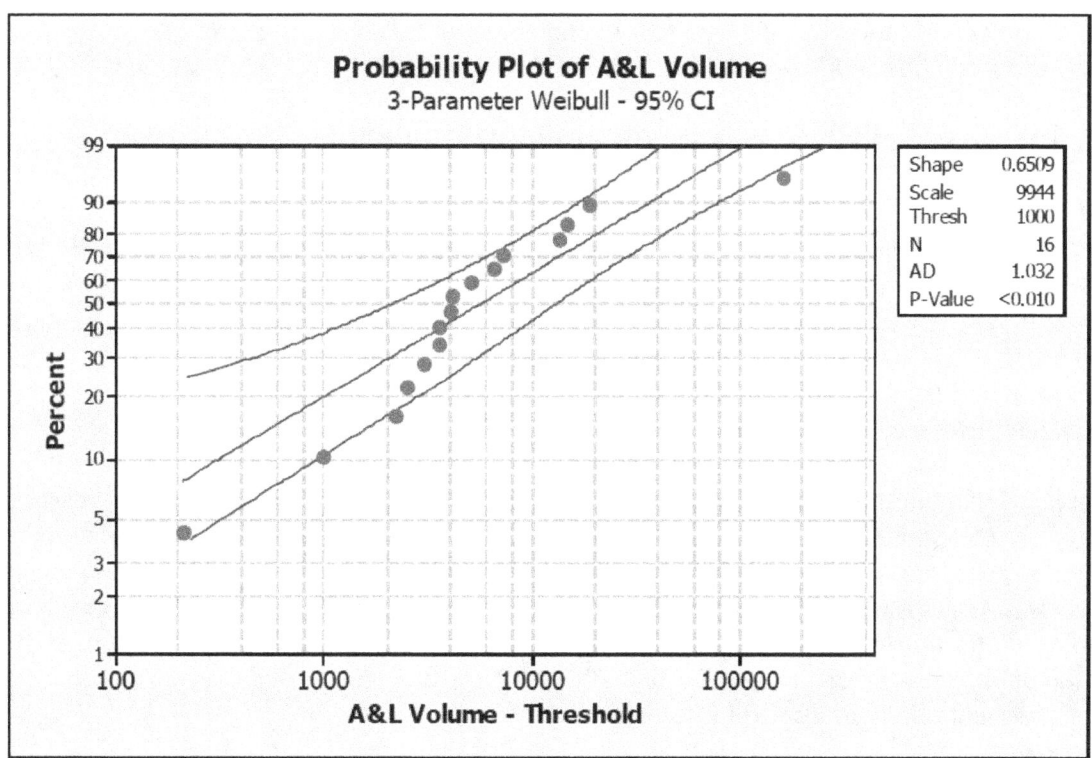

Figure 3.3 Weibull Probability Plot of Pipeline Spill Volumes Using Anderson & LaBelle (2000) Data

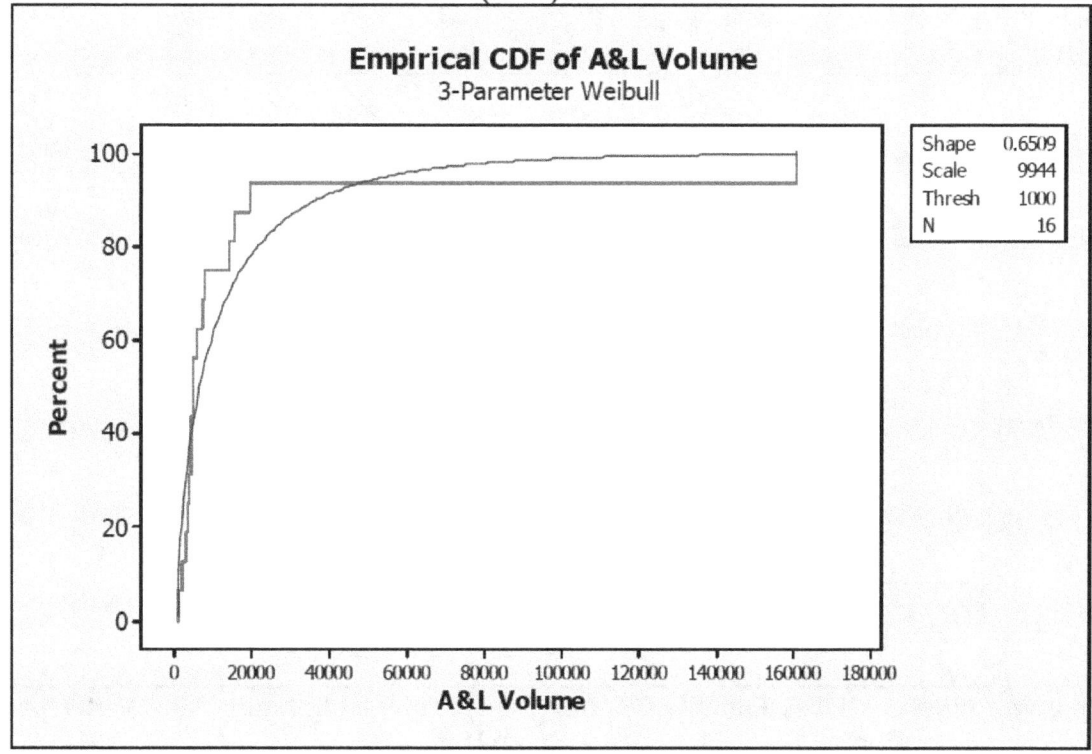

Figure 3.4 Weibull Empirical CDF Plot of Pipeline Spill Volumes Using Anderson & LaBelle (2000) Data

The Weibull distribution will be used considerably later in this chapter to provide linkages between various thresholds (e.g. 50 bbl, 100 bbl, 500 bbl, & 1000 bbl) choices in data sets.

3.4 Platform Spill Analyses Based on Spills ≥ 1000 bbl (1964 – 1999)

3.4.1 Platform Inter-Spill Distribution Analysis

The OCS Platform Inter-spill data are examined in this section using the data from Anderson & LaBelle (2000, p. 306) (also Table 2.6 in this report). Eleven platform spills occurred between 1964 and 1980. None occurred between 1980 and the publication of the Anderson & Labelle 2000 article. The assumption of a Poisson distribution for the frequency of spills based on time is tested in this section. This is addressed by examining if the exponential distribution adequately fits the inter-spill times.

Figures 3.5 and 3.6 show that the inter-spill times in days between 1964 and 1980 are reasonably fit by an exponential distribution implying the Poisson arrivals are reasonable over this time frame. In addition to the visual assessment, the Anderson-Darling goodness-of-fit test (p-value = 0.496) is not rejected. Thus modeling the process (at least based on time) by a Poisson distribution for this time period is justified, but there have been no platform spills between 1980 and the publication of Anderson & LaBelle (2000). How this lack of platform spills impacts the Poisson assumption is addressed in Section 3.4.2.

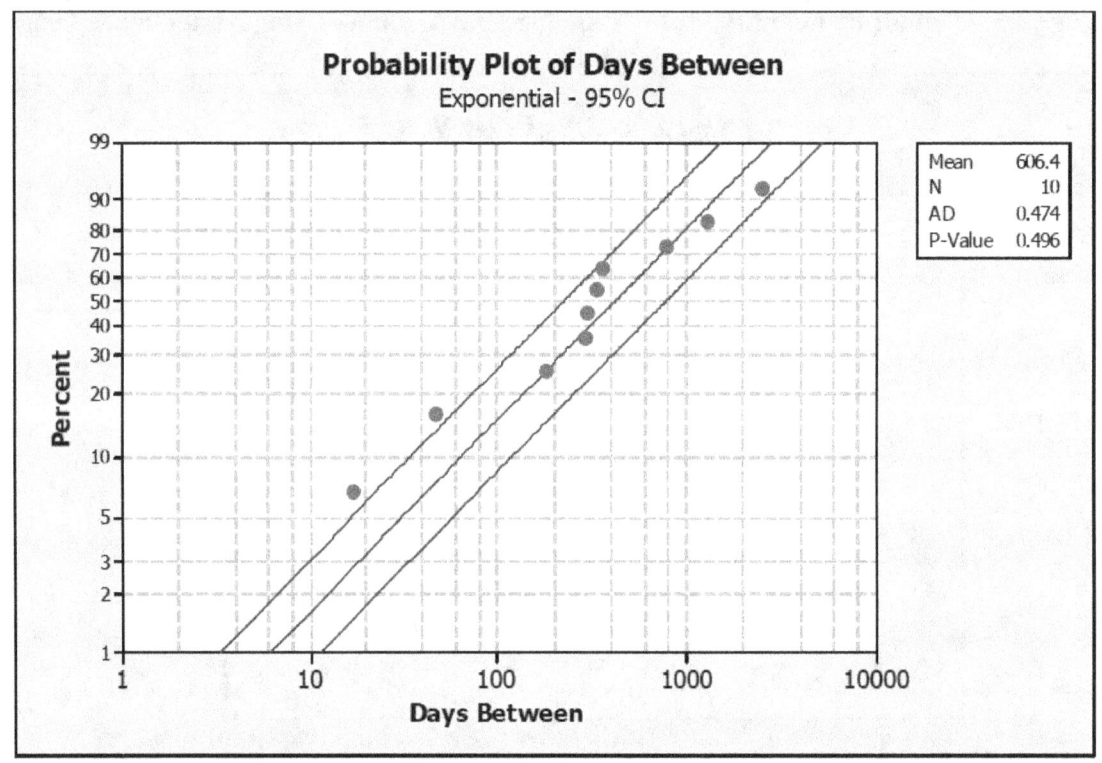

Figure 3.5 Exponential Probability Plot of Platform Inter-Spill times Using Anderson & LaBelle (2000) Data

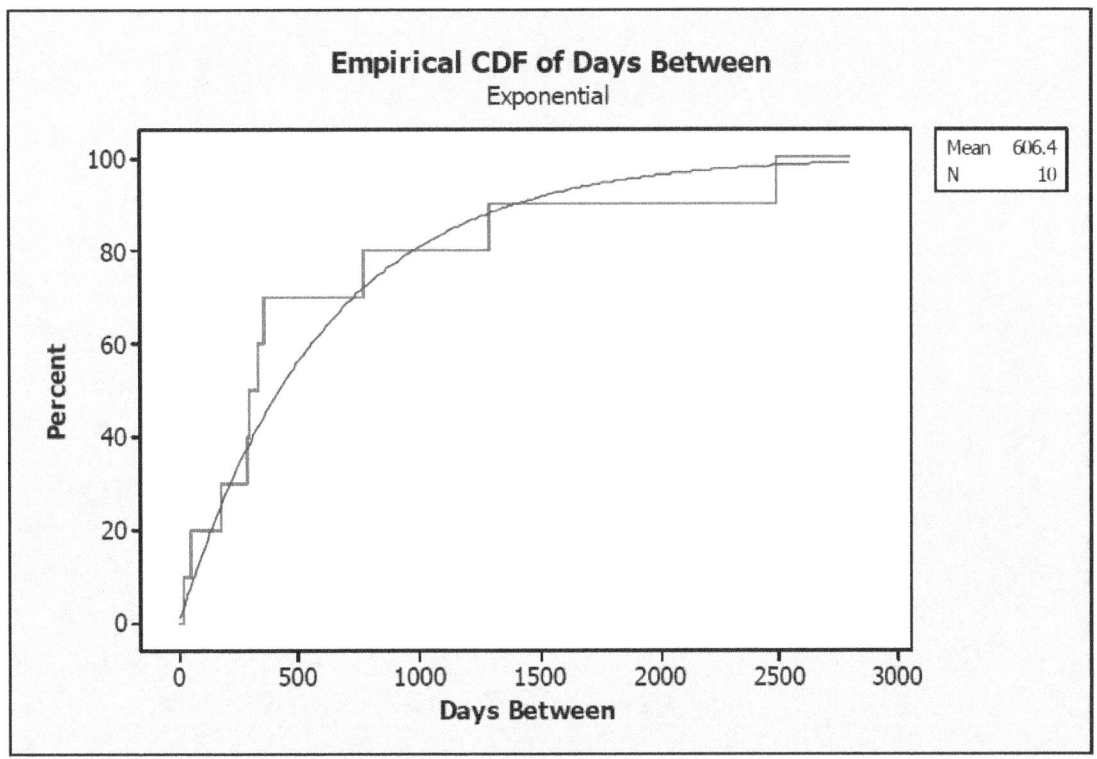

Figure 3.6 Exponential Empirical CDF Plot of Platform Inter-Spill times Using Anderson & LaBelle (2000) Data

3.4.2 Platform Inter-Spill Distribution Analysis with Hypothetical 1/1/1999 Spill

Given that no spills have occurred between 1980 and the publication of Anderson & LaBelle (2000), it is necessary to examine the applicability of a Poisson distribution. A hypothetical spill was added on 1/1/1999 to examine this issue. Figure 3.7 clearly shows that the exponential distribution no longer adequately fits the data with this hypothetical platform spill added. Supplemental statistical support is provided by the failing Anderson-Darling test (p-value = 0.017) though more weight should be given to failing the TLAR comparison.

Another way to approach this issue is to ask if a Poisson adequately fits the 1964-1980 data, what would that particular Poisson distribution tell us about the subsequent 19 years through 1999? For the 11 platform spills over the 16.61 year time frame in Anderson & LaBelle (2000) the annual spill rate is 0.662 platform spills/year. For a 19 year time period after this, the expected number of spills would be 12.58 spills versus the 0 spills observed. More specifically using a Poisson distribution with this mean, the probability of 0 spills in 19 years would be only 0.000003, i.e., a very unlikely situation. Thus it is concluded that the use of a single Poisson for platform spills over the time period from 1964 to 1999 is not currently justified (separate Poisson distributions for different intervals may be appropriate) for spills $\geq 1,000$ bbl.

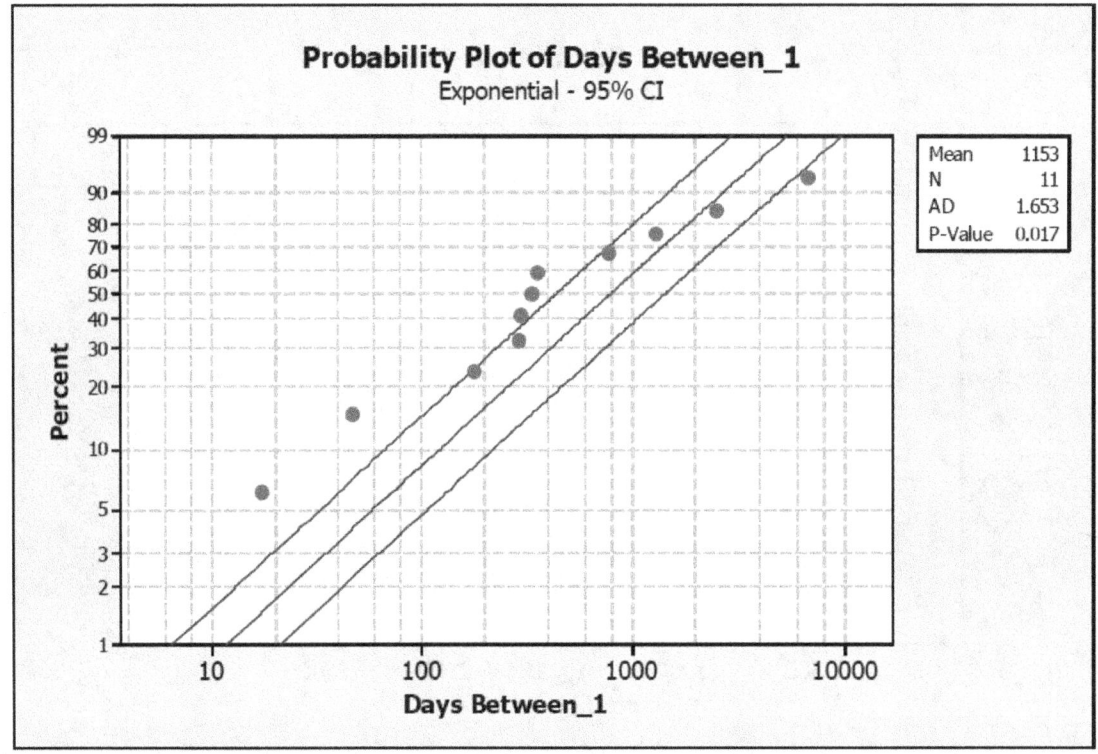

Figure 3.7 Exponential Probability Plot of Platform Inter-Spill times Using Anderson & LaBelle (2000) Data Supplemented with a Hypothetical Spill on 1/1/1999

3.4.3 Platform Volume Distribution Analysis

A Weibull distribution fits the platform spill volumes as illustrated in Figures 3.8 and 3.9. This is supplemented by the Anderson-Darling goodness-of-fit (p-value > 0.25) seen in Figure 3.8. The Weibull distribution is a flexible distribution compared to several common continuous distributions, and we use the Weibull distribution extensively (see Section 3.5) to generalize the work seen in Anderson & LaBelle (2000).

It is not uncommon to see p-values, such as in Figure 3.8, given as either > some value or < some value in goodness of fit applications. The underlying null hypothesis sampling distribution of the test statistic has not been fully solved for all potential statistical distributions being tested with goodness of fits tests such as the Kolmogorov-Smirnov and the Anderson-Darling. In such cases as seen in Figure 3.8 for a three parameter Weibull distribution current statistical methods are unable to give an exact p-value but can assess that the p-value is greater than 0.25 which is all that is needed for most hypothesis testing.

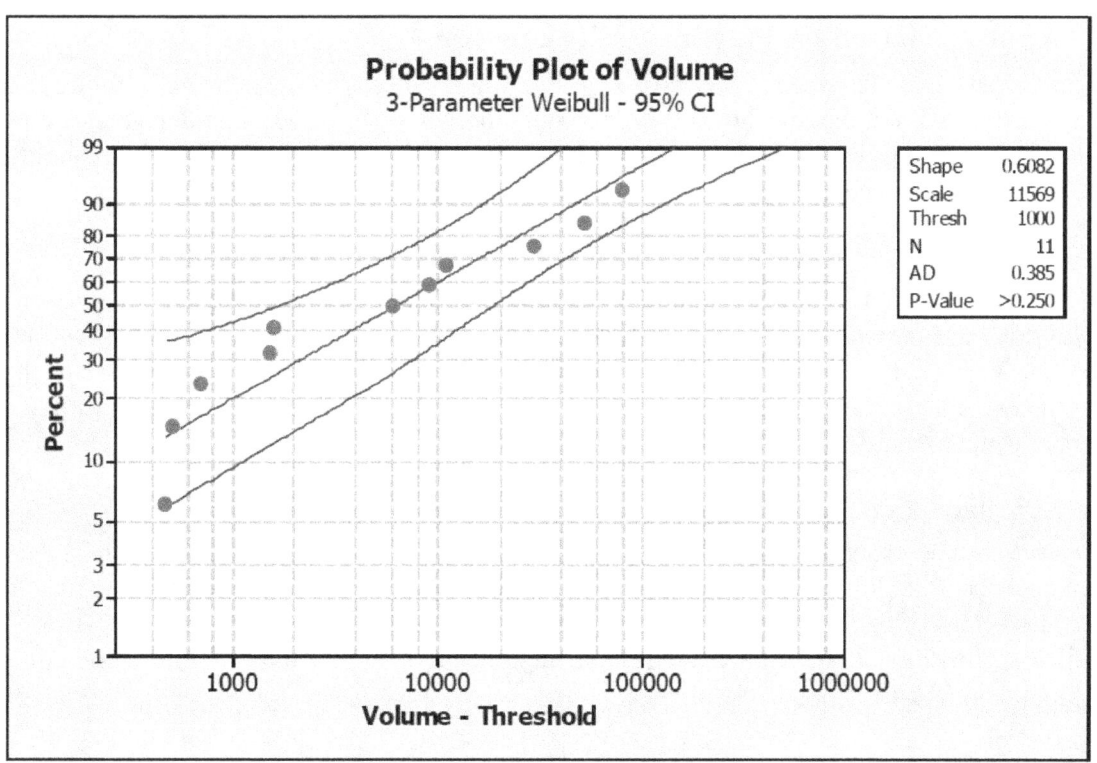

Figure 3.8 Weibull Probability Plot of Platform Spill Volumes Using Anderson & LaBelle (2000) Data

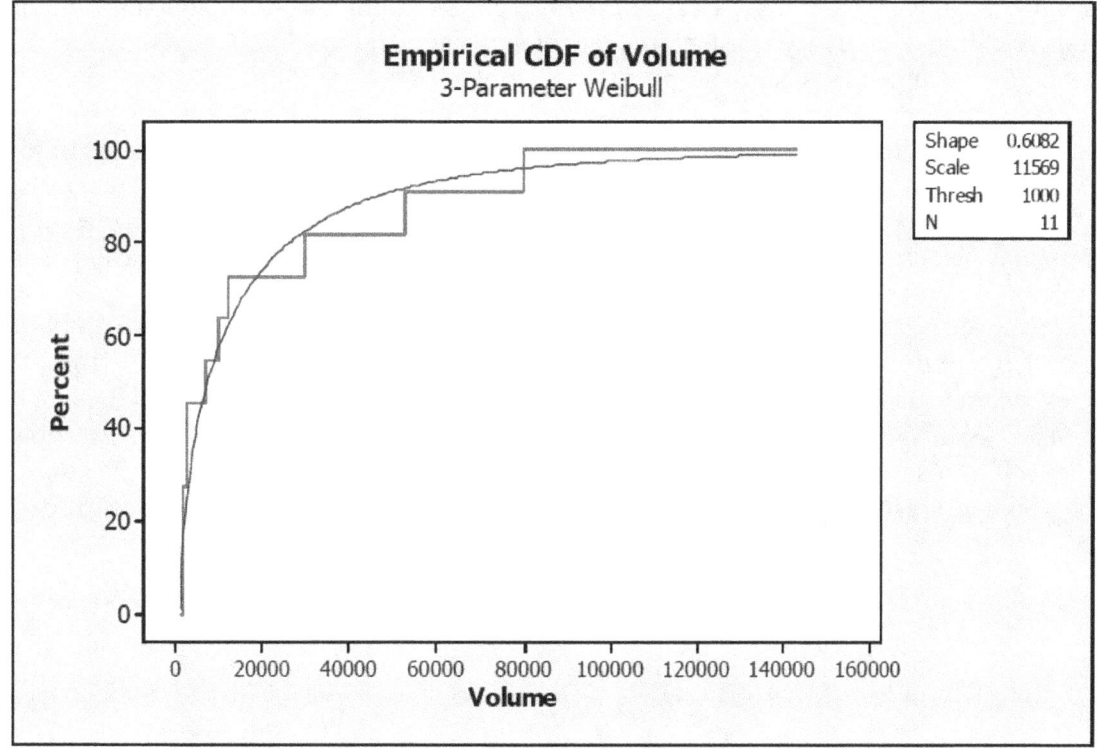

Figure 3.9 Weibull Empirical CDF Plot of Platform Spill Volumes Using Anderson & LaBelle (2000) Data

3.5 Analyses Based on Pipeline Spills ≥ 50 bbl

Section 3.5 extends published MMS work by including smaller spills. The reasons for adding extra data by lowering the threshold of 1,000 bbl include providing additional insights, testing if such extended data provides further support of the analyses based on the 1,000 bbl threshold, searching for other ways to estimate spill rate uncertainty, and examining the statistical value of a larger data set.

Another key extension is in the area of exposure variables. As mentioned before the Poisson distribution has tremendous flexibility, but it should be tested to see if it fits the actual observed data. Earlier in Chapter 3 this was examined only for the time between spill events. Does the Poisson assumption hold when the exposure variable is no longer time, but instead production volume or pipeline mile-years?

3.5.1 Pipeline Inter-Spill Analysis Based on Three Exposure Variables

A data set with 36 observations (Table 2.2 combined with Table 2.3) starting with June 13, 1972 was used to see if a Poisson process can be justified based on time, on production volume (Table 2.11) in millions of barrels (Mbbl), and from Table 2.12 on thousands of pipeline mile-years (KMiles). The rationale for this start date was due to the availability of both production volume and pipeline miles data.

This analysis required that the number of days in each year between each spill be computed. For example the first inter-spill time from June 13, 1972 to May 12, 1973 covered 333 days with 202 days in 1972 and the remaining 131 days in 1973. Then assuming that the production volume and pipeline miles were fairly constant throughout a given year, the total production volume and the total pipeline mile-years between spills were computed.

The inter-spill data for time, production volume, and pipeline mile-years are then tested to see if an exponential distribution fits the observed data. As before, if an exponential fits the inter-spill data for a given exposure variable (time, production volume, or pipeline mile-years) then a Poisson may be used to estimate the likelihood of the number of spills per unit of the exposure variable.

Figures 3.10 through Figure 3.15 illustrate that an exponential distribution adequately fits all three exposure variables (time, production volume, and pipeline mile-years) for this data set. Both visual assessments and the Anderson-Darling goodness-of-fit tests support this decision. Thus now it is possible to take advantage of the Poisson distribution for estimating the number of spills. Having said that a Poisson fit is acceptable, it is still necessary to examine the stationarity of the Poisson process (see Section 3.5.5).

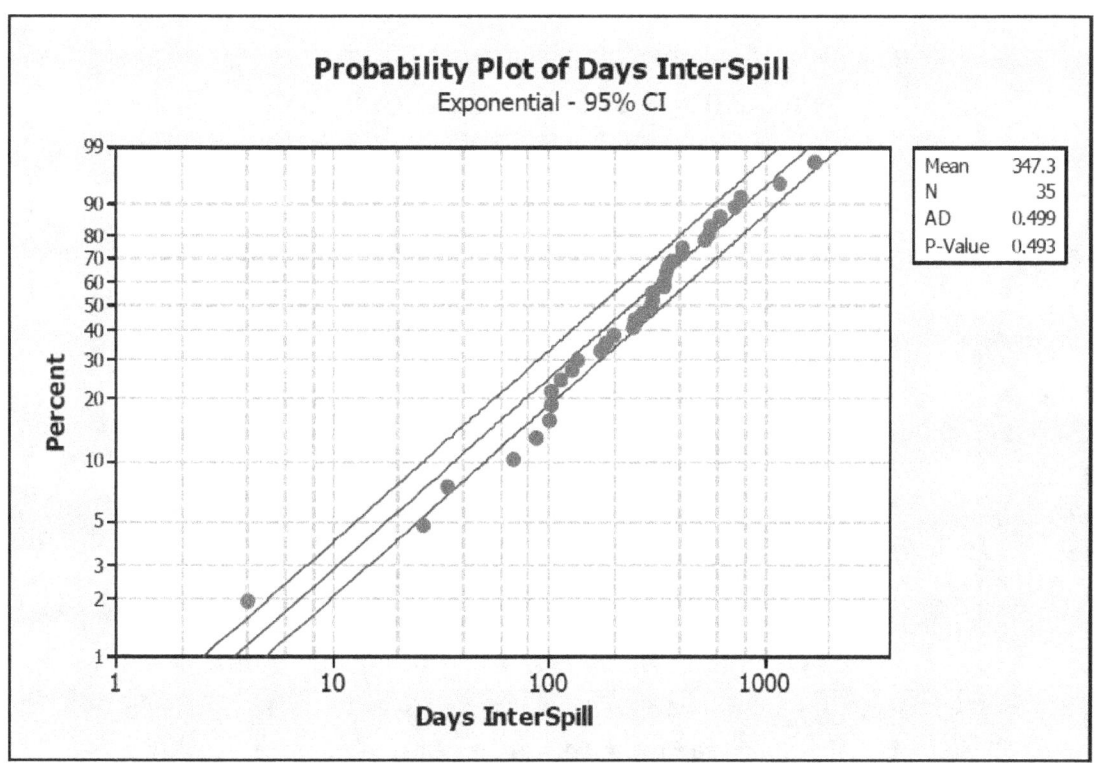

Figure 3.10 Exponential Probability Plot of Pipeline Inter-Spill (Spills ≥ 50 bbl) Times Using N = 36 Data Set

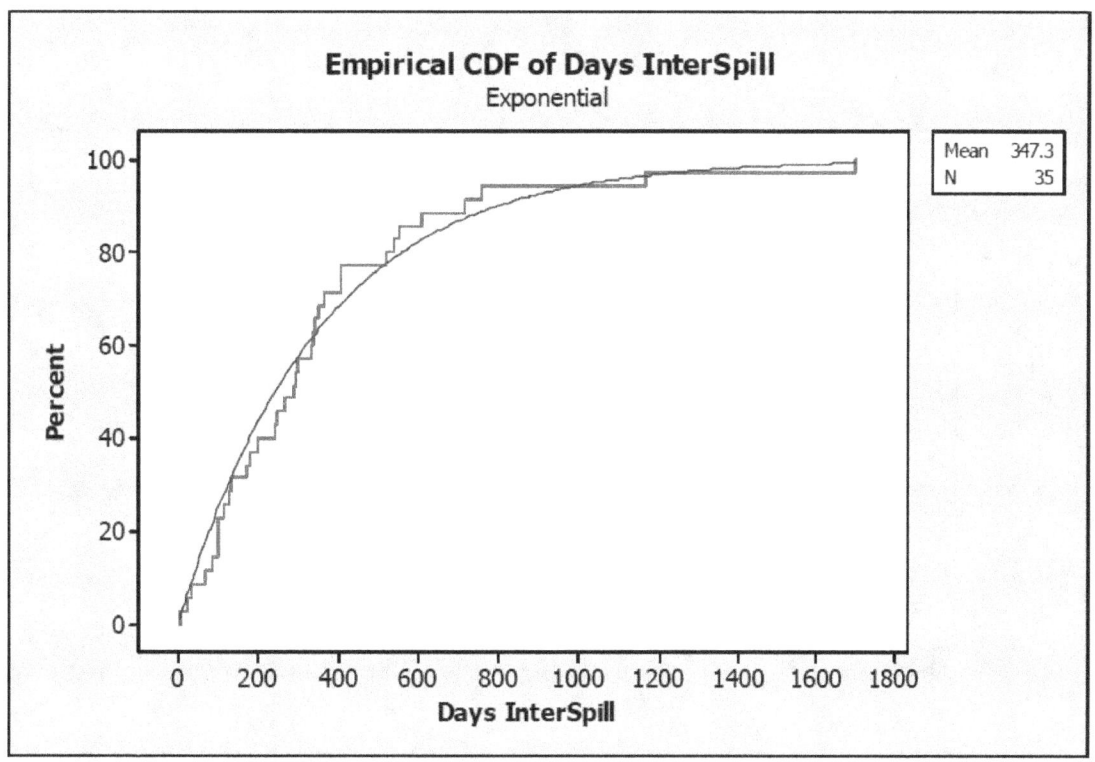

Figure 3.11 Exponential Empirical CDF Plot of Pipeline Inter-Spill (Spills ≥ 50 bbl) Times Using N = 36 Data Set

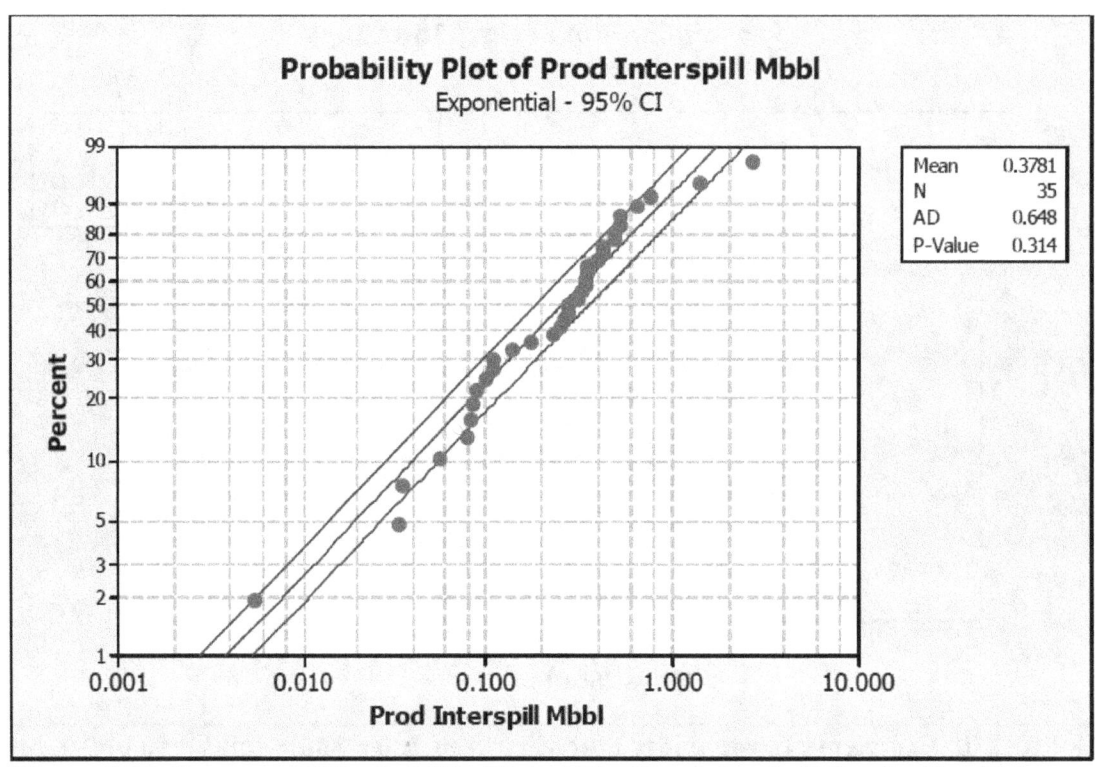

Figure 3.12 Exponential Probability Plot of Pipeline Inter-Spill Production Volumes (Mbbl) Using N = 36 Data Set (Spills ≥ 50 bbl)

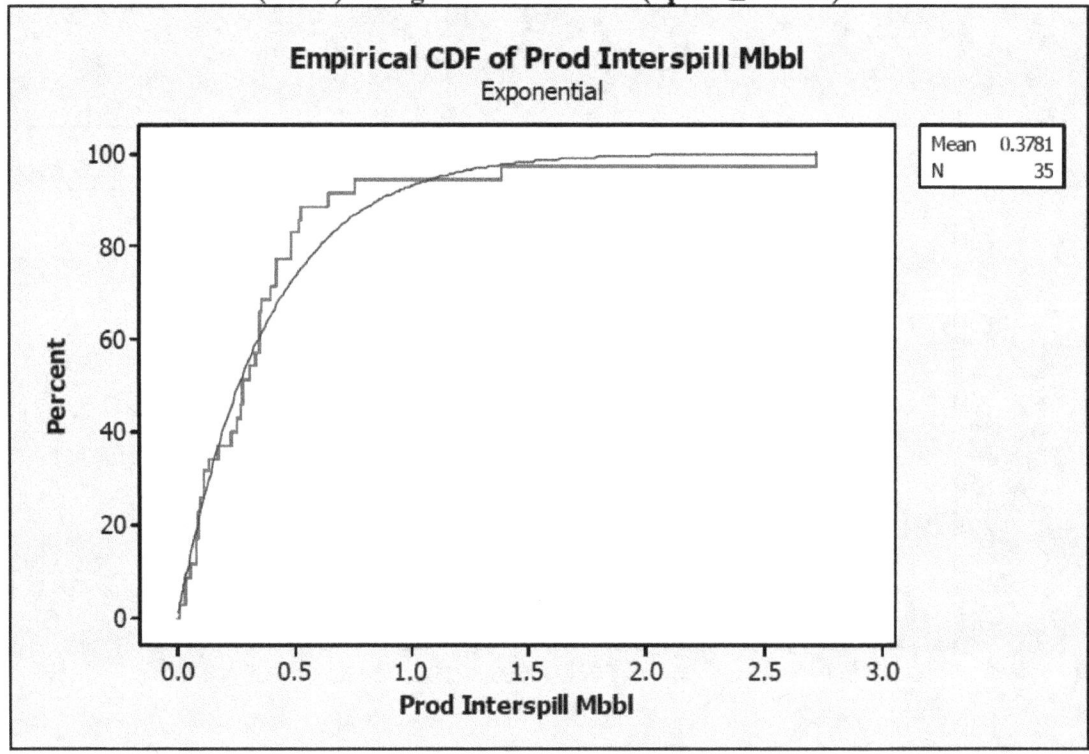

Figure 3.13 Exponential Empirical CDF Plot of Pipeline Inter-Spill Production Volumes Using N = 36 Data Set (Spills ≥ 50 bbl)

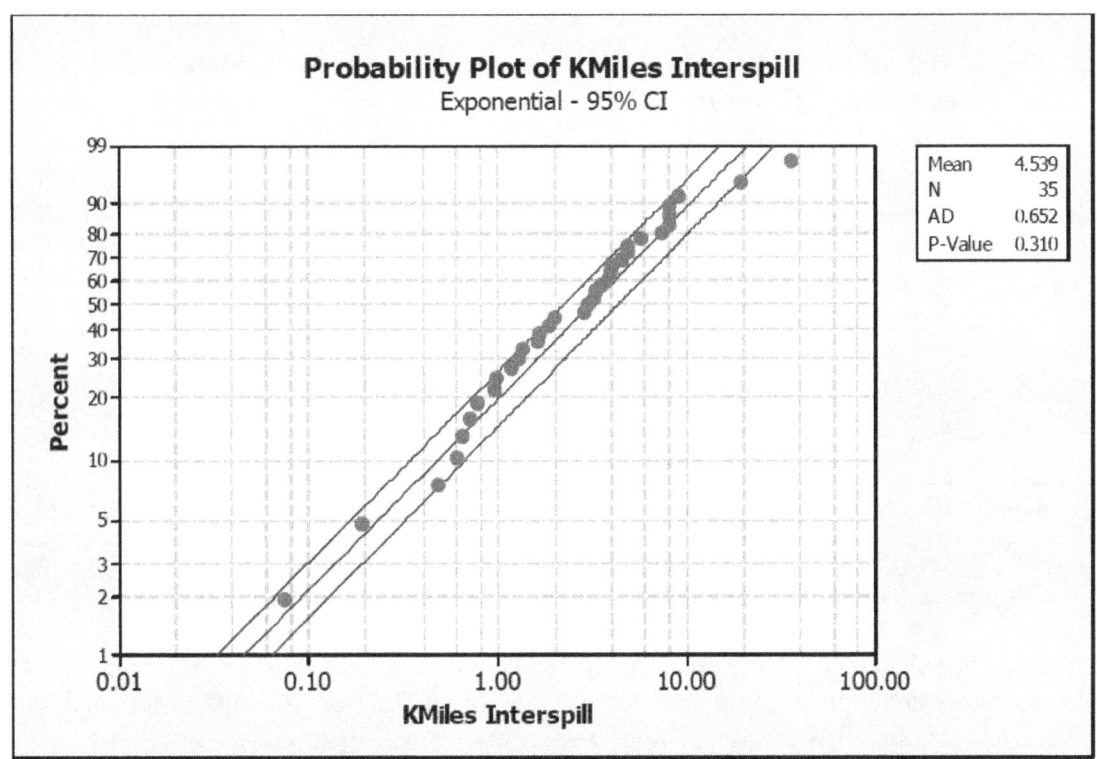

Figure 3.14 Exponential Probability Plot of Pipeline Inter-Spill Pipeline Mile-Years (KMiles) Using N = 36 Data Set (Spills ≥ 50 bbl)

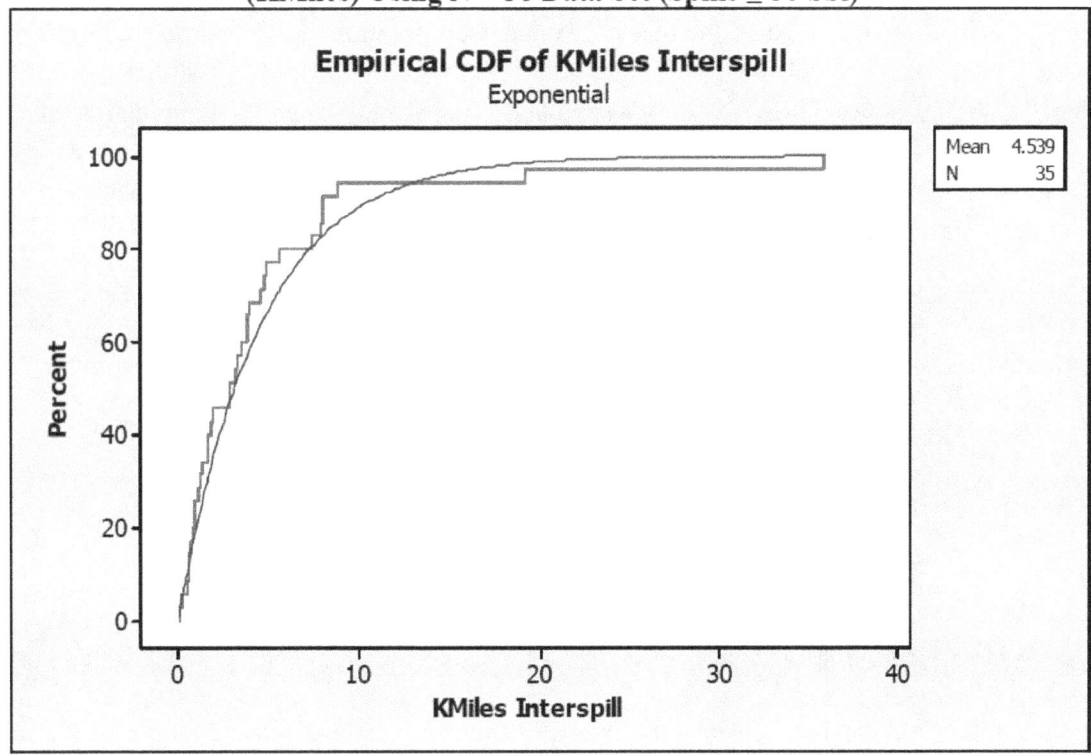

Figure 3.15 Exponential Empirical CDF Plot of Pipeline Inter-Spill Pipeline Mile-Years (KMiles) Using N = 36 Data Set (Spills ≥ 50 bbl)

3.5.2 Exposure Variable Poisson Confidence Intervals and an Introduction to the Poisson – Exponential Relationship

Once the Poisson assumption has been validated by testing exponential inter-arrival measures, it is possible to compute spill rates with exact Poisson confidence intervals (LCL, UCL) or (lower confidence limit, upper confidence limit) for each exposure variable. The results are shown in Table 3.3.

Table 3.3 Spill Rates for ≥ 50 bbl Spills (N = 36)

Label	Exposure Variable	Sum Exposure Variable	Rate	LCL	UCL
Pipeline Spills/KMile-year	KMile-years	161.80	0.223	0.156	0.308
Pipeline Spills/Bbbl	Bbbl Production	13.5	2.660	1.863	3.682
Pipeline Spills/year	Time, whole years	34	1.059	0.742	1.466

As detailed in earlier chapters, the relationship between the discrete Poisson distribution and the continuous exponential distribution allows the testing of the Poisson assumption for small data sets that could not directly be assessed from a discrete distribution approach.

Typically in modern statistics books λ is used to represent the true unknown Poisson mean and $\hat{\lambda}$ represents its estimate based on the observed data. Computationally $\hat{\lambda}$ is simply computed by dividing the number of events (spills) by the sum of the relevant exposure variable such as was done in Table 3.3 above. Since $\hat{\lambda}$ is only a sample estimate of the true population parameter λ it is critical to bound this estimate with a confidence interval as done in Table 3.3 to convey the uncertainty in the estimation. In what follows below the concern is not on the associated confidence interval but instead on using the Poisson and exponential relationship to provide an estimate of λ.

Each of the Minitab plots for the exponential distribution showed the value of the mean, $1/\lambda$. Examining these exponential means and inverting them, one might intuitively expect to get the same Poisson rates seen in Table 3.3. Instead the following is obtained.

Table 3.4 Rate Estimates using Exponential Distribution

Exposure Variable	Exponential Mean	Rate
Pipeline Spills/KMile-year	4.539	0.220
Pipeline Spills/Bbbl	0.3781	2.645
Pipeline Spills/year	347.3 days	1.051 per year

While the agreement is close between the two sets of rates shown in Tables 3.3 and 3.4, there are minor differences. These minor differences are based on the use of the data set. In this case the exponential analysis deals with the 35 intervals between the 36 spills used for the Poisson approach. Thus the exponential data set does not use the time (or amount of some other exposure variable) before the first spill or after the last spill which is part of the Poisson data set.

If the Poisson approach focuses in on these same data, that is the interval between the first and last spill, then an exact match to the exponential rate is found. This has one less spill, since "the clock starts" with the first spill (now spill 0) and ends with the last one. Thus, the rates in Table 3.5 match the rates in Table 3.4.

Table 3.5 Poisson Rates based on Inter-Spill Data (N = 35)

Label	# Spills	Exposure Variable	Sum Exposure Variable	Rate	LCL	UCL
Pipeline Spills/KMile-year	35	KMile-years	158.861	0.220	0.153	0.306
Pipeline Spills/Bbbl	35	Bbbl Production	13.235	2.645	1.842	3.678
Pipeline Spills/year	35	Time, years	33.304	1.051	0.732	1.462

Table 3.5 also allows a clear statement of how the exponential mean for the inter-arrival interval is estimated. It is simply the sum of the exposure variable divided by the number of spills. For KMile-year this is 158.861 divided by the 35 inter-spill observations. This gives the same exact exponential mean seen in Table 3.4 of 4.539. While this is straightforward, the goodness-of-fit statistics, empirical CDF, and probability plot require the computation of all the inter-spill exposure variables.

As there are large pipeline and platform spills near the end of the studied time frame (1972 – 2005), it is not true that the final data sets end with significant spans of time without spills. Thus, it is left to further research and other spill data sets whether it is desirable to consider a final long-period without spills as a "censored" application for the exponential distribution. For example, suppose the period of no platform spills exceeding 1000 bbl from 1980 were to have continued through 2005. This is the same issue faced in mortality estimation when some people in a study are still alive, which is handled by using censored data techniques. If a person is still alive, that period is known, even if their life span is not. It is a direct analogue to the last spill and thus the methods used on biostatistics could be applied to spill data.

3.5.3   Pipeline Spill Volume Models

In examining the pipeline spill volumes there are some ties for spills sizes ≤ 100 bbl and minor adjustments were made to break the ties. Of the 36 pipeline spill volumes, 31 (86%) were unchanged, 3 (8%) were increased by 1 bbl, 1 (3%) was increased by 2 bbl, and 1 (3%) was increased by 3 bbl. There were four spills listed as 50 bbl and two of these were the ones changed by 2 or 3 bbl. The average increase was 0.222 bbl. These changes are minor and do not impact the statistical results in this report. However, avoiding ties is important for some of the statistical work.

This section shows that Weibull distributions fit Pipeline spill volumes for draft spill volumes in the left-hand column of Table 2.2 with thresholds of 50 bbl, 100 bbl, 500 bbl, and 1000 bbl.

Subsequent sections use these results to present some conceptual approaches that extend the work of Anderson & LaBelle (2000). The dataset used here, based on data from 1972 to 2005, grows from 16 with a threshold of 1,000 bbl, to 19 with a threshold of 500 bbl, to 29 with a threshold of 100 bbl, and to 36 spills with a threshold of 50 bbl.

The authors believe that the more complete data set (spills ≥ 50 bbl) offers the opportunity for further insight and possibly better estimation. Even this larger (N = 36) data set ignores pipeline spills less than 50 bbl and hence cannot be considered a complete pipeline spill data set. What is the impact of ignoring spills less than 50 bbl? It depends on what proportion of the full population of pipeline spills are less than 50 bbl. The 50 bbl data set is used to estimate what conditional proportion of the ≥ 50 bbl population falls into the ≥ 1,000 bbl population. The results are encouraging.

Figure 3.16 through Figure 3.23 show that the Weibull distribution is a reasonable fit for all four thresholds shown. Visual TLAR assessments of both the probability plots and empirical cdf plots supplemented by the Anderson-Darling goodness-of-fit results in each probability plot support the selection of the Weibull distribution. Data sets with labels that include text such as 50_1 have been very slightly modified to break the lower level ties. For example rather than leaving say three values at 50 bbl, a label such as 50_1 implies that ties have been broken as discussed in the first paragraph of this section. Such modifications allow better visual distributional assessments as well as aiding the statistical goodness of fits tests.

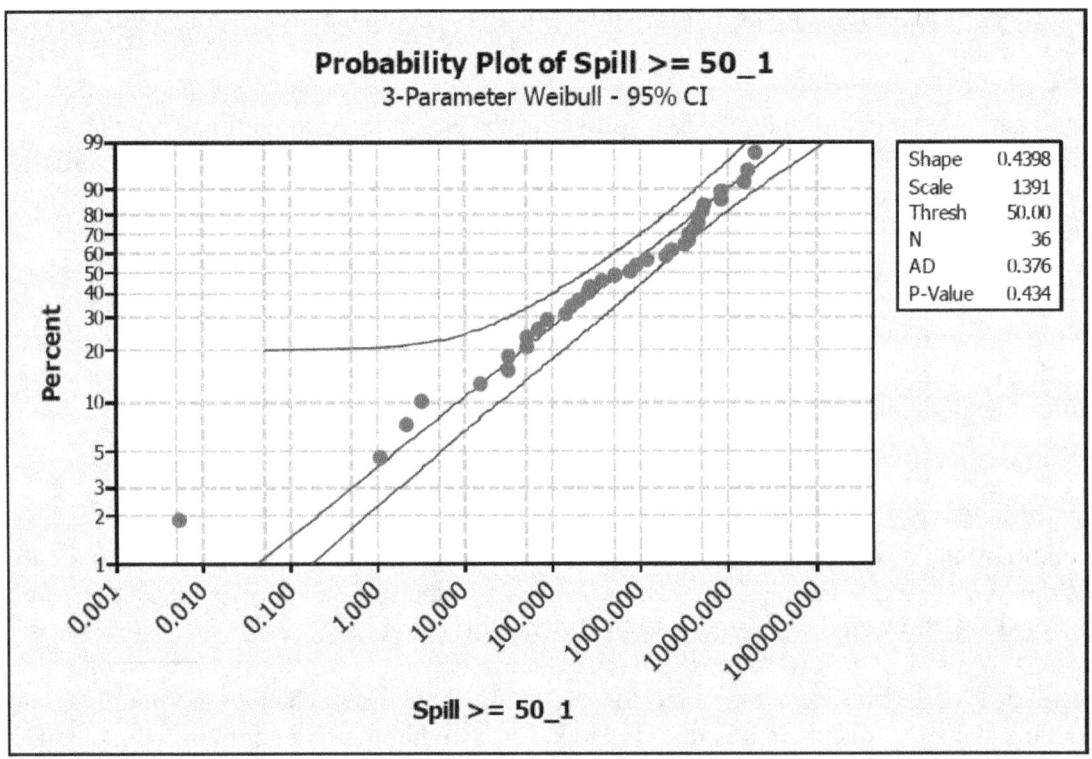

Figure 3.16 Weibull Probability Plot of Pipeline Spill Volumes for Spills ≥ 50 bbl

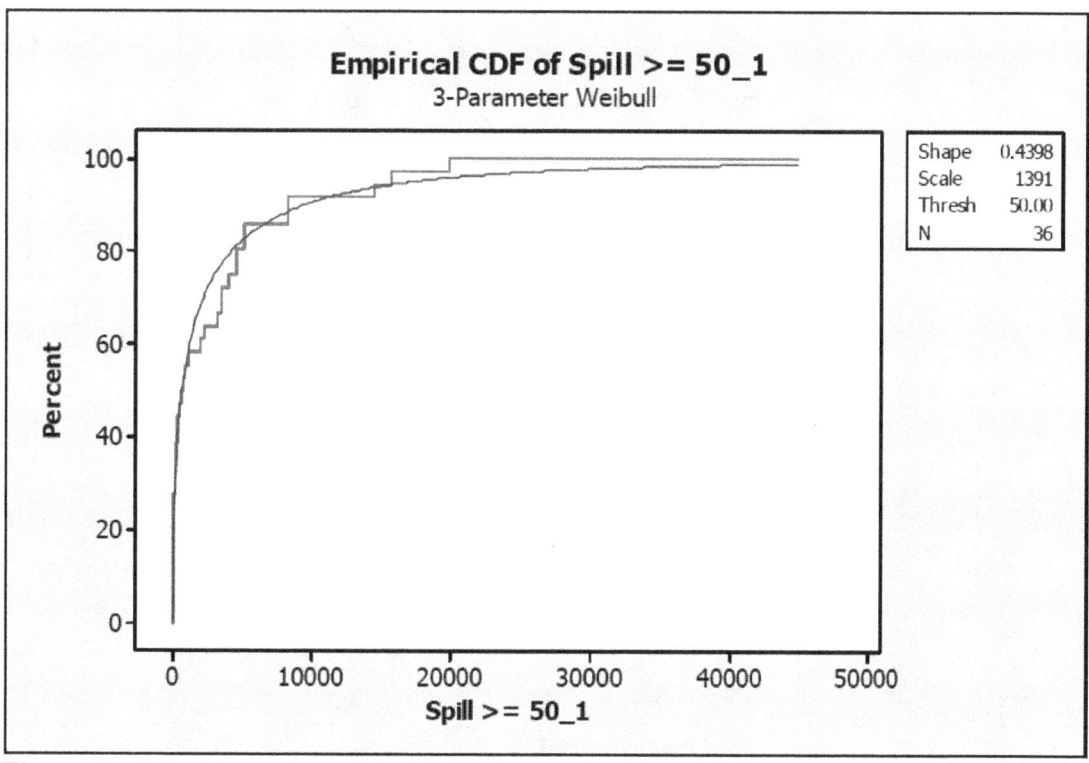

Figure 3.17 Weibull Empirical CDF Plot of Pipeline Spill Volumes for Spills ≥ 50 bbl

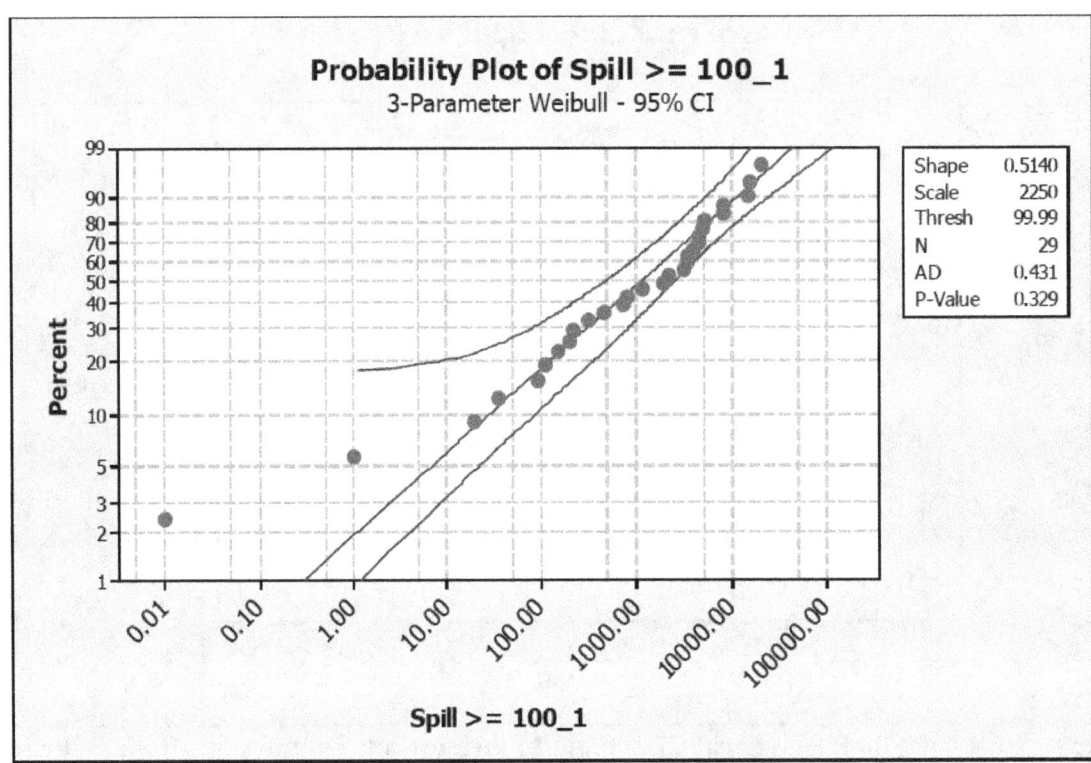

Figure 3.18 Weibull Probability Plot of Pipeline Spill Volumes for Spills ≥ 100 bbl

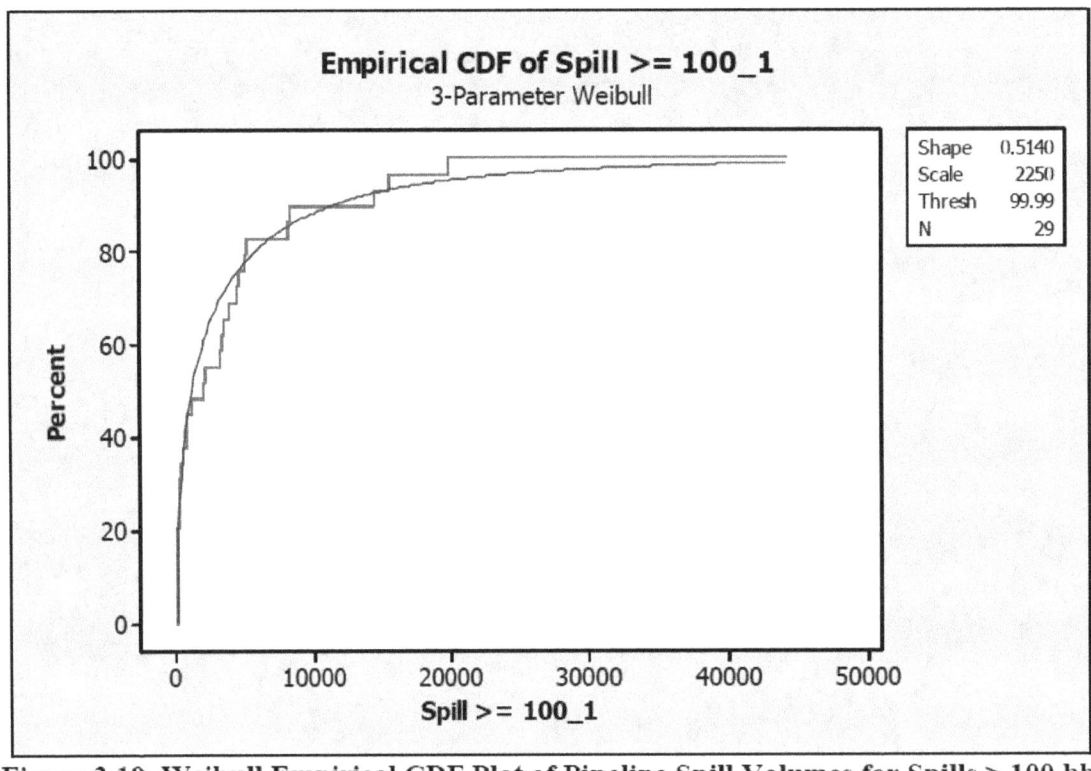

Figure 3.19 Weibull Empirical CDF Plot of Pipeline Spill Volumes for Spills ≥ 100 bbl

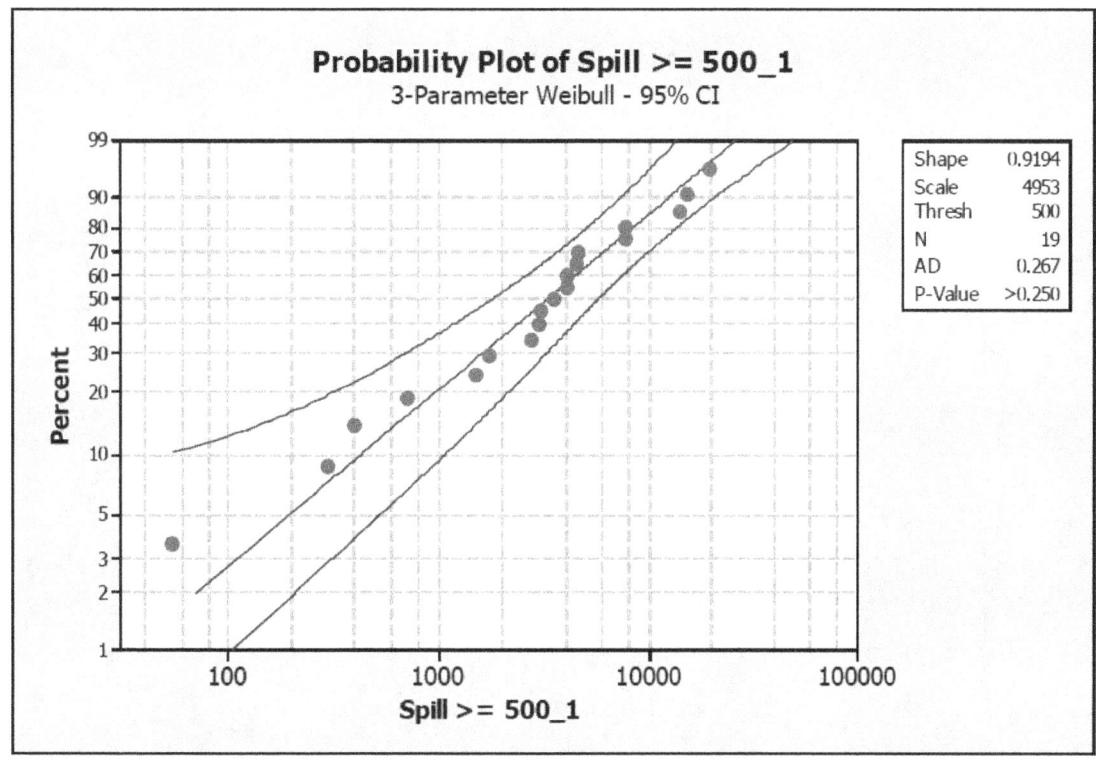

Figure 3.20 Weibull Probability Plot of Pipeline Spill Volumes for Spills ≥ 500 bbl

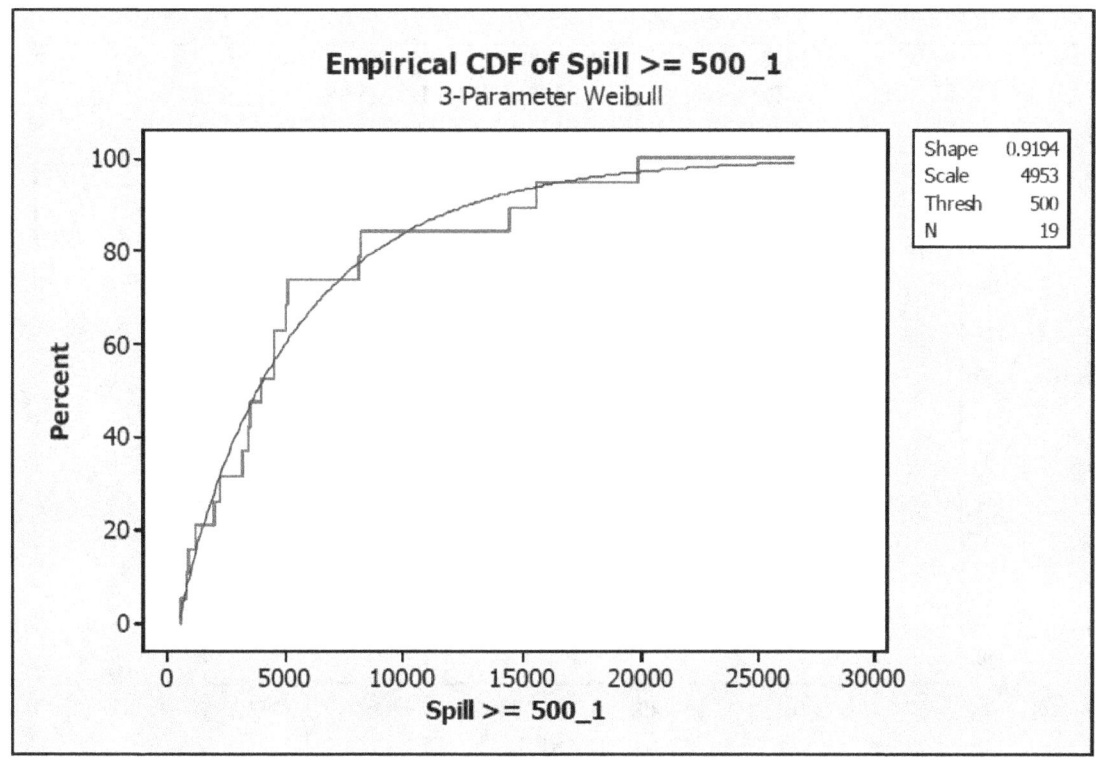

Figure 3.21 Weibull Empirical CDF Plot of Pipeline Spill Volumes for Spills ≥ 500 bbl

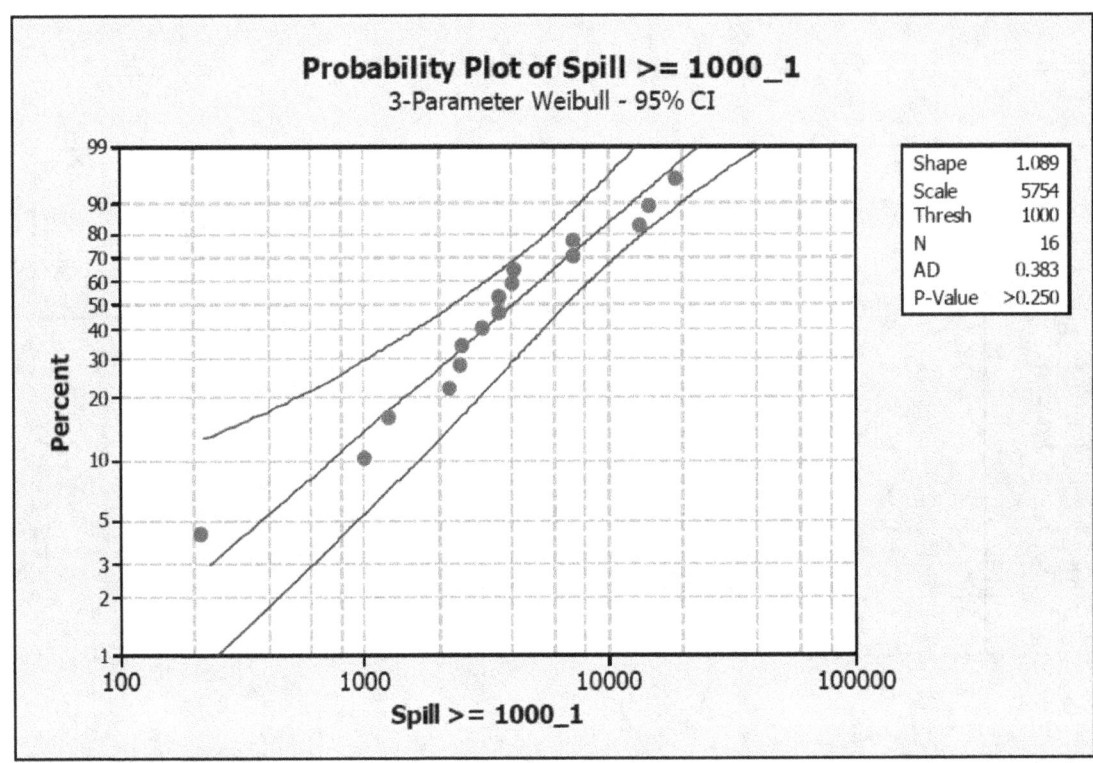

Figure 3.22 Weibull Probability Plot of Pipeline Spill Volumes for Spills ≥ 1000 bbl

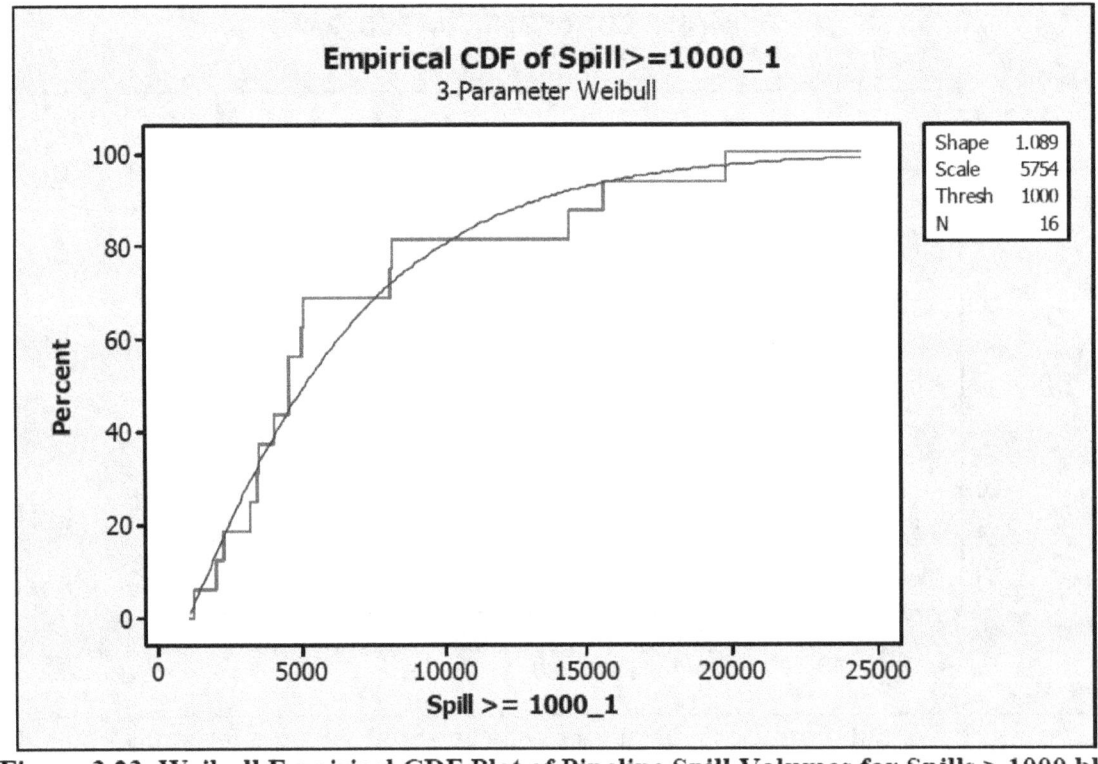

Figure 3.23 Weibull Empirical CDF Plot of Pipeline Spill Volumes for Spills ≥ 1000 bbl

3.5.4 Comparing Pipeline Spill Volume Models for Different Thresholds

Fitting the four Weibull (see Section 3.3.3 for explanation of Weibull) distributions to the four data sets, allows the computation of some measures of consistency. That is because with any of the spill distributions it is also possible to compute the probability of larger spills. For example, for the spill distribution for ≥ 50 bbls it is also possible to compute the probability of ≥ 100 bbls, ≥ 500 bbls, and ≥ 1000 bbls. Table 3.6 is a table of odds ratios comparing the four models. Notice that the blank cells correspond to size comparisons that cannot be made with a probability distribution at a higher threshold (e.g., the distribution for spills ≥ 500 bbl cannot be used to predict spills of ≥ 50 bbl).

For example, consider the row comparing 100 bbl spills vs. 500 bbl spills. In the ≥ 50 bbl column the odds ratio is 1.46 implying that the odds of spilling more than 100 bbl compared to 500 bbl is 1.46 to 1. In the ≥ 100 bbl column of this row, the odds of spilling more than 100 bbl compared to spilling more than 500 bbl is estimated to be 1.51. Note the consistency of the odds ratios in the ≥ 50 bbl and ≥ 100 bbl columns. This implies that these two Weibull models are providing similar predictions.

While the odds ratios for the ≥ 500 bbl and ≥ 1,000 bbl columns are similar to the other rows for some values, these two columns have much higher odds ratios for the last row 2000 vs. 15000 estimating the likelihood of spills exceeding 2000 bbl to spills exceeding 15,000 bbl. It is not unusual to find the extremes (tails) of a distribution having the largest uncertainty; however, it is believed that the smaller data sets available for the ≥ 500 and ≥ 1000 bbl models have led to less reliable results. It seems to be a better approach to use a larger data set (e.g., ≥ 50 bbl) to more completely estimate the spill distribution. Indeed if data were available for all spills regardless of size, then those data should be examined to assess their potential worth.

Table 3.6 Odds Ratios for the Four Different Threshold Weibull Distributions

Spill sizes compared	Thresholds for the four Weibull models			
	≥ 50 bbl	≥ 100 bbl	≥ 500 bbl	≥ 1,000 bbl
50 vs. 100	1.25			
100 vs. 500	1.46	1.51		
500 vs. 1000	1.27	1.24	1.13	
1000 vs. 2000	1.37	1.34	1.24	1.16
2000 vs. 15,000	5.37	5.62	10.50	12.00

Another way to compare these four Weibull distributions is to use the largest data set (≥ 50 bbl) to estimate the conditional proportion of how much of the ≥ 100 bbl distribution should represent given that the spill is ≥ 50 bbl. In a similar vein the ≥ 50 bbl distribution was used to do the same for the ≥ 500 bbl and ≥ 1000 bbl distributions. These conditional proportions (probabilities) are 0.793, 0.544, and 0.429, respectively. These conditional probabilities are then used to adjust the cumulative distribution functions of these three larger threshold distributions to allow a graphical overlay comparison of the four cdfs as given in Figure 3.24.

This paragraph and the next detail how this is done. The conditional probability of one event happening given another will happen is just the ratio of two probabilities. The numerator is the joint probability that both events will occur. The denominator is the probability that the event conditioned on will occur. For example, what is the conditional probability of a spill $\geq$ 1,000 bbl given that the spill is $\geq$ 50 bbl? The top half of the required ratio is P(x $\geq$ 1000 bbl and x $\geq$ 50 bbl) while the bottom probability is the probability that P(x $\geq$ 50 bbl) where x is the spill size. Unfortunately we have no way with the available data of assessing P(x $\geq$ 50 bbl). Instead we approach the problem from a different perspective. Our Weibull distribution for $\geq$ 50 bbl is not the full spill size distribution. It is a conditional distribution for only those spills $\geq$ 50 bbl. Thus when this model is used to compute P(x $\geq$ 1,000 bbl), it is instead computing the probability of a spill being $\geq$ 1,000 bbl given that the spill size is at least 50 bbl and hence a conditional probability. Jumping ahead to compute this probability which is one of three conditional probabilities in the next paragraph, 1- F(1000 bbl using the $\geq$ 50 bbl model) is the desired conditional probability. The math for this example is:

$$1 - F(1000) = 1 - \left\langle 1 - \exp\left[-\left(\frac{x-v}{\alpha}\right)^{\beta}\right]\right\rangle = \exp\left[-\left(\frac{1000-50}{1391}\right)^{0.4398}\right] = 0.429$$

The next paragraph provides such conditional probabilities for $\geq$ 100 bbl, $\geq$ 500 bbl, and $\geq$ 1,000 bbl thresholds given that the spill is $\geq$ 50 bbl. As another example, what happens to the conditional probability of a spill of $\geq$ 500 bbl when it is conditioned on the $\geq$ 100 bbl model? Conceptually consider what should happen, i.e., should this probability increase or decrease from a computed 0.544? What does the 0.544 represent? It represents the likelihood that a spill will be $\geq$ 500 bbl given that the spill is $\geq$ 50 bbl. The $\geq$ 50 bbl model covers any spills of at least 50 bbl. If a smaller range of potential spills is examined, such as at least 100 bbl, the proportion of this distribution that represents $\geq$ 500 bbl should be larger than the corresponding $\geq$ 500 bbl proportion of the $\geq$ 50 bbl distribution. Hence this new conditional probability should be larger than 0.544. Indeed it is larger and is 0.663 using the $\geq$ 100 bbl Weibull model as the base of this calculation.

One measure of how well the Weibull for $\geq$ 50 bbl fits the other data sets based on larger thresholds is that the theoretical conditional proportions (0.793, 0.544, 0.429) based solely on the $\geq$ 50 bbl Weibull distribution are close to the proportions based on the actual data which are 0.806, 0.528, 0.444 respectively. Given that the larger threshold data sets have progressively smaller sample sizes and these latter numbers are based on small integer values (number of observations in the data sets), these results are very encouraging. This supports the belief that the $\geq$ 50 bbl data set can be used to make predictions for larger thresholds.

Figure 3.24 shows that the $\geq$ 50 bbl and $\geq$ 100 bbl cdfs are similar, but with some differences from the curves for the 500 & 1000 bbl spills. Also the curve for the $\geq$ 500 bbl spills is "further away," for smaller spills so it is not a logical progression as the sample size is reduced. These differences are also seen in the comparison of 2000 vs. 15,000 bbl spills in Table 3.6.

The main implication of these results is that the reliability offered by a larger data set must be balanced with the reliability offered by a data set that has seen greater scrutiny. It is believed that it is prudent to examine the statistical results from both approaches.

CDF Comparison

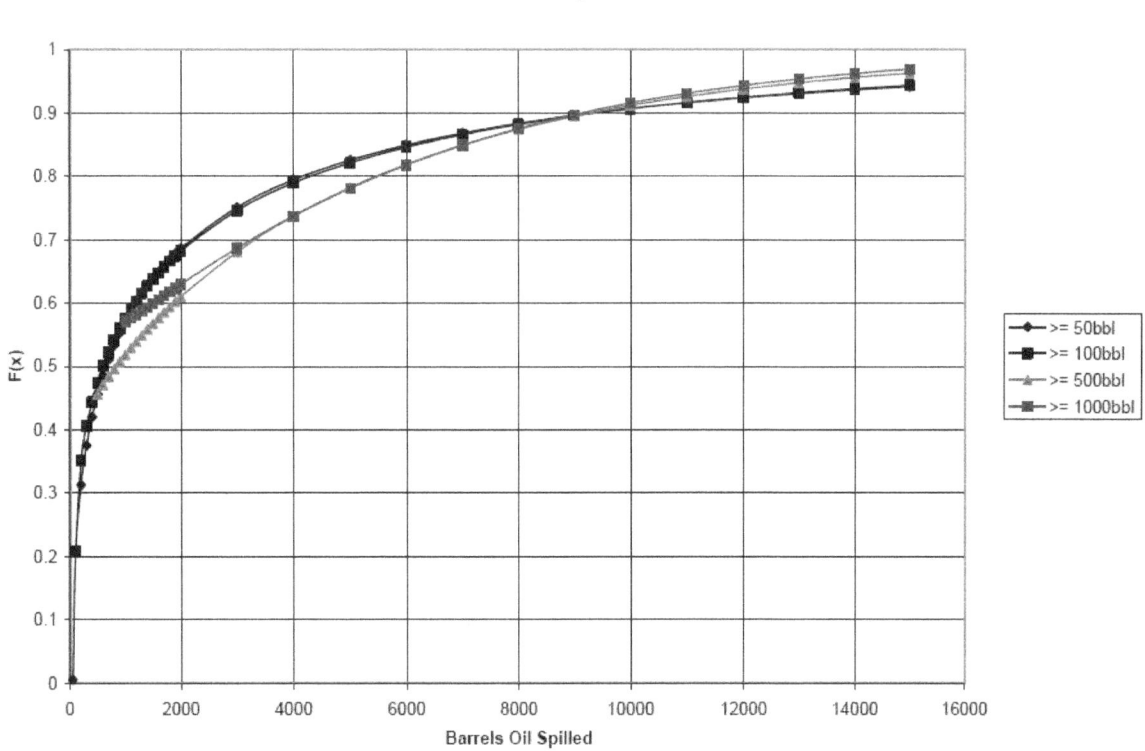

Figure 3.24 Overlay of Weibull Empirical CDFs

3.5.5   Concerns about Non-stationarity of the Poisson Process

Examination of various data sets over time visually seems to show a potential decrease in spill rates over time, Bbbl, and KMiles. Efforts using moving averages and regression with different exposure variables have yielded inconsistent results. For example a regression of inter-spill days versus spill year does not result in a statistically significant slope (p=0.155). While a trend may exist, the data is noisy enough that it cannot be confirmed for the GOM pipeline spills. When more evidence exists of a non-stationary process (as will be found for platforms) more sophisticated approaches are used to quantify the relationship of the changing rate.

3.5.6   Alternative Confidence Interval Approaches Applied to Pipeline Spills

This section examines the development of confidence intervals for spill rates using different methods. The analysis in this section is based on the 36 spills $\geq$ 50 bbl shown in Tables 2.2 and 2.3. Three subsets of these data using higher spill thresholds form the set of four models analyzed here. Spill rate confidence intervals are initially developed for all four thresholds as a function of production volume. The same methodology can be applied to other exposure variables.

One reason for pursuing this approach is to establish a statistically credible basis for estimating the probabilities of larger spills, such as $\geq$ 10,000 bbl or $\geq$ 100,000 bbl. At these spill levels

there are respectively only 3 pipeline spills and 0 pipeline spills, which are too small for any reliable estimation process.

Using the four thresholds with the exposure variable of Bbbl of production volume, Table 3.7 gives the four pipeline spill rates with their exact Poisson confidence intervals. These are based on the formulation given in Section 3.2.2. The confidence intervals below are based on smaller and smaller data sets as the threshold size increases. Thus, the Poisson spill rate falls faster than the upper limit on its value as the threshold increases.

These results are useful in estimating the probability of different size spills, but they can also be compared with results from other approaches that are based on the larger data set for spills ≥ 50 bbl. The disadvantage of the Table 3.7 results is the reduction in sample size as the spill thresholds increase.

Table 3.7 Exact Poisson Confidence Intervals for Different Pipeline Spill Thresholds with Production as Exposure Variable

Threshold	N	Poisson Rate for Bbbl	Exact Poisson CI Lower	Exact Poisson CI Upper
50	36	2.72	1.91	3.77
100	29	2.19	1.47	3.15
500	19	1.44	0.86	2.24
1000	16	1.21	0.69	1.96

Table 3.8 presents the fraction of the ≥ 50 bbl spills that are $\geq$ the higher thresholds using the previously developed Weibull probability distribution. More formally, the Weibull based model for pipeline spill volumes for ≥ 50 bbl is used to estimate the conditional probability of exceeding larger thresholds. Then assuming this probability represents a binomial proportion for the N = 36 observations in the ≥ 50 bbl data set, exact binomial confidence intervals are given in the last two columns. While the assumption that the conditional probability may be treated as a binomial in this manner may be questioned, it does provide one way of bounding the likely proportion of the ≥ 50 bbl population that would exceed the larger thresholds indicated and thus is useful information in its own right.

Table 3.8 Exact Binomial Confidence Intervals for the Proportion of the ≥ 50 bbl Model Spills Exceeding the Larger Threshold with Production as Exposure Variable

Threshold	P($\geq$ Threshold)	Lower Binomial Confidence Interval	Upper Binomial Confidence Interval	Actual Proportion
100	0.7932	0.6398	0.9181	0.8060 = 29/36
500	0.5440	0.3810	0.7206	0.5280 = 19/36
1000	0.4293	0.2551	0.5924	0.4440= 16/36

The models and the confidence intervals in Tables 3.7 and 3.8 can be used in three ways to estimate confidence intervals for spills ≥ the different thresholds. The three approaches are summarized in Tables 3.9 through 3.11.

Table 3.9 uses the values in Table 3.8 in two ways. First the P(≥ Threshold) column of Table 3.8 is used to estimate the spill rate per Bbbl for larger threshold based strictly on the ≥ 50 bbl Weibull model. This is done by multiplying the value in the P(≥ Threshold) column by the estimated spill rate based just on the ≥ 50 bbl data. For example, the estimated spill rate for ≥ 100 bbl spills is 2.16 (= 2.72*.79).

Note how closely these spill rates match the ones developed separately based on their individual data sets. This is encouraging and lends strength to the concept of basing spill probabilities for any threshold on the largest possible data set. The last two columns of Table 3.9 are the same 2.72 spills per Bbbl rate for the ≥ 50 bbl data multiplied by the corresponding lower or upper column in Table 3.8. Thus, this represents one way to bound uncertainty at any threshold level by using only the ≥ 50 bbl data.

One of the benefits of using the full data set is the ability to tighten the confidence intervals around the Poisson rates. While Table 3.7 does give exact Poisson confidence intervals for the four thresholds, each increasing threshold uses a smaller data set. This results in wide confidence intervals as the number of data points decreases. Using the full N = 36 data set in tables such as Table 3.9 does more than provide alternative confidence interval approaches for thresholds of interest. These tables more completely uses the larger data set resulting in the ability to reduce the width of the corresponding confidence intervals compared to the Table 3.7 intervals based on reducing sample sizes as the thresholds increase in magnitude.

Table 3.9 Spill Rate Estimates and Confidence Intervals Using 2.72 Spill Rate for ≥ 50 bbl Times Values in Table 3.8 with Production as Exposure Variable

Threshold	P(≥ Threshold)	Adjusted Poisson Rate per Bbbl	Adjusted LCL	Adjusted UCL
100	0.79	2.16	1.74	2.50
500	0.54	1.48	1.04	1.96
1000	0.43	1.17	0.69	1.61

Table 3.10 might be in some sense considered a worst case for the spill rate per Bbbl production volume in that it works with the exact Poisson confidence intervals in Table 3.7 for the ≥ 50 bbl spill and combines this information with the binomial proportion uncertainty given in Table 3.8. Table 3.10 has the widest intervals because it assumes for example, that the lower confidence interval rate for ≥ 50 bbl (1.91 in Table 3.7) and the lower confidence interval proportion for ≥ 100 bbl (0.64 in Table 3.8) occur simultaneously. Thus, 1.22 (= 1.91*0.64) is the tabulated value. While this is not the recommended approach for GOM volumes, the method has applicability in the extension from the GOM to the Arctic where both the proportion of GOM spills that may be applicable to the Arctic (the binomial component) and the rate (the Poisson component) are quite uncertain.

Table 3.10 Confidence Intervals for "Binomial Adjusted" Approach Using (1.91, 3.77) Table 3.7 Poisson Confidence Intervals from ≥ 50 bbl Model and the Binomial Confidence Intervals in Table 3.8

Threshold	Adjusted LCL Based on both Confidence Intervals	Adjusted UCL Based on both Confidence IntervalsI
100	1.219	3.457
500	0.726	2.714
1000	0.486	2.231

Table 3.11 also uses the (1.91, 3.77) exact Poisson confidence interval for ≥ 50 bbl. It multiplies this by the estimated proportion of the ≥ 50 bbl population that would exceed the larger thresholds (see Table 3.8). This provides a third approach to estimating the confidence interval for any threshold directly from the largest data set based on the 50 bbl threshold.

Table 3.11 Confidence Intervals Using (1.91, 3.77) Poisson Confidence Intervals from ≥ 50 bbl Model and P(≥ threshold) with Production as Exposure Variable

Threshold	P(≥ threshold)	Adjusted LCL	Adjusted UCL
50	1.0000	1.9052	3.7658
100	0.7932	1.5112	2.9872
500	0.5440	1.0364	2.0487
1000	0.4293	0.8179	1.6167

What is nice about the approaches summarized in Tables 3.9 to 3.11 is that a new subset of the data is not required each time a question arises about a different threshold. The quality of these estimates does depend on how well the ≥ 50 bbl data can be used to model the censored population above this threshold. These results are encouraging. While each approach has its own appeal, the Table 3.9 method is recommended for this section in which the proportions, i.e., P(≥ threshold), are thought to be reasonably estimated. If such proportions are more speculative than data based estimates, then the broader intervals of Table 3.10 are recommended. The Table 3.10 is related to the approach used in Chapter 4 for the extension from the GOM to the Arctic.

3.5.7 Comparison of Through 2005 versus Through 1999

Appendix A parallels the pipeline analysis in Section 3.5. In Section 3.5, analyses for pipeline spills ≥ 50 bbl are documented for data *through 2005*. Since the preliminary analysis submitted in the fall of 2005 analyzed data only through 1999, it was felt important to provide the reader an opportunity to see what has changed by adding six additional years of pipeline spill data. While some of the results in Appendix A are the same as given in the earlier preliminary analysis, others reflect changes due to corrected data. Appendix A gives analogous Figures and Tables to the pipeline information in Section 3.5 using a numbering scheme to make the matching of the through 1999 analysis figure/table to the through 2005 figure/table seen in the main body of the report obvious. For example Figure A3.10 is Appendix A may be compared to Figure 3.10 in Section 3.5.

The comparison between the Appendix A through 1999 and Section 3.5 through 2005 analyses may be summarized in the following areas:
- Pipeline Exposure Variable Goodness of Fit Distribution Analysis
    - All fits are very good and there are no major differences between the through 1999 and through 2005 data.
- Poisson Exposure Variable Rates
    - Spill rates have dropped somewhat in the through 2005 data.
- Weibull Distribution Volume Goodness of Fit Analysis
    - All fits are very good and there are no major differences between the through 1999 and through 2005 data.
- Comparison of the four Weibull Volume Threshold Data Sets
    - Results compare well between the through 1999 and through 2005 data with the through 2005 data visually showing a somewhat better match between the four curves at low spill thresholds.
- Alternative Spill Threshold Confidence Intervals
    - Following the pattern in the 2nd bullet above, spill rates have dropped somewhat in the through 2005 data. Slightly higher probabilities of larger spills are found in the through 2005 data though the reduction in spill rate dominates this.

The second and fifth bullets above mention the reduced spill rates in the through 2005 data versus the through 1999 data. This is not a major change and the resulting spill rates easily fall into the confidence intervals of the other time period's spill rates. Additionally the earlier mentioned regression analyses among other things in Section 3.5.5 do not point to a non-stationary system. The major conclusion that can be supported is that the methodology and the results are robust enough that the addition of 6 years of data has not led to significant changes.

3.5.8 Summary and Conclusions

Section 3.5 has analyzed pipeline spills $\geq$ 50 bbl from both an inter-spill perspective as well as spill volume. The three exposure variables studied (time, volume, and pipeline miles) were all found to be adequately fit by exponential distributions. Thus the Poisson assumption for the spill rates for each exposure variable is justified. This allows the creation of exact Poisson confidence intervals based on all three GOM exposure variables.

Pipeline spill volumes were well fit by a Weibull distribution. Four thresholds (50 bbl, 100 bbl, 500 bbl, and 1,000 bbl) were used to develop the approach given in this part of the report. The results of using a larger database of $\geq$ 50 bbl are very encouraging. Several methods were also derived for using the larger $\geq$ 50 bbl data to estimate spill rates and associated confidence intervals for the larger thresholds. These new methods make more complete use of the full N = 36 data set for spills $\geq$ 50 bbls, rather than depending on increasingly smaller subsets of spill data for larger thresholds.

The following conclusions may be made from the results in this section:

1. The use of the larger data set for pipeline spills ≥ 50 bbl adds remarkable modeling flexibility and improves the validation of the conceptual underpinnings of the statistical modeling.
2. Production and pipeline mile-years are useful exposure variables to help understand and model not only the GOM but will be advantageous in the Chapter 4 extension from the GOM to the Arctic.
3. Exploiting the relationship between the Poisson and exponential distributions provides a natural path to test whether the Poisson distributions is applicable to spill rates for an exposure variable.
4. The application of exact Poisson confidence intervals for differing exposure variables provides a more firm foundation for uncertainty quantification and prediction.
5. Table 3.3 for pipeline spill rates for all three exposure variables is the recommended source for spill rates ≥ 50 bbl. The rates are given separately for each of the exposure variables and are for ≥ 50 bbl rate estimates.
6. A Weibull distribution for pipeline spill volumes ≥ 50 bbl provides a more complete use of available data and reduces uncertainty of spill rate confidence intervals.
7. The Table 3.9 approach to assessing pipeline production spill rate confidence intervals for thresholds ≥ 50 bbl is recommended for GOM application, while the Table 3.10 approach that folds in other sources of uncertainty will be applied in Chapter 4 for the extension from the GOM to the Arctic. This table expands earlier work for just the exposure variable production that was based on ≥ 50 bbl predictions.
8. Table 3.9 allows the generalization to predictions for 100 bbl, 500 bbl, and 1,000 bbl as well as other desired thresholds.

3.6 Analyses Based on Platform Spills ≥ 50 bbl

Section 3.6 extends the published MMS work by including smaller platform spills. The reasons for adding extra data by lowering the threshold of 1000 bbl include providing additional insights, testing if such extended data provides further support of the analyses based on the 1000 bbl threshold, searching for other ways to estimate spill rate uncertainty, and examining the statistical value of a larger data set.

Another key extension is in the area of exposure variables, where three are tested – time, production volume, and the number of platforms. After the pipeline spill analyses were completed in Section 3.5, it was hoped that the platform spills would easily follow the same pattern. However platform spills have proved more difficult than envisioned.

3.6.1 Platform Inter-Spill Analysis Based on Three Exposure Variables

A data set with 86 observations (Table 2.6 + Table 2.8) starting with April 5, 1971 was constructed. The year 1971 had 8 spills and 1972 had none, and it was felt that some effort was needed to test the impact of including the 1971 data versus not including it. This analysis is documented in Section 3.6.2.

To be consistent with pipeline analysis that started with 1972 and the analysis in the Bercha reports (2002 & 2006), a subset with 78 spills was the focus of analysis. This includes examination of whether a Poisson process can be justified based on time, on production volume in Mbbl, and on number of platform-years. This analysis required that the number of days in each year between each spill be computed. Then assuming that the production volume and number of platforms were fairly constant throughout a given year, the total production volume and the number of platform-years between spills were computed.

The inter-spill data are then tested to see if an exponential distribution fits the observed data. As before, if an exponential fits the inter-spill data for a given exposure variable then a Poisson may be used to estimate the likelihood of the number of spills per unit of the exposure variable.

While the exponential distribution did pass relevant goodness of fit statistical measures and visual TLAR approaches some of the time, a Weibull distribution often fit the inter-spill data better. A Weibull distribution is a generalization of the exponential distribution. Unlike the censored (each had a lower threshold of 50 bbl, 100 bbl, 500 bbl, or 1000 bbl) Weibull distributions used for the pipeline spill volumes in Section 3.5, most Weibull distributions for inter-spill time have a lower bound of 0 and not some higher value. In such cases the threshold parameter $v = 0$.

In reliability theory the hazard function (defined further below) is often used to assess the failure rate as a function of time. The hazard function may increase or decrease dynamically (i.e., showing time dependence) indicating a rising or dropping failure rate. A horizontal hazard function is time independent (i.e., static) so the failure rate is not changing. This static or constant hazard function is the special case of the Weibull distribution that is the exponential distribution. The Weibull (Weibull, 1951) distribution allows a non-constant failure rate (or hazard function), so that the Weibull distribution is one of the major tools used in reliability assessments.

The hazard function or conditional failure function is defined as:

$$h(t) = \frac{f(t)}{1 - F(t)}$$

where $h(t)$ is the hazard function, $f(t)$ is the probability density function, and $F(t)$ is the cumulative distribution function. Thus $1 - F(t)$ is the probability that the component will survive to time t.

When the Weibull distribution shape parameter $\beta = 1$ we have a constant hazard function and thus an exponential distribution. When $\beta < 1$, the Weibull has a hazard function that is decreasing with time. When $\beta > 1$, the Weibull has a hazard function that is increasing with time. In the Weibull analyses that follow in this section, the shape parameter $\beta < 1$ and thus a decreasing spill rate is indicated. This also matches the Anderson and Labelle platform data discussion for platforms in Section 3.4.2.

3.6.1.1 Platform Inter-Spill Analysis Based on Time

Figure 3.25 shows an exponential distribution fit to the inter-spill exposure time in days. The p-value of 0.304 is not rejected by the Anderson-Darling goodness of fit test; however, the initial left hand portion of the curve shows a common (in this section) problem. There were numerous ties especially among the smaller values. Out of the 77 inter-spill days, 62 (81%) were unchanged, 8 (10%) were lengthened by 1 day, 5 (6%) were lengthened by 2 days, and 2 (3%)

were lengthened by 3 days to remove all the ties. The maximum change was 3 days and the average change was 0.31 days. A revised version based on tie breaking adjustments results in Figure 3.26. The p-value is higher (improved) though the main improvement is visual. Similar changes would be possible for other exposure variables but were not done as it is more difficult to adjust them.

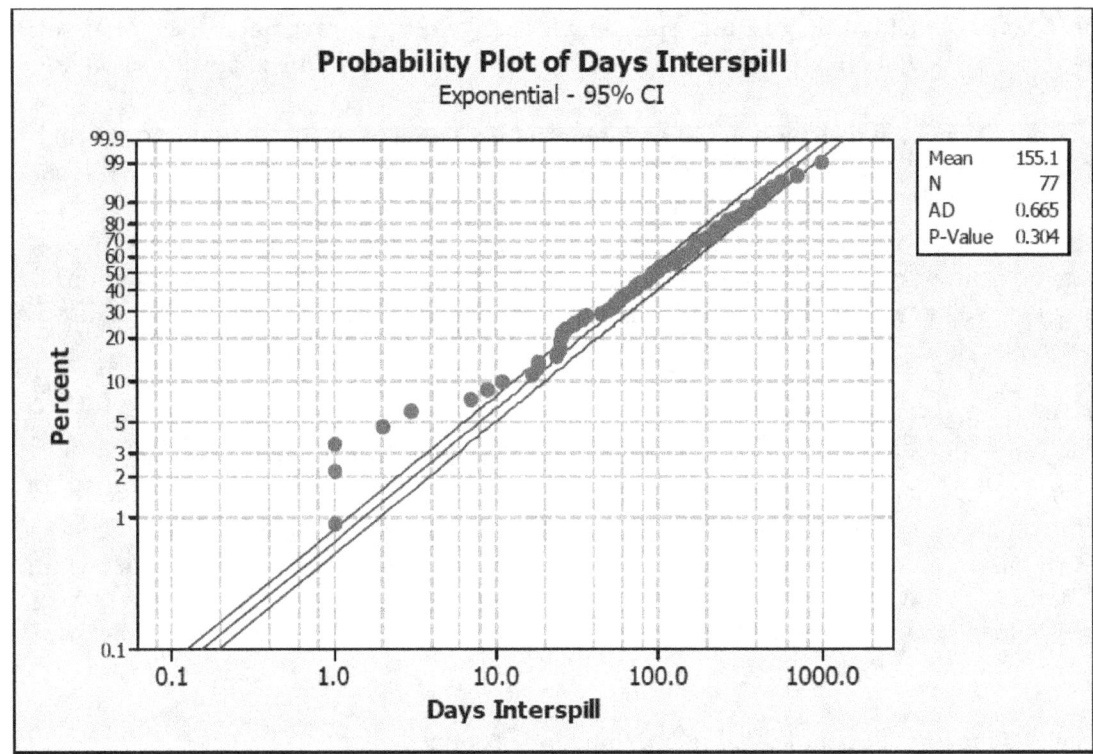

Figure 3.25 Exponential Probability Plot of Platform Inter-Spill (Spills ≥ 50 bbl) Times using 1972-2005 Data Set

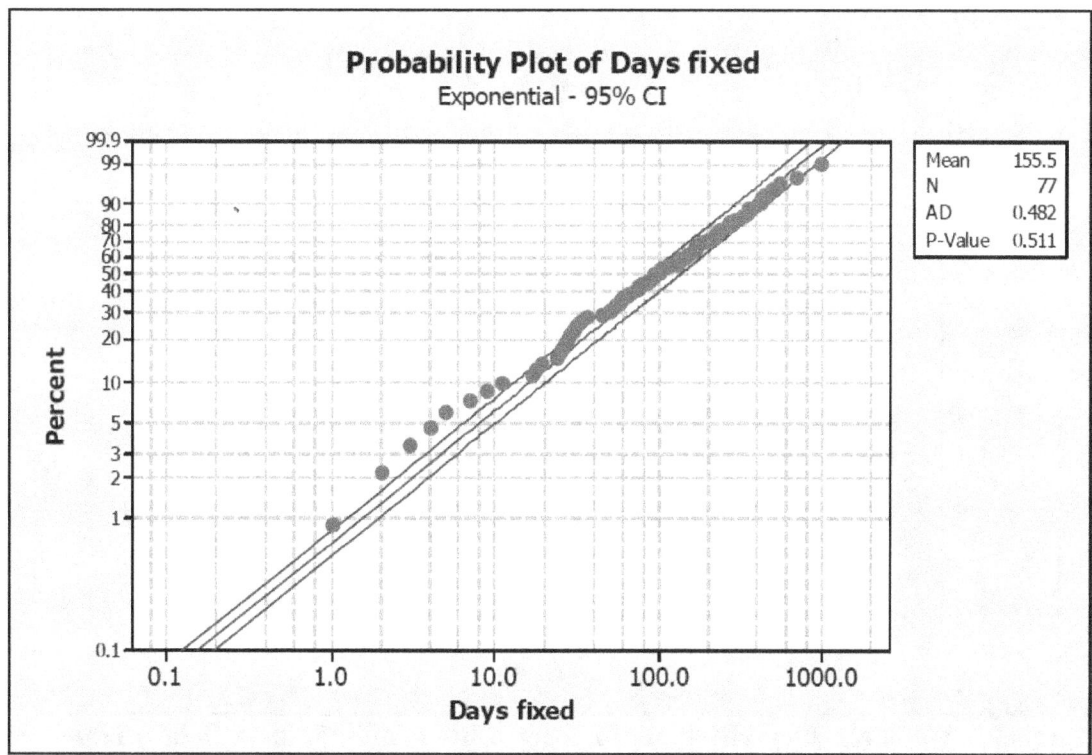

Figure 3.26 Exponential Probability Plot of Tie-breaking Adjusted Platform Inter-Spill (Spills ≥ 50 bbl) Times using 1972-2005 Data Set

Figure 3.27 fits a Weibull distribution to the same data as used in Figure 3.25, i.e., not adjusted for ties. Two things are worth noting: 1) more of the data points are within the 95% confidence limits; 2) the shape parameter (labeled β in the mathematics given earlier) is $0.8756 < 1.0$. Again, this shape parameter implies that the inter-spill time is increasing and that the spill rate is decreasing.

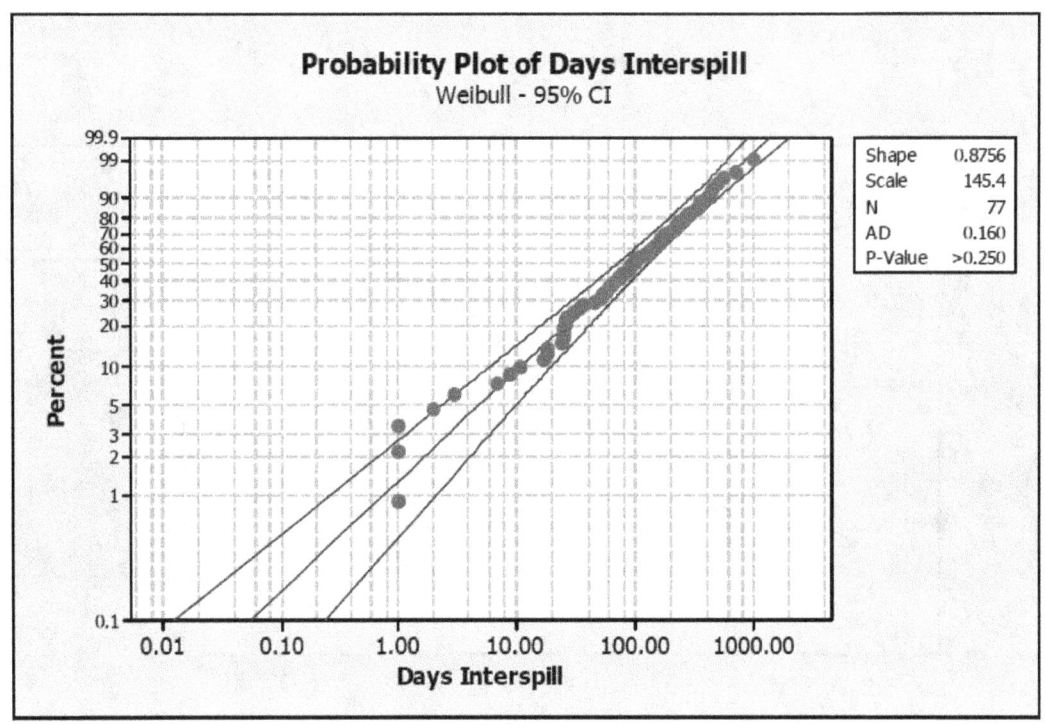

Figure 3.27 Weibull Probability Plot of Platform Inter-Spill (Spills ≥ 50 bbl) Times using 1972-2005 Data Set

Figures 3.28 and 3.29 show good empirical distribution function fits of the exponential and Weibull, respectively. A better fit for the Weibull is seen for smaller spill sizes.

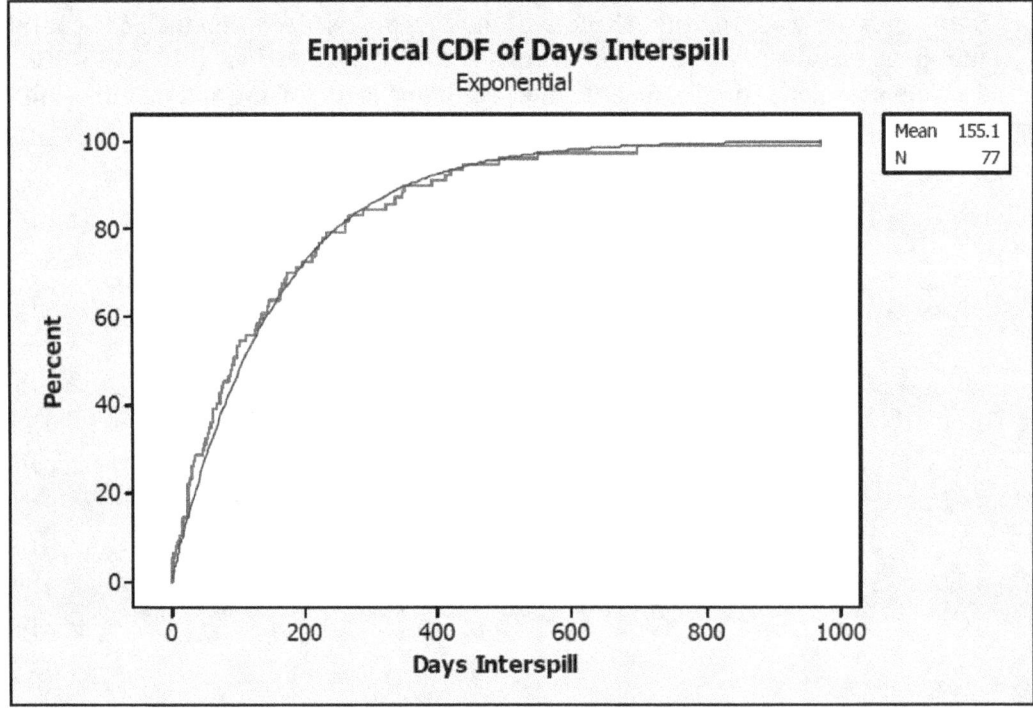

Figure 3.28 Exponential Empirical Distribution Function Fit of Platform Inter-Spill (Spills ≥ 50 bbl) Times using 1972-2005 Data Set

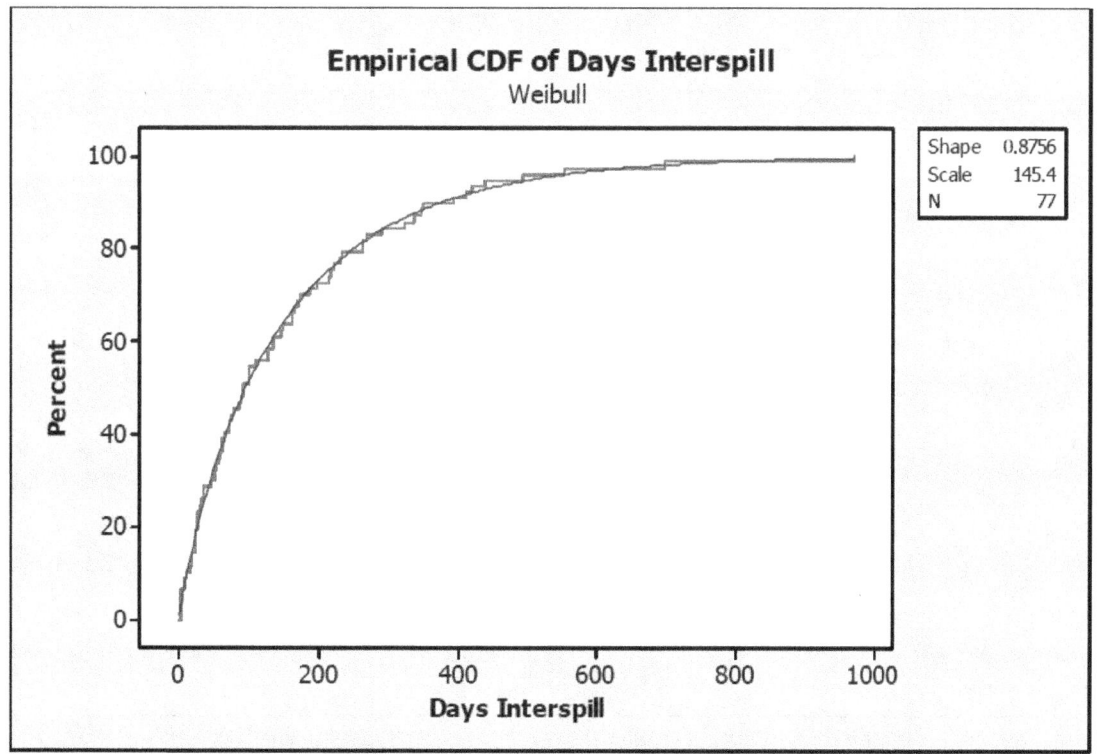

Figure 3.29 Weibull Empirical Distribution Function Fit of Platform Inter-Spill (Spills ≥ 50 bbl) Times using 1972-2005 Data Set

While the exponential distribution does not fare too badly in this section for time as the exposure variable, its performance is not as good for the other two platform exposure variables. This in turn led to the analysis that follows in this section. Even with time, Figure 3.29 shows a better fit for the Weibull than Figure 3.28 for the exponential. The major discussion of a new approach based on the Weibull and a dropping failure rate will be detailed in this section but relevant applications for production volume and the number of platforms as exposure variables will be given in Sections 3.6.1.2 and 3.6.2.2.

The shape parameter for the Weibull fit for all three exposure variables is < 1. This means the hazard of spills is declining over time. The significance of the decline is demonstrated through linear regression, and by dividing the time span into two parts.

Figure 3.30 is a straight line regression of the inter-spill days versus spill year. While the R^2 is small the regression slope is statistically significant (p-value 0.009). The positive slope says that over the time period the average increase in inter-spill days is 5.774 each year. This is not a high rate but over periods of 5 to 10 years or more, it adds up.

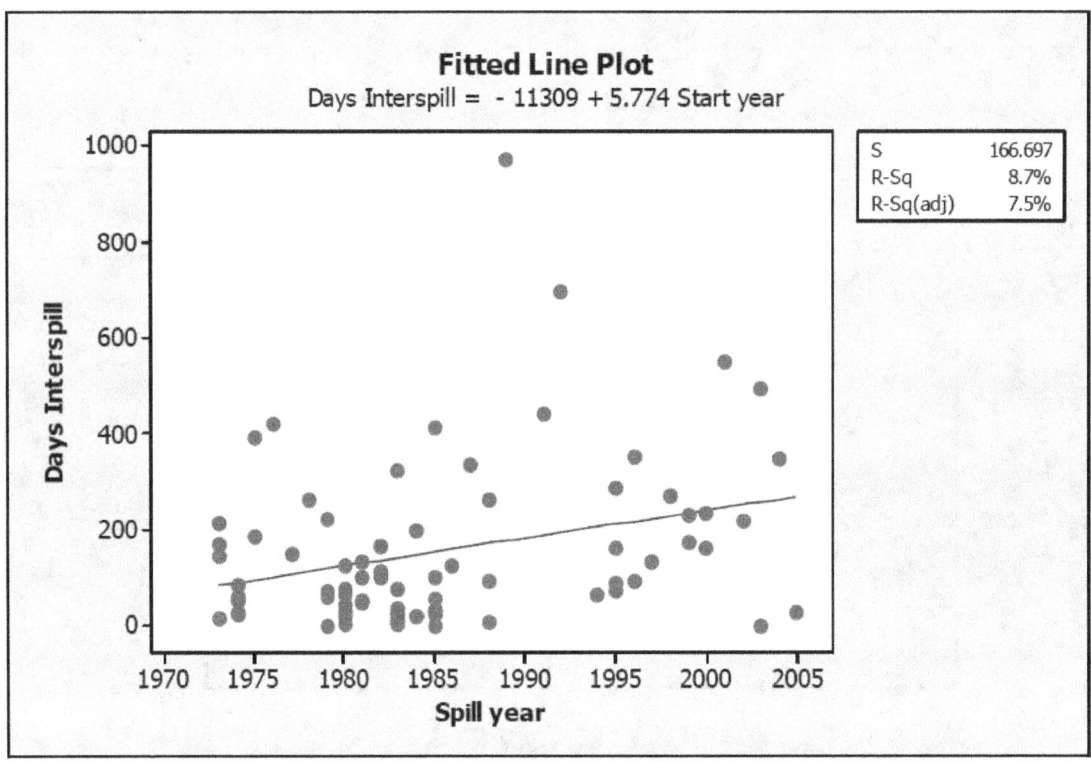

Figure 3.30 Regression of Inter-Spill time versus Spill Year

Table 3.12 summarizes the predicted inter-spill time, which is found by using the equation at the top of Figure 3.30. The table also lists 95% confidence limits for the *average* inter-spill time and 95% upper and lower prediction limits (LPL, UPL) for a *single* inter-spill time in that year. The confidence limits make it clear that the interval is increasing by enough to matter on average. The prediction intervals are so broad that it is clearly impossible to expect to see the improvement by looking at individual inter-spill times.

Table 3.12 Predicted Average Inter-spill Times (days) with 95% Confidence and Prediction Intervals

Year	Inter-spill	LCL	UCL	LPL	UPL
2000	239.0	166.1	311.9	0.0	579.0
2005	267.9	176.0	359.7	0.0	614.4
2010	296.7	184.9	408.5	0.0	647.1

While potentially very useful for prediction in the GOM, this technique is clearest using time as the variable. It is possible that similar results might be obtained if inter-spill intervals are measured in production units or platform-years. To convert these calculated inter-spill values and limits to spill rates they are simply inverted. This may be a desirable approach for longer-range predictions.

Given the difficulty of implementing and explaining this approach, a better starting point for analyzing changes in platform spill rates is to simply divide the 1972 to 2005 interval into two

parts. Without examining the data, it was decided that 1990 would be a good break point for analysis purposes. It was felt that this was a nice round year to work with and broke the full time interval into fairly equal parts. Thus the question is: Is there a statistically significant difference in the inter-spill data for 1972 to 1989 versus 1990 to 2005? To avoid losing a data point the inter-spill time between 1989 and 1990 was included in the earlier interval. This is one of the longest inter-spill times; thus including it in the earlier interval is a conservative approach to estimating the rate of improvement.

Figure 3.31 is an Analysis of Means (ANOM) comparing the 1972 – 1989 average inter-spill days to the 1990 – 2005 average. The centerline shows an overall average over the full 1972 – 2005 time frame of 155.1 inter-spill days. The "stairstep" lines represent upper or lower bounds around this grand average. The interval is tighter for the earlier data due to more data points falling into the earlier time period. Since both averages fall outside the bounds, both are significantly different from the overall grand average. Hence we have a non-stationary system without a constant failure rate over time.

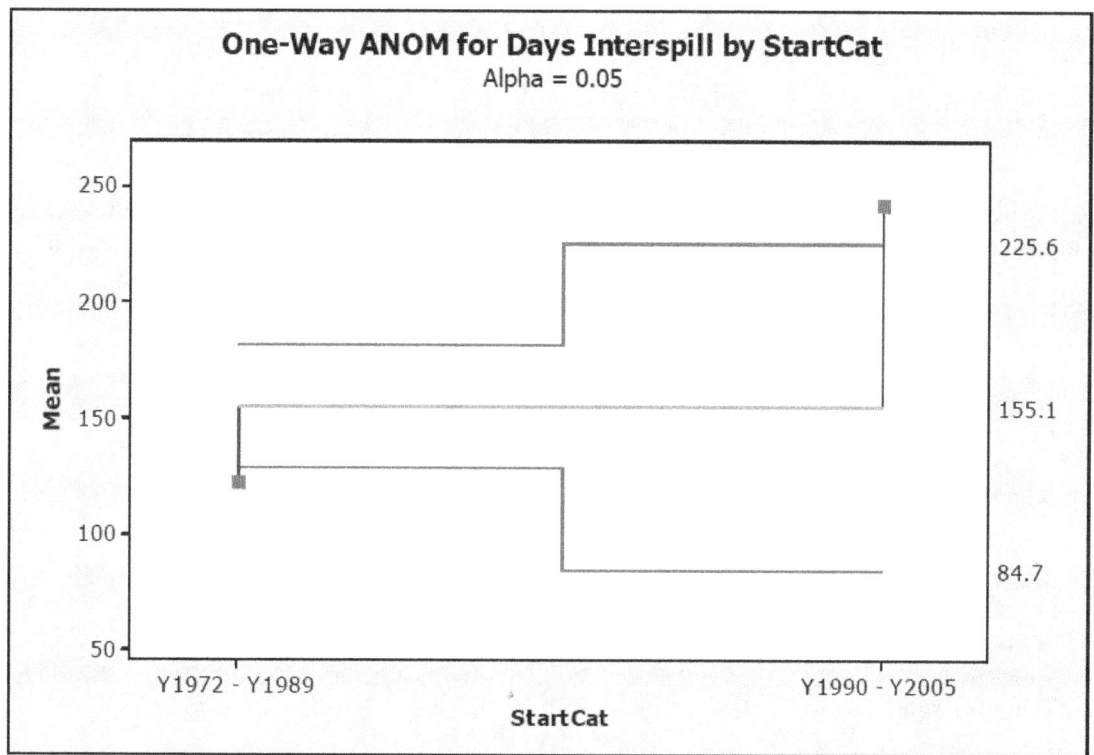

Figure 3.31 Analysis of Means Comparing Inter-Spill Averages between Data for 1972-1989 versus 1990-2005

Similar statistical result may be seen in the two sample t-test (p-value of 0.012) comparing the two means and the nonparametric Kruskal-Wallis test (p-value of 0.001) comparing the two corresponding medians. The two rounded inter-spill sample means of 122 days for 1972 – 1989 and 243 days for 1990 – 2005 are seen below in the two sample t-test output. The inter-spill days have approximated doubled in the latter time interval implying that the spill rate is roughly one half of the 1972 – 1989 time interval. This will be further quantified later with a confidence interval for the ratio of these two rates. The Kruskal-Wallis shows the median inter-spill days are approximately three times (218 days versus 69.5 days) for the 1990 – 2005 versus 1972 – 1989 time intervals.

Table 3.13 Comparing 1972-1989 and 1990-2005 Platform Inter-Spill Times

Two-sample T-test

	N	Mean	Std. Dev.	SE Mean
Y1972-Y1989	56	122	159	21
Y1990-Y2005	21	243	183	40
Estimate for difference	-120.280	95% Conf. Int.	(212.688, -27.871)	
T-test	t = -2.65	P-value = 0.012	DF = 31	

Kruskal-Wallis Test of Median Inter-spill Times

	N	Median	Average Rank	z
Y1972-Y1989	56	69.50	34.0	-3.23
Y1990-Y2005	21	218.00	52.4	3.23
Overall	77		39.0	
H = 10.40	DF = 1	P = 0.001		
H = 10.41	DF = 1	P = 0.001	(adjusted for ties)	

All of this implies that the rate of spills varies significantly across these two time periods. Thus, the next step is to test if the two time periods can be shown to be adequately modeled separately by exponential distributions. If so, then separate Poisson distributions could be fit to each time interval. There is also a statistical test to directly compare the two Poisson rates.

Figures 3.32 and 3.33 show the two different exponential fits to the inter-spill days for the two time intervals. The main point to be made is that both exponential distributions adequately fit each interval based on the p-values. Hence there is no reason here to discard the Poisson assumption. For the other two exposure variables only the panel display style of Figure 3.33 is used.

Figure 3.34 can be compared with Figure 3.33 to examine how "breaking ties" (as in Figure 3.26) improves the resulting fits. This is shown primarily for illustration and to hopefully convey the idea that the ties in the lower end of the distributions are not as important as they may visually appear to be.

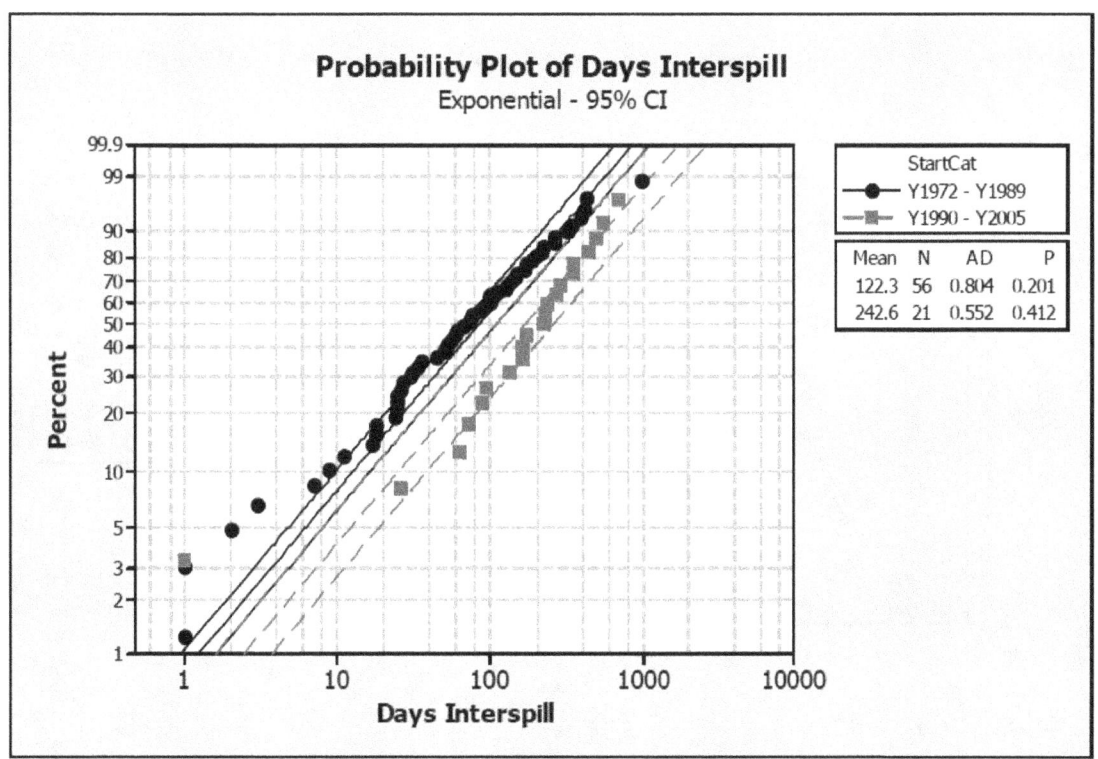

Figure 3.32 Overlaid Exponential Distribution Fits to Platform Inter-Spill Time for 1972-1989 versus 1990-2005

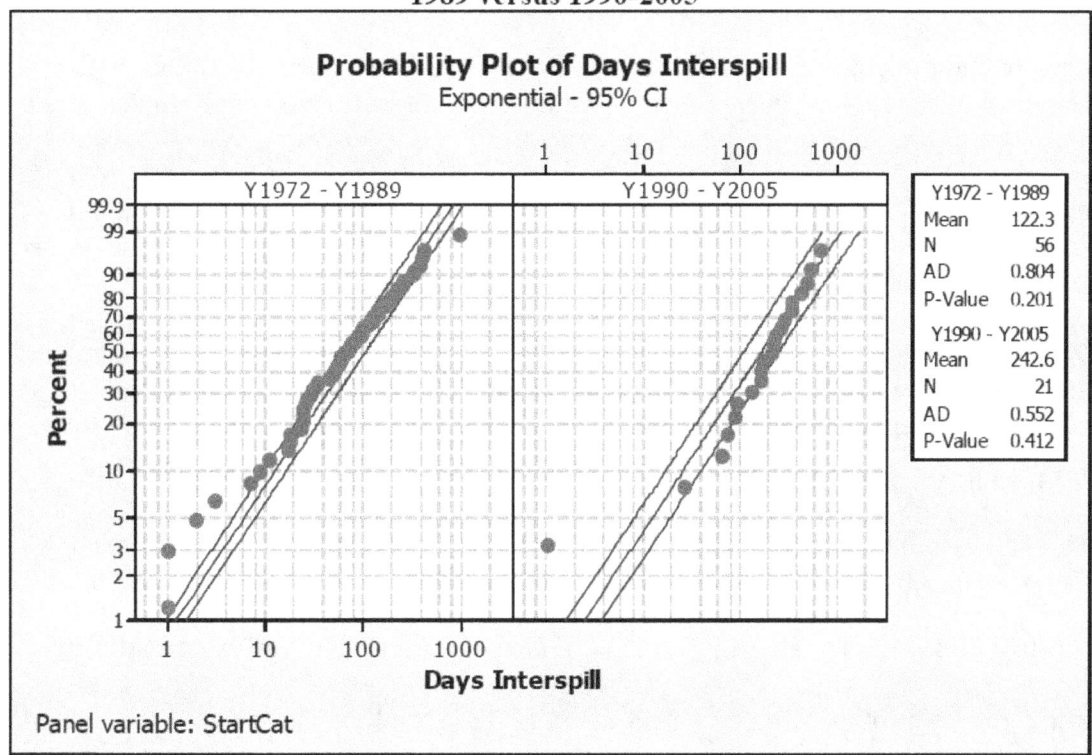

Figure 3.33 Panel Displayed Exponential Distribution Fits to Platform Inter-Spill Time for the 1972-1989 versus 1990-2005

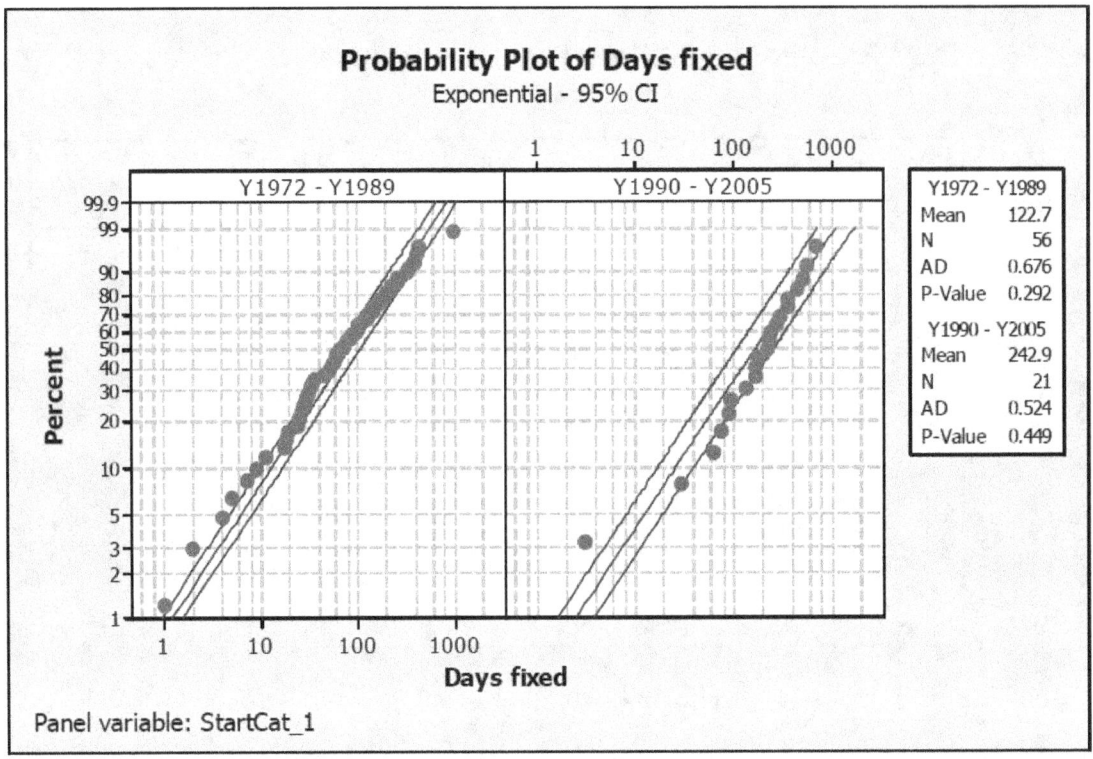

Figure 3.34 Panel Displayed Exponential Distribution Fits to Adjusted (Tie Breaking) Platform Inter-Spill time for the 1972-1989 versus 1990-2005

Building on the work of Przyborowski and Wilenski (1940), Chapman (1952) illustrates the development of an exact confidence interval for the ratio of two Poisson rates. In this case it is desired to know how the Poisson rate drops going from 1972 – 1989 to 1990 – 2005. First keep in mind that the higher average inter-spills days for the exponential distribution for 1990 – 2005 versus 1972 – 1989 implies the Poisson rates will vary in the opposite direction. The exponential gives the mean inter-spill time, while the Poisson rate is the number of spills per time (or per unit of another exposure variable).

Let X and Y be two Poisson random variables with x and y spills, respectively. Let the Poisson mean rate for X be λ and let the Poisson mean rate for Y be $\gamma\lambda$. The total sample size will be the sum of x and y where there are x inter-spill and y inter-spill values in the 1972 – 1989 and 1990 – 2005 time intervals, respectively. Let $\tau = \lambda(1+\gamma)$ *and* $\rho = \dfrac{1}{1+\lambda}$. Then X has a binomial (n, ρ) distribution. Using the exact Excel binomial confidence interval function described in Section 2.5.5, $(\rho, \overline{\rho})$ may be developed. As given in Chapman (1952), a confidence interval for the ratio γ of the two Poisson mean rates is $\left(\dfrac{1}{\overline{\rho}} - 1, \dfrac{1}{\underline{\rho}} - 1 \right)$. Thus we can compute an exact confidence interval for the ratio of the two Poisson mean rates. If the resulting interval does not contain the value 1.0 at a given level of confidence, then the two Poisson rates are significantly different.

Implementing this results in a 95% two sided confidence interval for the Poisson mean rate ratio γ of (0.3051, 0.8330) with the point estimate of 0.5041 for γ. Since 1.0 is not in this Poisson mean rate ratio confidence interval, this implies at the 95% confidence level that the two rates are significantly different and the 1990 – 2005 rate is significantly lower. Thus we have statistical backing for claiming that platform spill rates have dropped from the 1972 – 1989 to 1990 – 2005 time interval. Indeed the rate is roughly ½ of the earlier time period rate as indicated early in the exponential results. But now this ratio is bounded by confidence limits.

3.6.1.2   Platform Inter-Spill Analysis Based on Production Volume (Mbbl)

This section analyzes production volume in millions of barrels (Mbbl) as an exposure variable for platform spills. As seen in Figures 3.35 through 3.38, the Weibull distribution fits inter-spill production better than an exponential. Indeed in this section the exponential fails the Anderson-Darling goodness of fit test (p = 0.017) at the 95% confidence level. Hence even more reason to move away from fitting an exponential to the full time period. Also note the Weibull shape is 0.8224 < 1. Again, this shape parameter implies that the inter-spill production volume is increasing and that the spill rate is decreasing

This section with production volume follows an abbreviated version of the same procedure given in Section 3.6.1.1 for time as the exposure variable. A more direct approach is used in this section as the major concepts and concerns have been given in the prior section. The 1972 – 1989 versus 1990 – 2005 comparison is also presented. Fundamentally, the conclusion is the same. Modeling the entire interval with one distribution is better done with the Weibull, but the increasing inter-spill production volume and decreasing spill rate can be modeled with two exponential distributions for the two time periods.

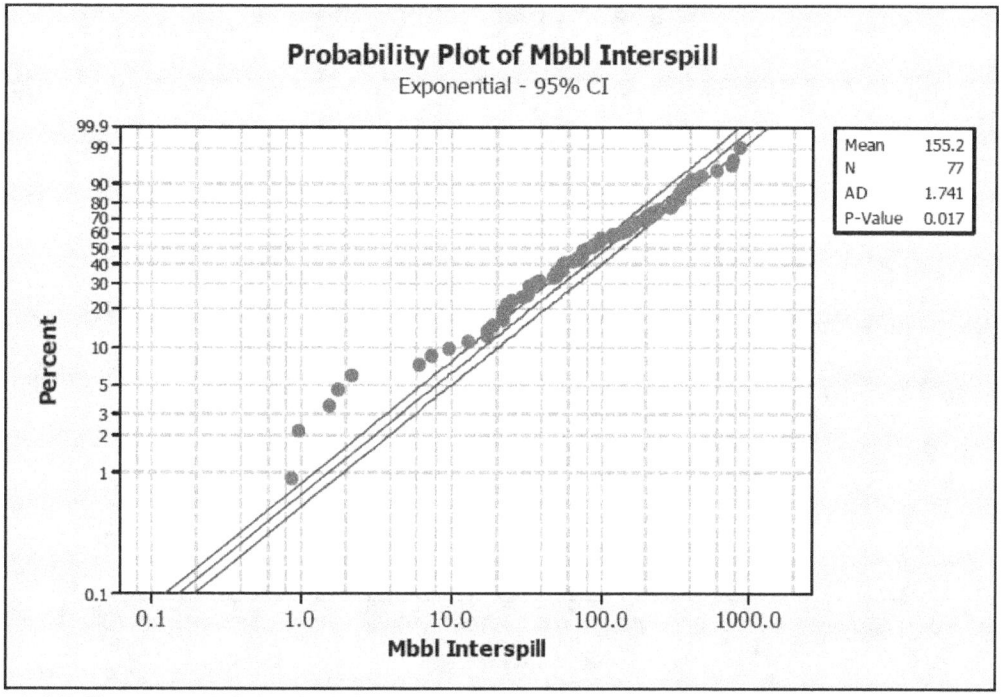

Figure 3.35 Exponential Probability Plot Platform Inter-Spill (Spills ≥ 50 bbl) Production (Mbbl) using 1972-2005 Data Set

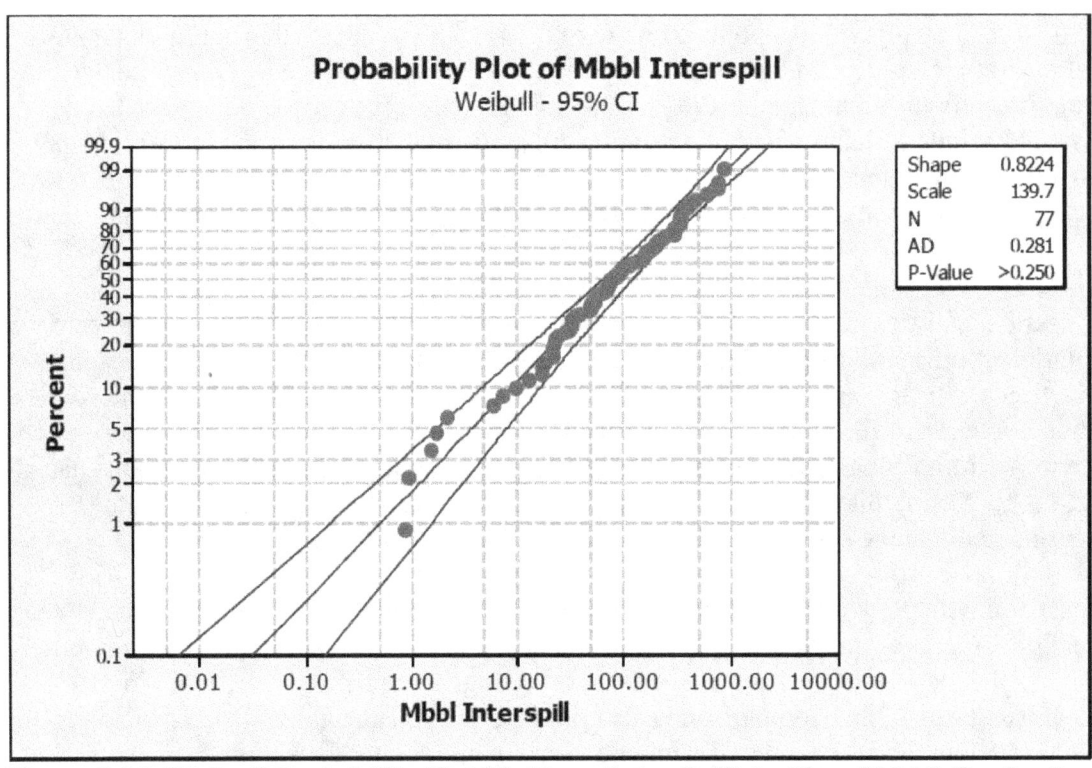

Figure 3.36 Weibull Probability Plot Platform Inter-Spill (spills ≥ 50 bbl) Production (Mbbl) using 1972-2005 Data Set

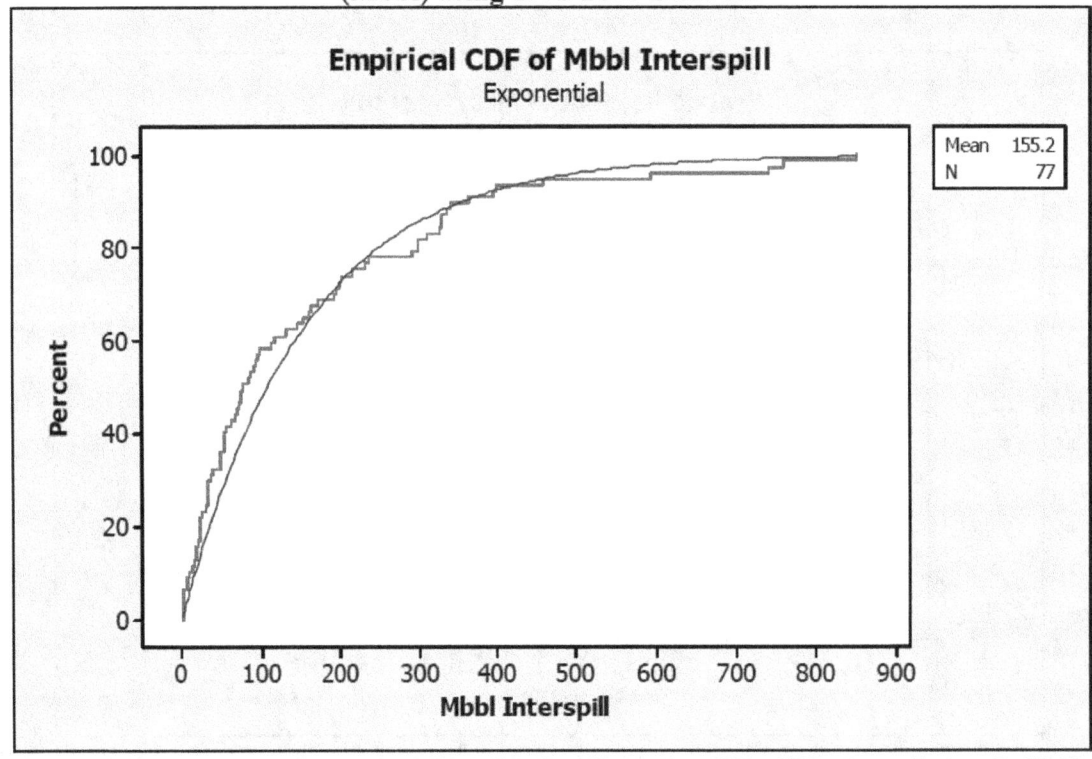

Figure 3.37 Exponential Empirical Distribution Function Fit of Platform Inter-Spill (Spills ≥ 50 bbl) Production (Mbbl) using 1972-2005 Data Set

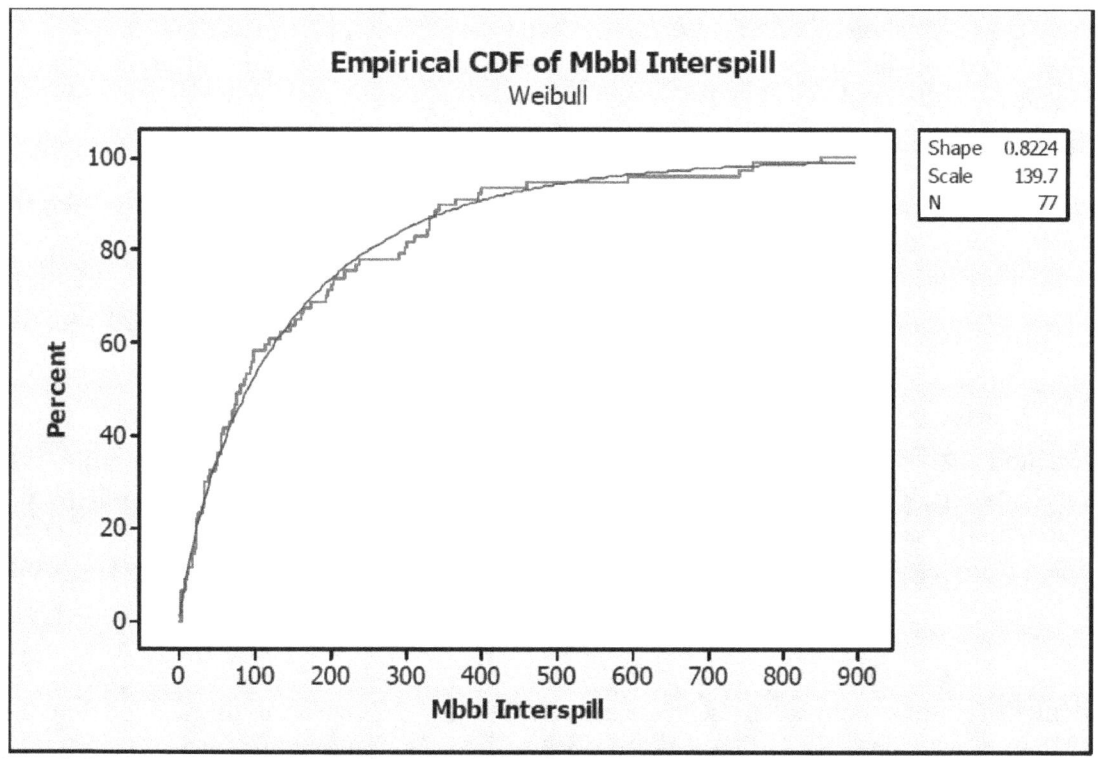

Figure 3.38 Weibull Empirical Distribution Function Fit of Platform Inter-Spill (spills ≥ 50 bbl) Production (Mbbl) using 1972-2005 Data Set

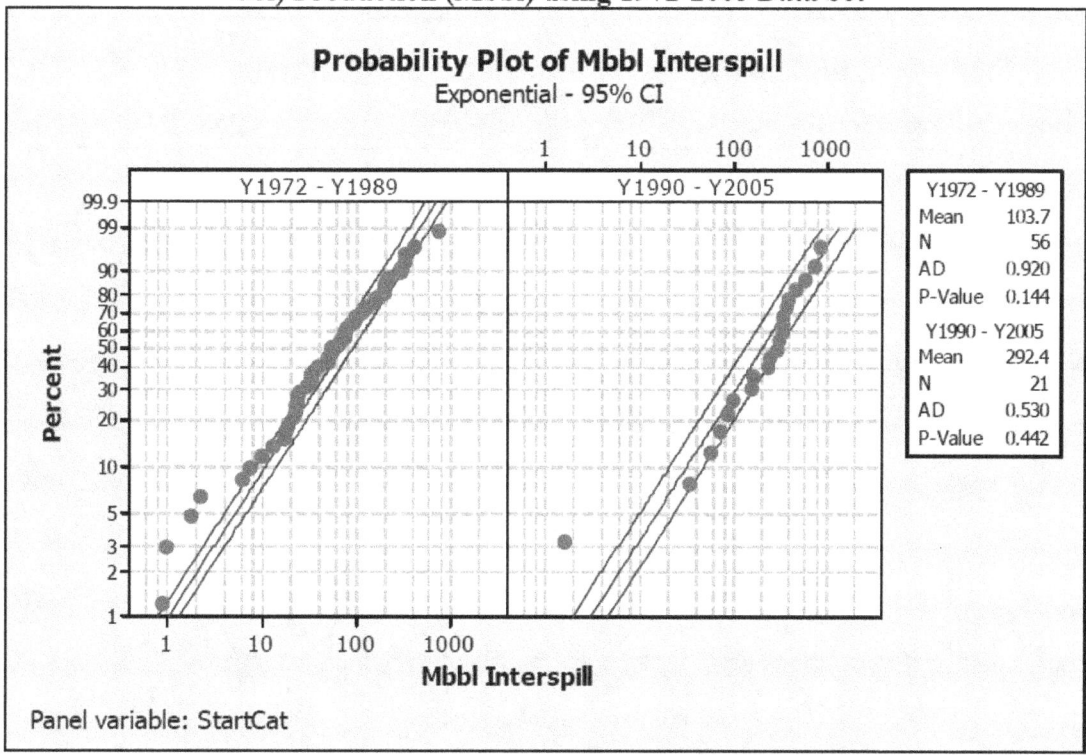

Figure 3.39 Panel Displayed Exponential Distribution Fits to Platform Inter-Spill Production (Mbbl) for 1972-1989 versus 1990-2005

Separate exponential distributions fit the to the two time periods 1972 – 1989 and 1990 – 2005 pass the Anderson-Darling Goodness of fit test as seen in Figure 3.39. The corresponding inter-spill means are 103.7 Mbbl and 292.4 Mbbl. This is even more evidence that the time based results that the spill rate has dropped in the 1990 – 2005 time interval.

The point estimate for the ratio of the two Poisson means rate is 0.3547 indicating the rate over the 1990 – 2005 time interval is only around 1/3 that of the 1972 – 1989 time interval. The corresponding 95% confidence interval for this ratio is (0.1997, 0.5930). With 1.0 not falling into the confidence interval it is seen that the two Poisson mean rates are significantly different.

3.6.1.3   Platform Inter-Spill Analysis Based on Number of Platforms

This section analyzes the number of platforms as an exposure variable for platform spills. As seen in Figures 3.40 through 3.43, the Weibull distribution fits inter-spill production better than an exponential. As seen with production the exponential distribution fails the Anderson-Darling goodness of fit test (p = 0.011) at the 95% confidence level. Hence even more reason to move away from fitting an exponential to the full time period. Also note the Weibull shape is 0.8007 < 1. The 1972 – 1989 versus 1990 – 2005 comparison is presented below.

Fundamentally, the conclusion is the same as with the other exposure variables. Modeling the entire interval with one distribution is better done with the Weibull, but the increasing inter-spill platform-years and decreasing spill rate can be modeled with two exponential distributions for the two time periods.

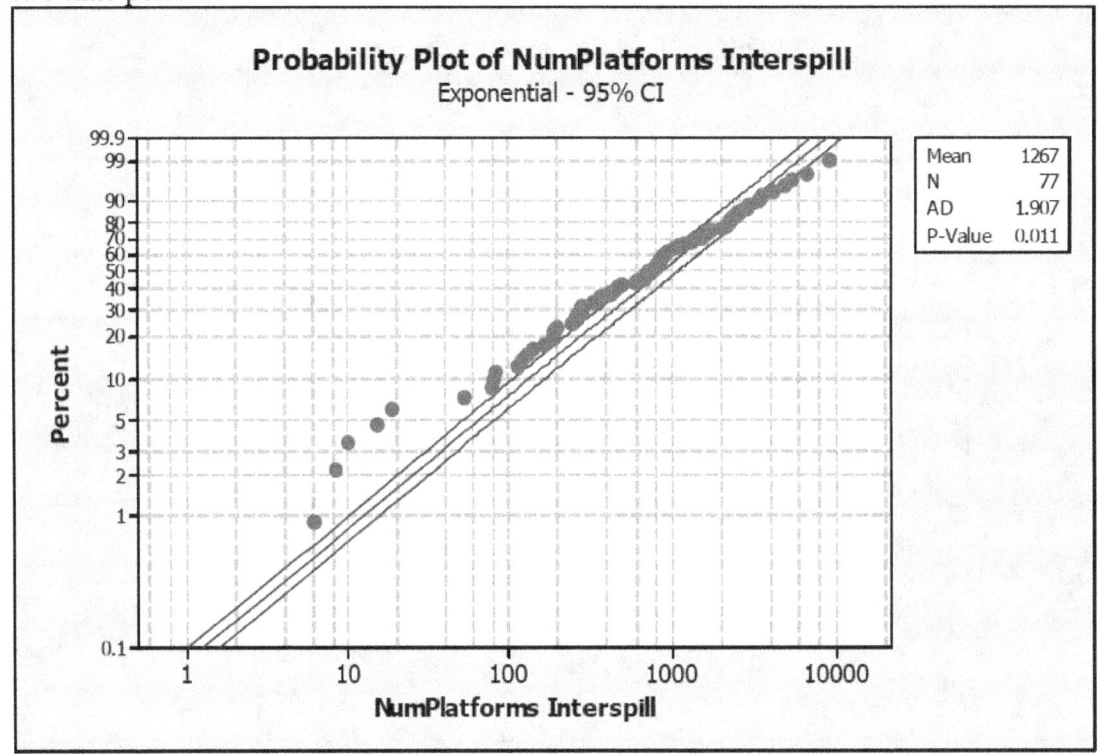

Figure 3.40 Exponential Probability Plot Platform Inter-Spill (spills ≥ 50 bbl) Number of Platforms using 1972-2005 Data Set

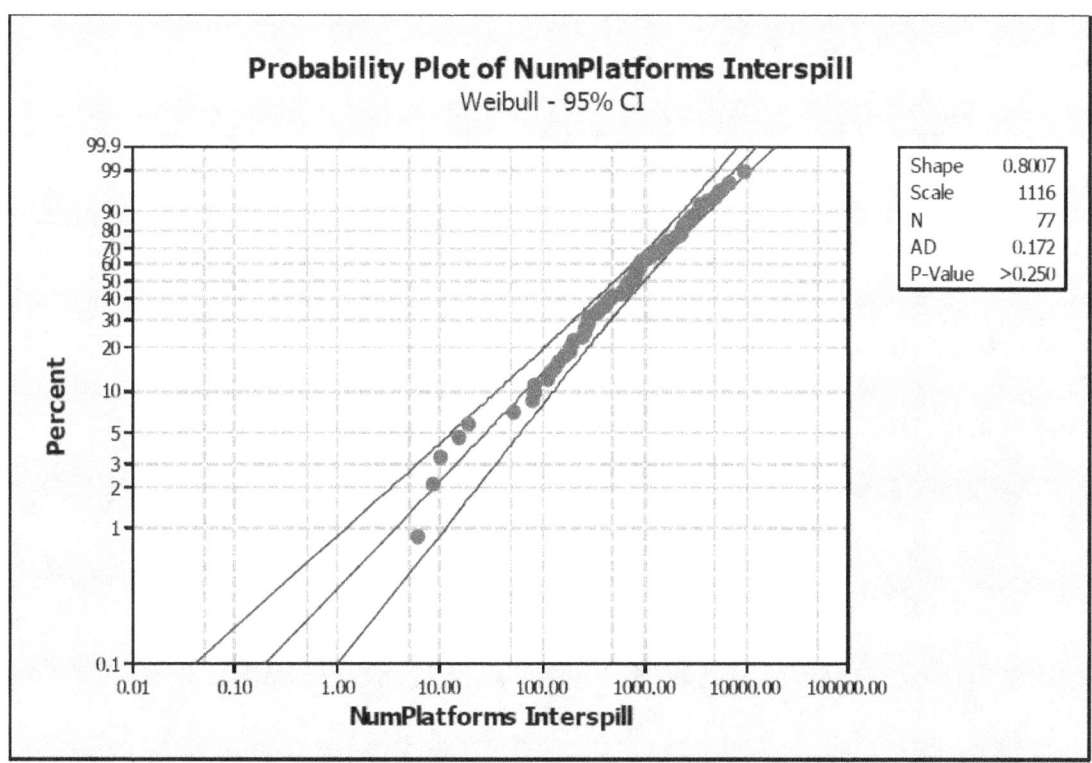

Figure 3.41 Weibull Probability Plot Platform Inter-Spill (Spills ≥ 50 bbl) Number of Platforms using 1972-2005 Data Set

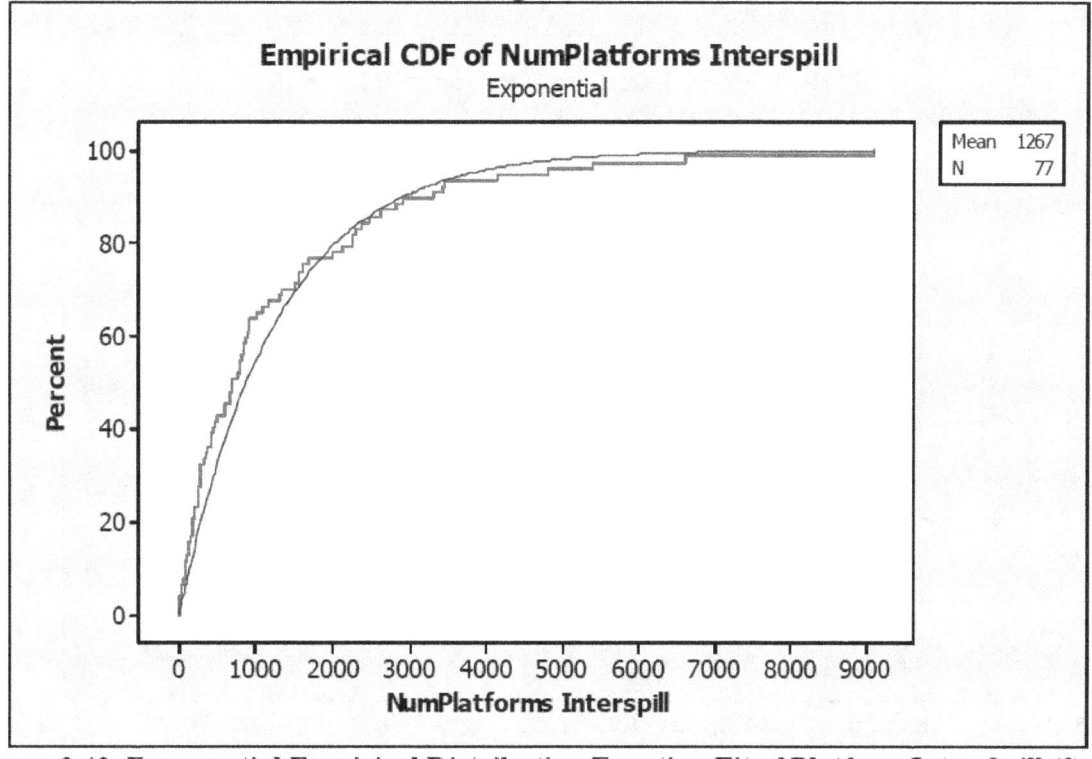

Figure 3.42 Exponential Empirical Distribution Function Fit of Platform Inter-Spill (Spills ≥ 50 bbl) Number of Platforms using 1972-2005 Data Set

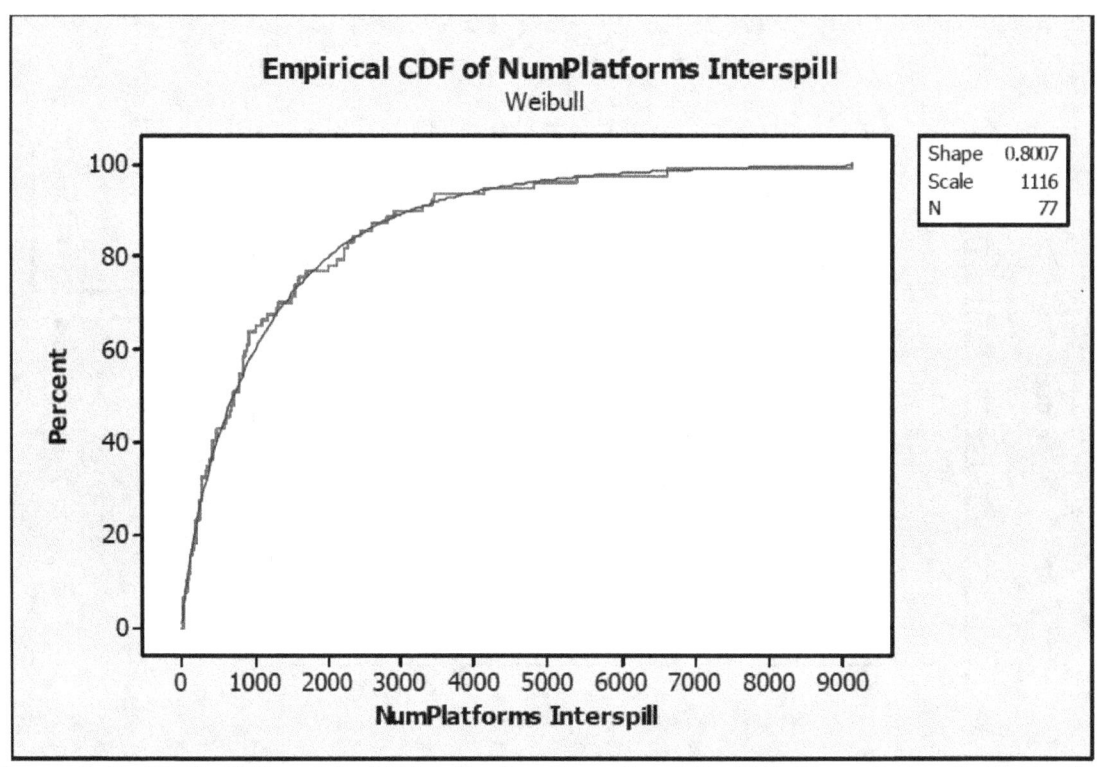

Figure 3.43 Weibull Empirical Distribution Function Fit of Platform Inter-Spill (Spills ≥ 50 bbl) Number of Platforms using 1972-2005 Data Set

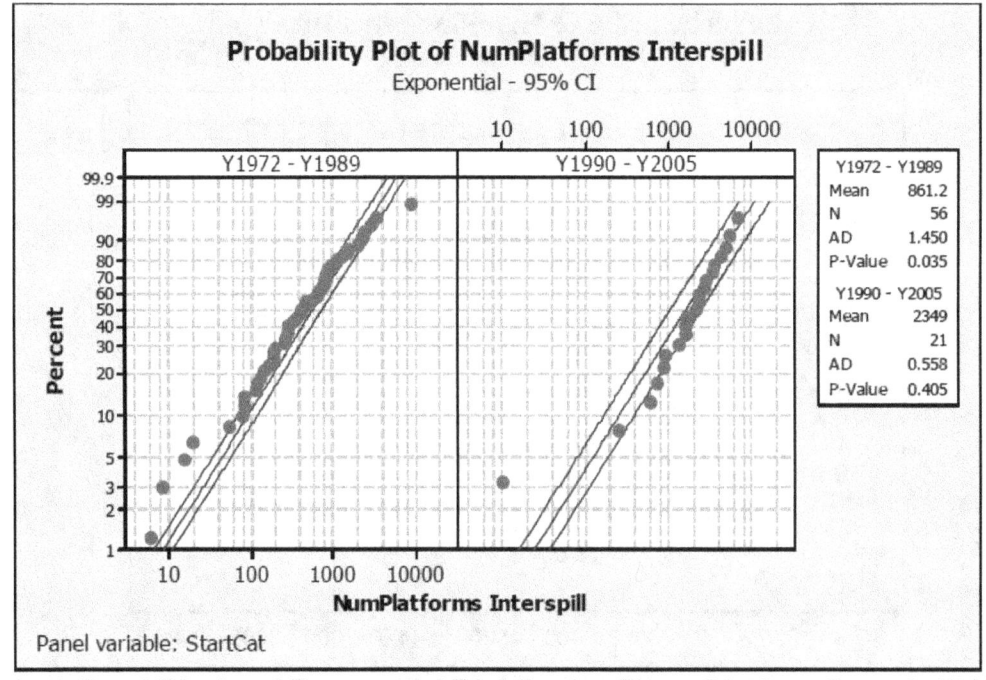

Figure 3.44 Panel Displayed Exponential Distribution Fits to Platform Inter-Spill Number of Platforms for 1972-1989 versus 1990-2005

Separate exponential distributions fit the to the two time periods 1972 – 1989 and 1990 – 2005 are seen in Figure 3.44. Technically the 1972 – 1989 time period does not quite pass the Anderson-Darling goodness of fit test at the 95% confidence level since its p-value is < 0.05. However the visual TLAR assessment is reasonable. Keep in mind also that if the ties were adjusted (as was illustrated for time as the exposure variable) both the visual fit and the Anderson-Darling results would improve. Using Arena's Input Analyzer the exponential distribution passes the Kolmogorov-Smirnov Test with a p-value > 0.15. Hence an exponential distribution can be used for the 1972 – 1989 interval. The corresponding inter-spill means are 861.2 platform-years and 2349 platform-years. This indicates that spill rate has dropped in the 1990 – 2005 time interval since the average number of platform-years between spills has increased.

The point estimate for the ratio of the two Poisson means rate is 0.3666. The corresponding 95% confidence interval for this ratio is (0.2157, 0.6292). With 1.0 not falling into the confidence interval it is seen that the two Poisson mean rates are significantly different with the 1990 – 2005 time frame having the lower spill rate with number of platforms as the exposure variable.

The above binomial based confidence intervals provide an exact confidence interval for the ratios of the two Poisson rates. Table 3.14 based on inter-spill data shows the exact Poisson confidence intervals for each time period and for all exposure variables. An inexact approach to testing whether the Poisson mean rates are different would be to see if the UCLfor the 1990 – 2005 falls below the LCLof the 1972 – 1989 time period. This does occur for production and number of platforms, but not quite for time as an exposure variable. Such a method (commonly used but incorrect) for comparing Normal means is well documented to be ad hoc and not powerful; however, it is still used in practice by many.

Table 3.14 GOM Platform Spill Rates (Spills ≥ 50 bbls) for 1972-1989 and 1990-2005

Platforms 1972-1989 Using Inter-Spill Exponential Distribution

Label	# Spills	Exposure Variable	Sum Exposure Variable	Rate	LCL	UCL
Spills/Bbbl	56	Production Bbbl	5.806	9.645	7.286	12.52
Spill/(Number of Platforms)	56	KPlatforms-Years	48.23	1.161	0.8771	1.508
Spills/year	56	Time, years	18.77	2.984	2.254	3.874

Platforms 1972-1989 Using Full Years

Label	# Spills	Exposure Variable	Sum Exposure Variable	Rate	LCL	UCL
Spills/Bbbl	56	Production Bbbl	5.680	9.860	7.448	12.80
Spill/(Number of Platforms)	56	KPlatforms-Years	43.72	1.281	0.9677	1.663
Spills/year	56	Time, years	18	3.111	2.350	4.040

Platforms 1990-2005 Using Inter-Spill Exponential Distribution

Label	# Spills	Exposure Variable	Sum Exposure Variable	Rate	LCL	UCL
Spills/Bbbl	21	Production Bbbl	6.141	3.420	2.117	5.227
Spill/(Number of Platforms)	21	KPlatforms-Years	49.34	0.4257	0.2635	0.6507
Spills/year	21	Time, years	13.96	1.504	0.931	2.300

Platforms 1990-2005 Using Full Years

Label	# Spills	Exposure Variable	Sum Exposure Variable	Rate	LCL	UCL
Spills/Bbbl	22	Production Bbbl	6.766	3.252	2.038	4.923
Spill/(Number of Platforms)	22	KPlatforms-Years	56.37	0.3903	0.2446	0.5909
Spills/year	22	Time, years	16	1.375	0.862	2.082

3.6.2 Platform Spills Comparing a 1971 Start with a 1972 Start

A data set with 86 observations (Table 2.6 + Table 2.8) starting with April 5, 1971 was constructed. The year 1971 had 8 spills and 1972 had none, and it was felt that some effort was needed to test the impact of including the 1971 data versus not including it. This section analyzes the impact on including versus dropping 1971 using time as the only exposure variable. It is expected that the other two exposure variables would respond in similar fashion.

Figures 3.45 and 3.46 show that an exponential distribution is not rejected by the Anderson-Darling goodness of fit test since all p-values are > 0.05. Figure 3.46 has broken the ties found in the original data resulting in better fits both visually and based on p-values. The difference in the exponential inter-spill mean days is small with the 1971 – 2005 inter-spill mean slightly smaller. The difference is NOT statistically significant, as is detailed at the end of this section.

While the difference might be significant if comparing 1971 – 1989 with 1972 – 1989, that comparison does not matter because the earlier time period is not used for any projections to the Beaufort and Chukchi Seas which is the focus of this study. Thus, only analysis for the entire time span was done.

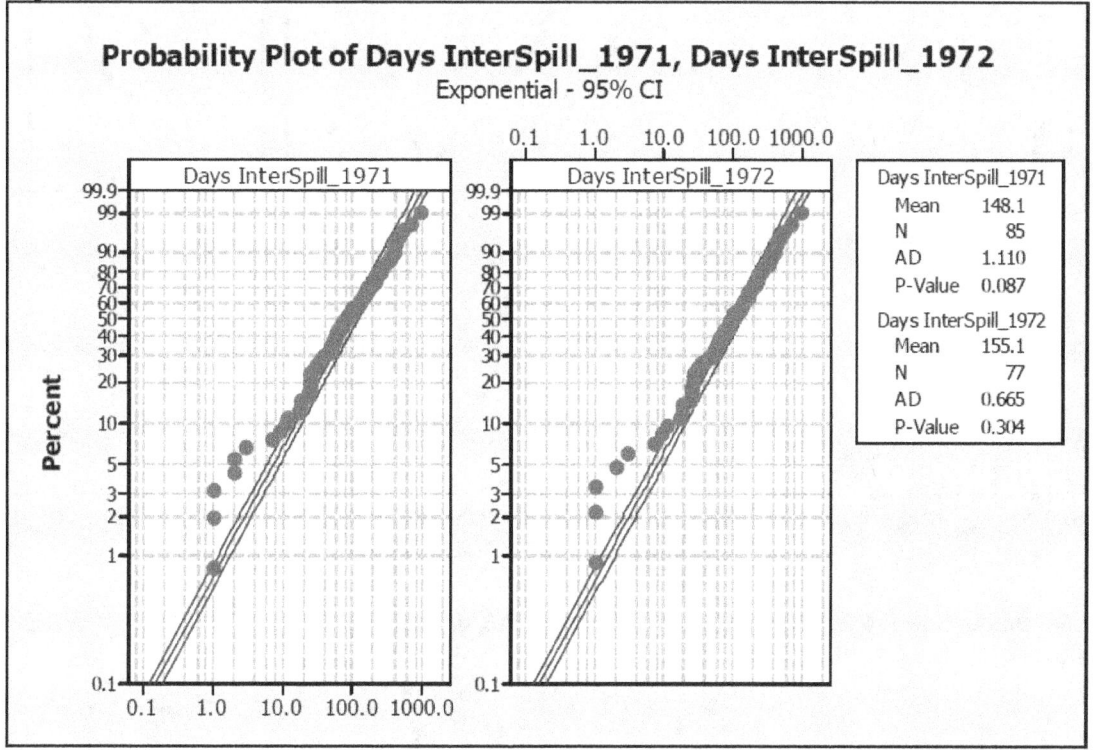

Figure 3.45 Panel Displayed Exponential Distribution Fits to Platform Inter-Spill Time for 1971-2005 versus 1972-2005

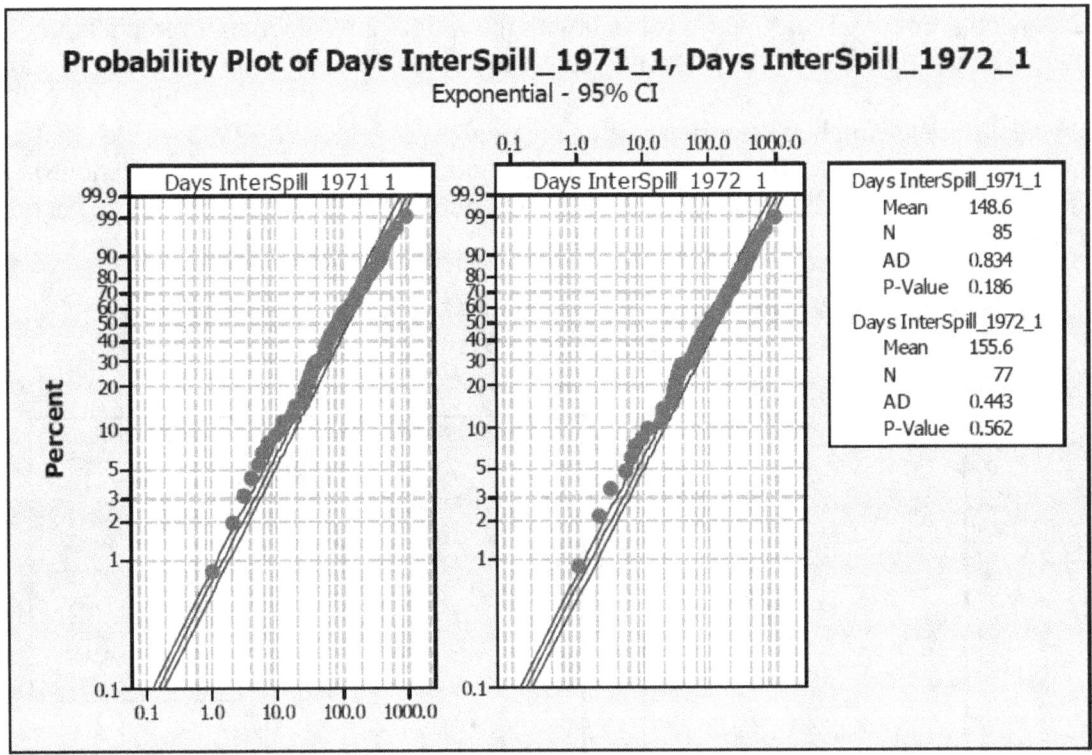

Figure 3.46 Panel Displayed Exponential Distribution Fits to Platform Inter-Spill Adjusted (Tie Breaking) Time for 1971-2005 versus 1972-2005

The point estimate for the ratio of the two Poisson means rate is 0.9550. The corresponding 95% confidence interval for this ratio is (0.6066, 1.56338). With 1.0 falling into the confidence interval it is seen that the two Poisson mean rates are not significantly different.

Since exponentials fit both the 1971 – 2005 and the 1972 – 2005 time intervals and there is no statistically significant difference in the corresponding Poisson rates, it is felt that there is no reason to further analyze platform data using a 1971 start. The platform volume spill analysis that follows uses the 1972 – 2005 data.

3.6.3   Platform Spill Volume Models

This section shows that three parameter lognormal distribution fits platform spill volumes with thresholds of 50 bbl, 100 bbl, 500 bbl, and 1000 bbl. Subsequent sections use these results to present some conceptual approaches that extend the work of Anderson & LaBelle (2000). A three parameter Weibull distribution (as was used for the pipeline spills) fit the two larger thresholds well, but did not fit as well as the lognormal distribution for the smaller two thresholds.

It is our belief that the more complete data set (spills ≥ 50 bbl) offers the opportunity for further insight and possible better estimation. Even this larger data set ignores pipeline spills less than 50 bbl and hence cannot be considered a complete pipeline spill data set, but as discussed earlier it is a reasonable choice given data quality issues.

Figure 3.47 through Figure 3.50 show that the three parameter lognormal distribution is a reasonable fit for all four thresholds shown. Visual TLAR assessments of the probability plots supplemented by the Anderson-Darling goodness-of-fit results in each probability plot support the selection of the three parameter lognormal distribution. In this section all the ties were broken along the lines of breaking volume ties for pipeline spills.

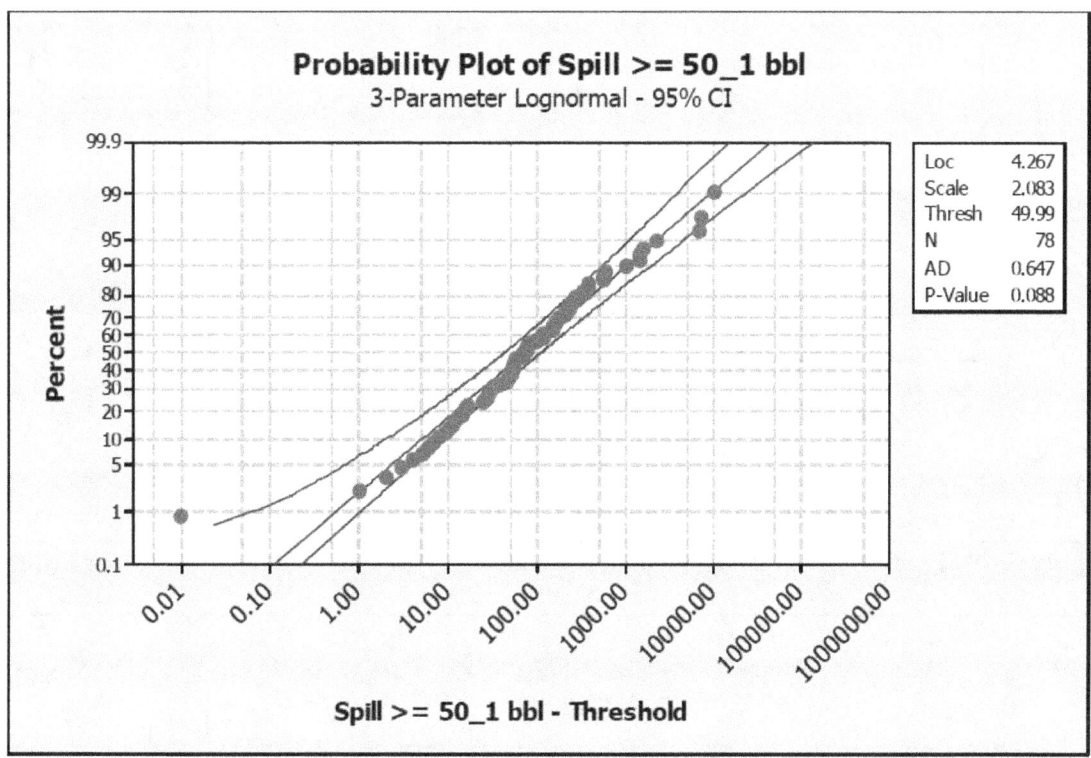

Figure 3.47 Three Parameter LogNormal Probability Plot of Platform Spills for Spills ≥ 50 bbl

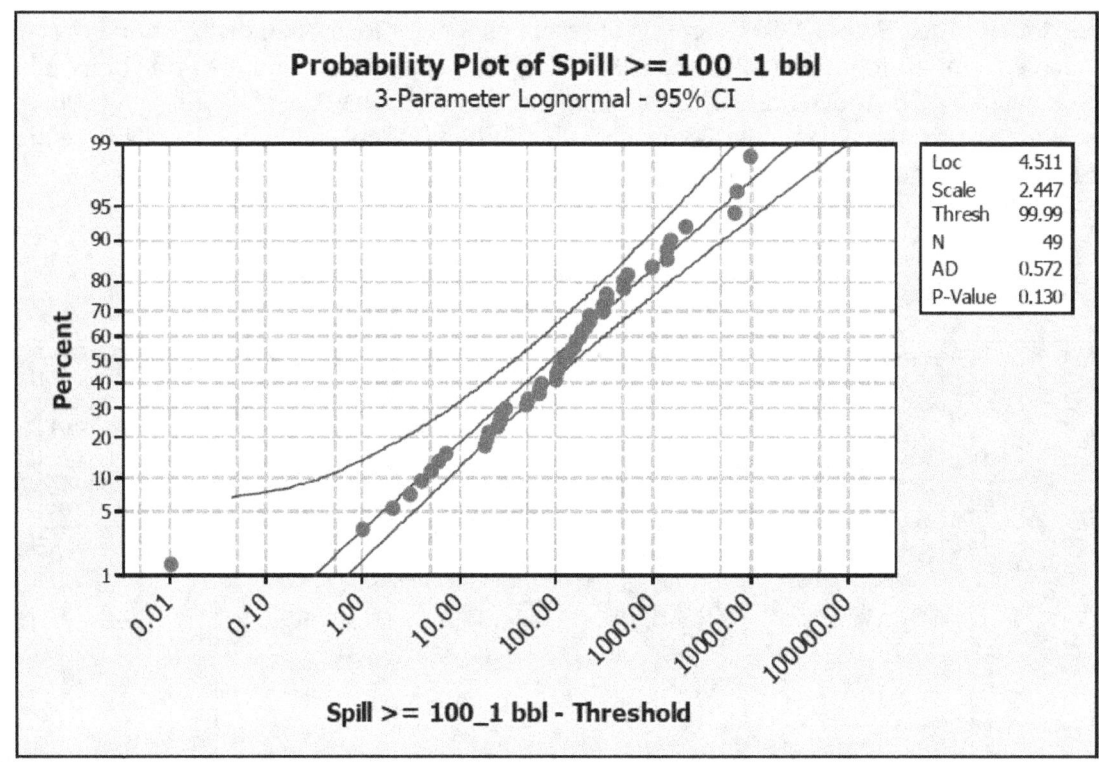

Figure 3.48 Three Parameter LogNormal Probability Plot of Platform Spills for Spills ≥ 100 bbl

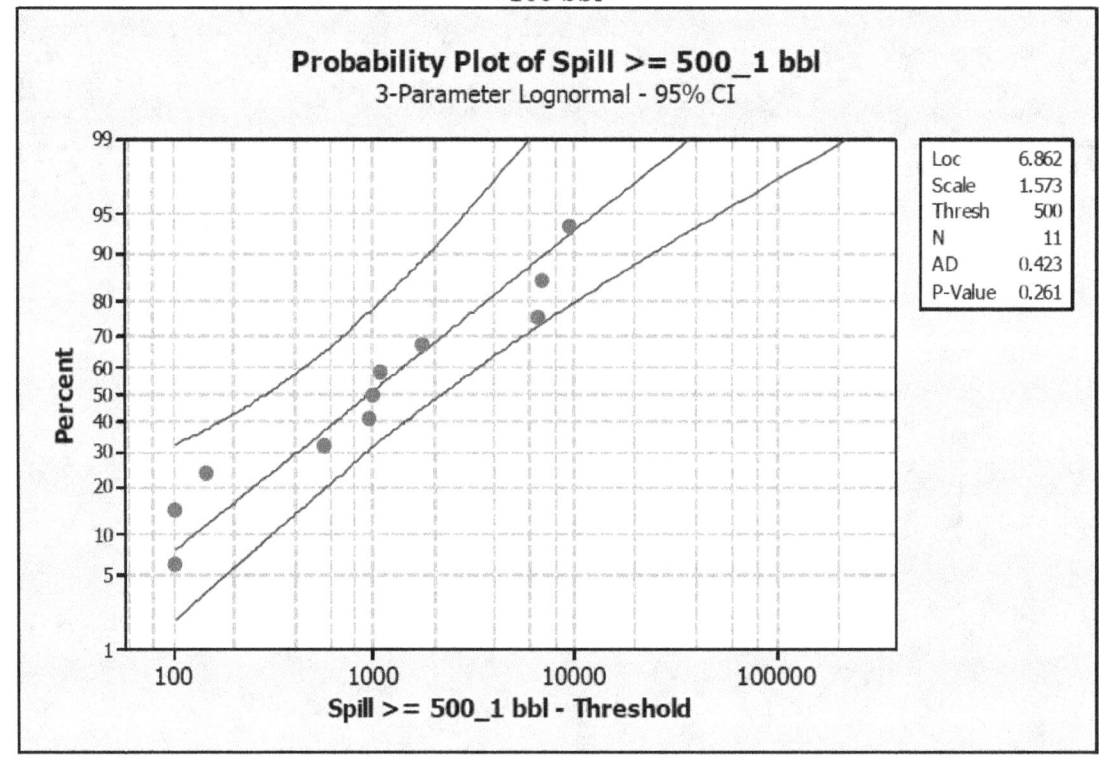

Figure 3.49 Three Parameter LogNormal Probability Plot of Platform Spills for Spills ≥ 500 bbl

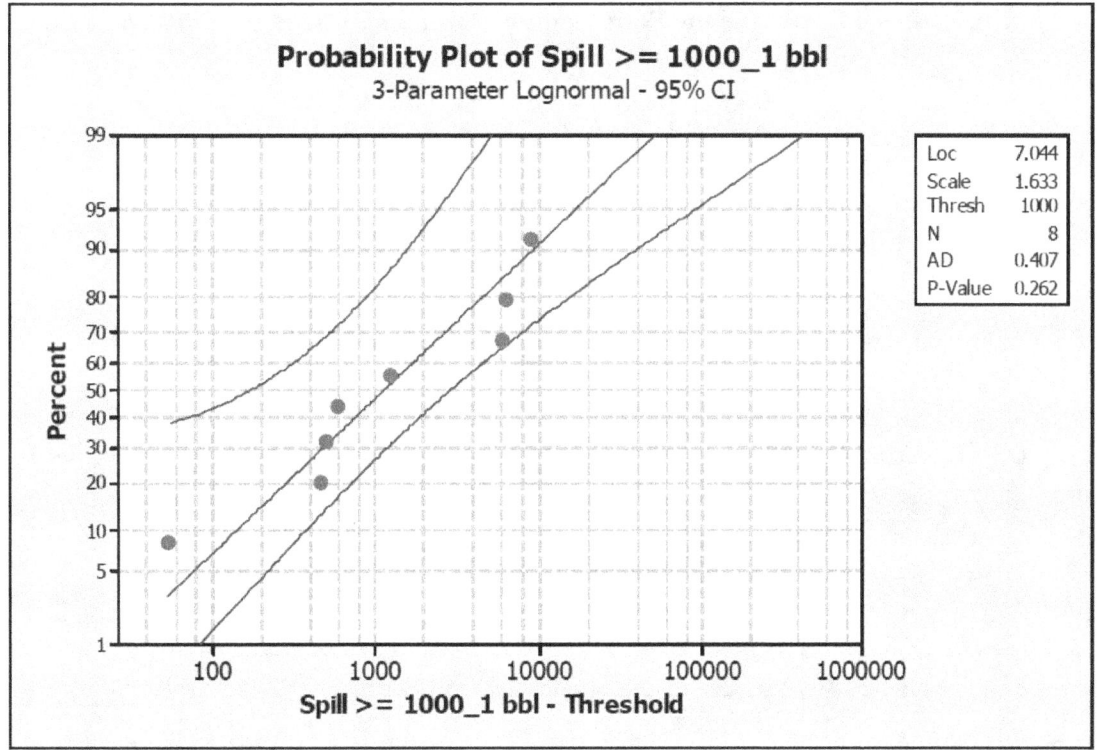

Figure 3.50 Three Parameter LogNormal Probability Plot of Platform Spills for Spills ≥ 1000 bbl

3.6.4 Comparing Platform Spill Volume Models for Different Thresholds

Fitting the four lognormal distributions to the four data sets, allows a comparison of consistency across the models. Table 3.15 presents the odds ratios comparing the four models. Notice that the blank cells correspond to size comparisons that cannot be made with a probability distribution at a higher threshold (e.g., the distribution for spills ≥ 500 bbl cannot be used to predict spills of ≥ 50 bbl).

For example, consider the row comparing 100 bbl spills vs. 500 bbl spills. In the ≥ 50 bbl column the odds ratio is 3.02 implying that the odds of spilling more than 100 bbl compared to 500 bbl is 3.02 to 1. In the ≥ 100 bbl column of this row, the odds of spilling more than 100 bbl compared to spilling more than 500 bbl is estimated to be 3.67. With the minor exception of the 5.76, note the consistency of the odds ratios in the all columns. This is done by looking at each row separately. If the values in the row are in the same ballpark, then the models are predicting similar outcomes. The results in this table imply that these lognormal models are providing similar predictions. Thus the value of a larger data set (e.g., ≥ 50 bbl) may be used to reasonably predict the likelihood of larger platform spill sizes.

The consistency of the four lognormals is rather striking. Following the approach that led to the pipeline Figure 3.24, Figure 3.51 illustrates the excellent match between the four cumulative distribution functions based of the conditional probability approach detailed in Section 3.5.4 for pipelines.

Table 3.15 Odds Ratios for the Four Lognormal Distributions for Platform Spills

Thresholds for the four lognormal models

	> 50 bbl	> 100 bbl	> 500 bbl	> 1,000 bbl
50 vs. 100	1.76			
100 vs. 500	3.02	3.67		
500 vs. 1000	1.76	1.56	1.52	
1000 vs. 2000	1.91	1.63	1.70	1.88
2000 vs. 15000	10.91	5.76	9.24	8.51

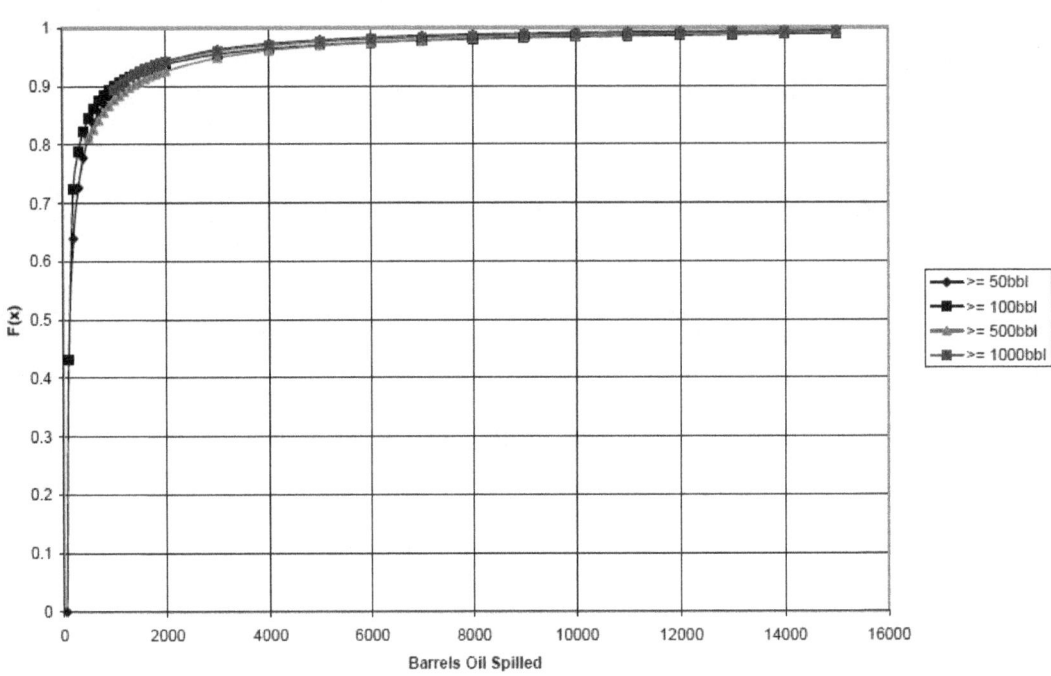

Figure 3.51 Overlay of Lognormal Empirical CDFs for Platform Spill Data

3.6.5   Platform Spill Volume Confidence Intervals

Section 3.5.6 on pipeline spills presents alternative ways to develop confidence intervals. As explained in that section the recommended approach for confidence intervals for varying volume thresholds is the one given in Table 3.9. Thus in this section it is the only approach applied. As in the pipeline Section 3.5.6 the approach is given here only for the production exposure variable.

The volume was well modeled by the lognormal distribution, but this was based on the full set of spills independent of which time frame the spill fell into. The two volume means for the time periods are not be significantly different (p-value = 0.591) in a two sample t-test. Thus the full volume data set is used regardless of the spill date.

While the full set of volumes is used, this section focuses on applying that data only to the 1990-2005 production volume exposure variable. The 1990 – 2005 production spill rate is 3.420 spills/Bbbl production as given in the earlier Table 3.13. To implement the confidence interval approach recommended the binomial confidence intervals first need to be computed. Table 3.16 does that below and then the results are used to get the desired Poisson based confidence intervals for higher thresholds in Table 3.17.

Table 3.16 Exact Binomial Confidence Intervals for Various Platform Spill Volume Thresholds

Threshold	P(≥ Threshold)	Lower Binomial Confidence Level	Upper Binomial Confidence Level
100	0.57	0.45	0.68
500	0.19	0.11	0.30
1000	0.11	0.05	0.19

Table 3.17 Recommend Rate Estimates and Confidence Intervals for Various Platform Volume Spill Thresholds (using the 1990 – 2005 Rate)

Threshold	P(≥ Threshold)	Adjusted Poisson Rate per Bbbl	Adjusted LCL	Adjusted UCL
100	0.57	1.94	1.53	2.31
500	0.19	0.64	0.38	1.02
1000	0.11	0.37	0.16	0.66

The above Table 3.17 is useful for estimating spill volumes for the thresholds given above. It is based on the larger ≥ 50 bbl data set. Other thresholds of interest can easily be examined in the same manner. In addition to providing rate estimates for the 100 bbl, 500 bbl, and 1,000 bbl thresholds, this table bounds the rate with the recommended approach to establishing confidence intervals when the P(≥ Threshold) is relatively well estimated. This is felt to be the case for platform spills using the three parameter lognormal distributions developed.

3.6.6   Summary and Conclusions

Section 3.6 analyzed platform spills ≥ 50 bbl from both an inter-spill perspective as well as a volume perspective. Inter-spill analyses used three different exposure variables: time, production, and platform-years. This analysis showed that platform spill rates have significantly dropped over time for all exposure variables. The data was divided into two fairly equal time intervals 1972 – 1989 and 1990 – 2005. Exact Poisson rate ratio analysis provided confidence intervals for the declining rates between the two time intervals.

Three parameter lognormal distributions fit the platform volume data very well. Using the larger ≥ 50 bbl data set, it was shown how to estimate the likelihood of spills exceeding over thresholds, e.g., 100 bbl, 500 bbl, and 1,000 bbl. Confidence intervals were developed to bound these rates. This methodology can be applied to any desired spill threshold.

In summary, it is believed that the use of a larger data set such as used in this section can add considerable value. In addition to being able to estimate rates for other spill thresholds, this larger data set conclusively showed that platform spill rates have indeed fallen over time. This was not evident in earlier analyses based on data ≥ 1,000 bbl.

The following conclusions are drawn from the results in this section:
1. The use of the larger data set for platform spills ≥ 50 bbl adds remarkable modeling flexibility and improves the validation of the conceptual underpinnings of the statistical modeling. Without the larger data set, it is unlikely that the statistically significant drop in platform spill rates would have been detectable.
2. Production and platform-years are useful exposure variables to help understand and model not only the GOM but will be advantageous in the GOM to Arctic extension of Chapter 4.
3. The application of exact Poisson confidence intervals for differing exposure variables provides a more firm foundation for uncertainty quantification and prediction.
4. The application of exact Poisson rate ratio confidence intervals allows quantification of the uncertainty in the relative change in platform spill rates for the two time periods used.
5. Table 3.13 provides platform spill rates for all three exposure variables for spill rates ≥ 50 bbl for both the 1972 – 1989 and 1990 – 2005 time intervals.
6. A three parameter lognormal distribution for platform spill volumes ≥ 50 bbl provides a more complete use of available data and reduces the width of spill rate confidence intervals.
7. Table 3.17 presents the recommended production spill rate confidence intervals for thresholds ≥ 50 bbl.

3.7   Chapter Summary

Chapter 3 examines inter-spill distributions and spill volume distributions for pipelines and platforms. Section 3.2 introduces exact Poisson confidence intervals. Sections 3.3 and 3.4 examine the Anderson and Labelle (2000) data for pipelines and platforms, respectively. The data in these two sections are limited to spills ≥ 1,000 bbl. Exponential distribution analysis shows that the Poisson distribution assumption is valid for the exposure variable time for this data. Weibull distributions fit the spill volumes for both pipelines and platforms.

Section 3.5 expands the pipeline data to include spills ≥ 50 bbl. Three exposure variables are used: time, production, and pipeline miles. The inter-spill data for all pipeline exposure variables are found to be adequately fit by exponential distributions. Therefore a Poisson distribution can be used to assess spill rates for these exposure variables as well as quantifying the associated uncertainty. This section also highlights the relationship between the exponential and Poisson and illustrates their relationship. Pipeline spill volumes are modeled well by a Weibull distribution and ways to estimate rates for spills of varying thresholds are given along with alternative confidence interval approaches. The recommendation approach is documented. There was no statistical evidence of a spill rate change over time for pipelines.

Section 3.6 performs a similar analysis for platform spills $\geq$ 50 bbl, but complications arose in that the spill rates cannot be modeled by a single Poisson distribution for the full $\geq$ 50 bbl data set for any of the three platform exposure variables (time, production, and platform-years). Several statistical techniques were used to examine spill rates from 1972 – 1989 versus 1990 – 2005. All techniques strongly showed that platform spill rates are significantly lower in the latter time period. Each of these two time periods separately is well modeled by Poisson distribution and confidence intervals are provided for all three exposure variables separately for the time periods. Three parameter lognormal distributions fit the platform spill volume data and methods were presented to estimate spill rates for other thresholds from the $\geq$ 50 bbl data.

4 Extending to Alaska

4.1 Introduction

Rather than repeating discussions about the similarities and differences between the GOM and the Beaufort and Chukchi Seas, this section will simply describe the organization of this chapter and the methodology used to construct oil-spill probabilities for OCS areas north of Alaska.

However, it is appropriate to begin with a description of the uncertainties that must be addressed so that the level of accuracy of the results can be placed in a realistic context. These uncertainties include:

1. What is the best mix of drivers by which to measure oil spill probabilities?
2. What is the average rate of oil spills within the existing OCS infrastructure?
3. What is the best way to deal with GOM oil spills with GOM specific causes, such as hurricanes and third party damage from fishing trawlers?
4. What is the relationship between spill rates at the different spill thresholds of 50, 100, 500, or 1000 bbl?
5. Since different values will be calculated depending on the exact data set and methodology, how should the uncertainty over which is best be reflected?
6. Is the average rate shifting over time, and if so what is it now and what is it projected to be?
7. How should this average rate be extended to new regions, such as Alaska?
8. What is the mix of infrastructure that will be used to produce oil in the OCS region of Alaska?
9. What spill probabilities are linked to Alaska specific spill causes and how do probabilities for existing causes such as human error change with increased cold and darkness?
10. What reductions in oil spill probabilities are possible through regulatory requirements for design and operations?

Many of these uncertainties are beyond the scope of this study, and some may in fact be unknowable. However, they collectively enforce the humble recognition that the uncertainties defined in this study are only the starting point for where other uncertainties begin.

Oil spills in Alaskan waters can occur for reasons such as corrosion and human error that operate anywhere. The probabilities of these spills detailed in Section 4.3 are estimated using GOM data. The results are built upon, but distinct from the material of Chapter 3, as some spills included in the spill rates of Chapter 3, such as those from hurricanes and third party impacts, are extremely unlikely or impossible in the Arctic.

One of the sets of spill rate estimates derived for the GOM is clearly unusable for extension to the Arctic. These are the spill rates based on time. For example, Table 3.13 includes platform spill rate estimates for 1990 to 2005 of 1.375 or 1.504 spills per year, depending on approach. This is for an average of 3523 platforms, thus applying it to a development scenario with a maximum of 8 platforms would clearly be absurd. Thus, rates per year derived for the GOM should only be applied within the GOM.

The spill rates developed in this chapter, like the ones in Chapter 3, are stated as x pipeline spills per pipeline mile-year or y platform spills per platform-year. Thus, it is necessary to have a development scenario of how many pipeline miles and platforms in each year to produce what volume of production. Since any development is some time in the future, any scenario is in some sense speculative. However, for its own planning purposes and in conjunction with Bercha (2002 and 2006) MMS has constructed a Beaufort Sea development scenario. This is detailed in Section 4.2. While it is unlikely to match development if it occurs, it is certainly a realistic representation of one possibility. As such, it is a solid example of how the spill rates can be used, and a useful test case as to what methodologies are the most realistic.

Sections 4.4 and 4.5 addresses what is known about Arctic specific causes that can be linked respectively with pipeline and with platform oil spills. Not surprisingly, some of this cannot currently be stated in statistical terms because not enough is known.

Section 4.6 applies the spill rates to the Beaufort development scenario in order to calculate life-of-field (LOF) probabilities where possible. This can be compared with results in Section 4.7 for the data in Bercha (2006). This is done in order to examine the level of agreement and disagreement between the two reports on oil spill occurrence estimators for the Beaufort/Chukchi Sea OCS.

Section 4.8 summarizes this chapter.

4.2 Development Scenario

Table 4.1 summarizes a hypothetical development scenario for the Beaufort Sea. This is a simplification of data supplied by MMS for Bercha (2006, Table 3.2) and also directly for this study. As this study does not for example generally consider the water depth for pipelines or platforms, nor the diameter for pipelines; the scenario is simplified so that only the total rows and columns from the more detailed scenario are repeated in Table 4.1. While not part of the original scenario, the final row for total exposure has been created by simply counting the years or summing the platforms, pipelines, or production.

One of the uncertainties described in Section 4.1 concerned the mix of infrastructure that will be used to produce oil in the OCS region of Alaska. This uncertainty includes both the details for each category, and the relationships between them. Obviously, the precise mix of miles of pipelines, numbers of platforms, and numbers of wells will not be known until and if they are built. This uncertainty means that probabilities derived from spill rates for each driver are combined in an uncertain way. Perhaps the most important of these uncertainties is how much production will come from the infrastructure, as fundamentally it is the level of production which produces the benefits and justifies all costs of development – economic, environmental, and social. This study can only recognize this uncertainty; this study cannot quantify it.

The scale of the Beaufort development introduces another source of uncertainty. Unlike the GOM which has a large infrastructure that forms a sizeable statistical universe, the Beaufort development would be an example of small sample statistics – where greater variability in average outcomes is expected. While the GOM of Mexico has a platform spill rate for $\geq$ 50 bbls of about 1.5 per year, it is not unexpected to have 5 spills in some years, but 15 spills in 1 year (or 10 times the average) would be extremely unlikely. On the other hand, if Alaska were to have a platform spill rate of 1 every 30 years; the year with a spill is 30 times the average. Predicting the average spill rate is not significantly affected by this scale difference, but the uncertainty over the reasonable range of possible outcomes for an Alaskan scenario is heavily affected. Thus, it should be emphasized that it is average rates that are being estimated in this study.

Table 4.1 Beaufort Sea Development Scenario

Year	Cumulative Production Platforms	Cumulative Production Wells	In-use Pipeline Length [miles]	Production Mbbl
2009	1	3		
2010	1	13	10	7.9
2011	2	26	10	15.7
2012	3	39	20	23.6
2013	3	59	30	39.4
2014	4	72	30	44.4
2015	4	82	50	55.3
2016	5	95	50	59.5
2017	6	108	80	74.5
2018	7	132	80	76.1
2019	8	156	115	102.5
2020	8	176	115	103.5
2021	8	196	115	97.9
2022	8	206	115	93.1
2023	8	206	115	85.6
2024	8	206	115	79.2
2025	7	183	105	67.5
2026	7	183	105	59.0
2027	6	160	95	49.9
2028	5	137	80	42.2
2029	5	137	80	37.0
2030	5	137	70	32.4
2031	5	137	70	28.5
2032	5	137	70	25.0
2033	5	137	70	21.9
2034	4	114	60	17.0
2035	4	114	60	14.9
2036	2	68	40	8.3
2037	2	68	40	7.3
2038	2	68	40	6.5
	Total exposure for variable			
30	148	3555	2035	1375.6

4.3 Extension of Non-GOM Specific Spills to the Arctic

4.3.1 Methodology

This section focuses on how the extension to the Arctic of GOM based models can be done. This allows the large data base of past experience to be used, but the results are expected to be less reliable predictors for the Arctic than they are the GOM.

Two ways are envisioned to extend the GOM results to the Arctic:
1. Use estimated spill rates from Chapter 3 for the GOM by exposure variable. To estimate rates for spills exceeding the threshold, use information from the spill size modeling sections of Chapter 3. Adjust these rates by using binomial probabilities for "applicable spills." These binomial probabilities would be based on the best estimates as to which of the GOM spills above each spill threshold might be applicable to the Arctic.
2. Discard GOM spill data that is thought to be not applicable to Arctic. Apply methodology similar to Chapter 3 to derive spill rates for the "applicable spills." To calculate rates for spills exceeding the threshold, count the number spills exceeding threshold in the data.

This section relies on the statistical foundation of Chapter 3, and some of the results are used here. There is a difference which affects the rates for pipeline spills with the production exposure variable. Chapter 3 analyses of pipeline spills used total OCS production, while chapter 3 analyses of platform spills used GOM production. In this chapter, GOM production has been used for both pipeline and platform spills.

Method 1 is presented in Section 4.3.2.1 and 4.3.3.2, respectively for pipelines and platforms, for spills sizes ≥ 50 bbl. Since it starts with the full data set of spills ≥ 50 bbl, its statistical reliability is maximized. It is applied to spill rates exceeding size thresholds with three exposure variables – production, pipeline mile-years, and platform-years. Extensive work has gone into carefully analyzing the GOM data for each of the relevant exposure variables for pipelines and platforms. In addition, various approaches to defining confidence intervals for spill size thresholds were examined in detail with production as the exposure variable.

There has not been detailed examination within the GOM data of spill size thresholds with pipeline mile-years and platform-years as the exposure variable. However, the basic work on what proportion lies within above each spill size threshold does not depend on the exposure variable. Thus, the authors believe that method 1 can be applied with the same validity to the exposure variables of production, pipeline mile-years, and platform-years.

Method 1 allows the uncertainty in the selection of what is applicable or not applicable from the GOM to the Arctic to be directly folded into the analysis. Method 1 results in conservative estimates for the lower and upper confidence limits (LCL, UCL). Consider the LCL for method 1. It is found by multiplying (1) the LCL for the Poisson rate times (2) the LCL for the binomial proportion of the ≥ 50 spills above each threshold times (3) the LCL for the binomial proportion of the spills within above each threshold that are applicable. Because it is relatively unlikely for

MMS   113   TGE Consulting

the Poisson rate, the threshold binomial proportion, and the applicable binomial proportion to be simultaneously at their respective LCLs, the resulting computation is conservative. That is, the confidence interval is wider than it needs to be to account for the combination of these three uncertainties.

The results of method 2, which considers only data from applicable spills at each spill size threshold, are presented respectively in Sections 4.3.2.2 and 4.3.3.3 for pipeline and platform spills. The calculation of Poisson rates and confidence intervals is relatively straight-forward given the number of spills and the exposure variable. Detailed testing of exponential inter-spill quantities for "applicable spills" has not been possible within the constraints of this study. Nor is it obvious that such testing (the equivalent of much of Chapter 3) is warranted, since the focus is on the predicted spill rate parameter. Under method 2, it is not possible to consider the two uncertainties in the fraction of spills to be included. Under this method, a spill is either dropped (GOM specific) or not dropped (applicable). There is no uncertainty about it. Similarly, there is no uncertainty in the proportion of spills exceeding any size threshold. The exact number is counted in the data.

Before applying these methods, it is appropriate to look again at the scale issue briefly discussed in Section 4.1 for the extension of GOM results to the Arctic. The scale issue is an analog of the distribution of the sample mean. A particular time period (or quantity of other exposure variable) may be used to develop an estimate of the spill rate which is an average of the number of spills divided by the quantity of exposure variable (time, production, pipeline mile-years, or number of platforms). Fewer spills are expected for the Arctic than for GOM. Thus the inter-spill times will likely be more uncertain resulting in the exponential distribution taking longer to stabilize on a good estimate (assuming the system is time homogeneous). Thus, the numerator of the spill rate is more variable. For the denominator the number of pipeline-miles (platforms) may be as much 60 (400) times larger in the GOM than in the Arctic. In some sense these exposure variables may be thought of as volumes. In geostatistics (Clark and Harper, 2000, chapter 11) the volume variance relationship explains the phenomena. As volumes increase the resulting standard deviation decreases. With increased variability in the Arctic, the resulting confidence intervals should be wider for the Arctic than for GOM.

Method 2, which uses only data for applicable spills to derive estimates, is equivalent to another intuitively appealing, but limited approach. If one simply used portion ρ of the GOM spills (pipeline or platform) for an Arctic analysis, one gets a simple but possibly misleading Poisson approach. While intuitively appealing, it underestimates the uncertainty in the Arctic rate.

The difficulty is that for a Poisson process, the rate parameter λ is the mean and variance of the distribution. Hence a lower mean implies a lower variance and thus a lower standard deviation. This is not a justifiable procedure for extending the GOM results to the Arctic. While the rate for "applicable spills" is lower, the confidence intervals must recognize the uncertainties in the binomial proportions of "applicable spills" and of "spills above the threshold."

In addition to the work presented here, analysis has also been done for two other approaches. The first is similar to method 1, but it used a single binomial proportion applicable for all spills, instead of using a different proportion applicable for each spill size threshold. While

conservative, this approach ignored the apparent relationship between spill size and "applicability." Its usefulness was clearly surpassed by the method 1 presented here. An ad hoc modification to method 2 is also not presented, as the improved method 1 made it less necessary and because its complexity made it difficult to explain and validate.

Method 2 represents a lower bound on the uncertainty involved in the extension from the GOM data to the Arctic, while method 1 provides an upper bound for the sources of uncertainty consider. This analysis deals with the known statistical uncertainties as completely as possible and method 1 does so in conservative way that overestimates that statistical uncertainty. However, the results in Sections 4.3.2 and 4.3.3 do not address some of the different uncertainties summarized in Section 4.1 – in particular the uncertainties related to the Arctic. Thus, the confidence intervals for both methods are most likely still an underestimation of the overall uncertainty in any Arctic predictions. As more data and better methods of estimation become available, Arctic predictions can be improved.

4.3.2   Pipeline Spills

4.3.2.1   Pipeline Spills using Method 1

Method 1 starts with the basic uncertainty in the Poisson rate which was detailed for GOM pipeline spills in Table 3.3. However, in Table 4.2 the value for the production exposure variable is based upon GOM rather than OCS production from 1972 to 2005. Since the exposure volume is lower, the spill rate is slightly higher than in Table 3.3.

Table 4.2 Method 1 Arctic Pipeline Spill $\geq$ 50 bbl Poisson Based Rate and 95% Confidence Intervals

Label	# Spills	Exposure Variable	Sum Exposure Variable	Rate	LCL	UCL
Spills/Bbbl	36	Production Bbbl	12.445	2.8927	2.0260	4.0048
Pipeline Spills /KMile-year	36	KMile-years	161.796	0.2225	0.1558	0.3080

The second source of uncertainty that must be addressed by method 1 is the proportion of spills at each spill size threshold. Chapter 3 examined spill rates for varying spill thresholds using the rates per Bbbl of production for $\geq$ 50 bbl spills and the distribution of spill volumes. For pipelines a Weibull distribution fit the GOM spill volumes. Table 3.8 (relevant part reproduced below) describes the proportion and the exact binomial confidence intervals for the proportion of a spill data set above the thresholds of 100, 500, and 1000 bbl. Multiplying Table 3.8 times the Poisson rates and confidence limits was the conservative procedure in Chapter 3 to estimate pipeline spill rates at higher spill thresholds with production volume as the exposure variable. Exactly the same approach can be applied for pipeline mile-years using the last row of Table 4.2 times the proportion and exact binomial confidence intervals for spill size thresholds shown in Table 3.8.

**Table 3.8 Proportion of ≥ 50 bbl Pipeline Spills above Different Thresholds with 95%
Binomial Confidence Limits**

Threshold	P(≥ Threshold)	LCL	UCL
50	1	1	1
100	0.7932	0.6398	0.9181
500	0.5440	0.3810	0.7206
1000	0.4293	0.2551	0.5924

The third source of uncertainty is the proportion of spills above each threshold that are applicable to the Arctic vs. those with a GOM-specific cause. Table 4.3 details that the spill sizes are on average larger for GOM-specific spill causes than the non-GOM or applicable spill causes. The number of GOM-specific pipeline spills is about the same for each threshold, while the number of applicable spills falls sharply as the threshold increases.

**Table 4.3 GOM and Applicable Pipeline Spills at Different Thresholds with 95% Binomial
Confidence Limits (Based on Table 2.17)**

Spill Threshold	GOM Specific	Applicable or Non-GOM	Total	Proportion Applicable	LCL	UCL
≥ 50 bbl	15	21	36	.5833	0.4076	0.7449
≥ 100 bbl	15	14	29	.4828	0.2945	0.6747
≥ 500 bbl	13	6	19	.3158	0.1258	0.5655
≥ 1000 bbl	11	5	16	.3125	0.1102	0.5866

The estimated Arctic pipeline spill rate for each spill threshold is simply the Poisson rate times the size proportion times the applicable proportion for that size threshold. For conservative estimates of the lower and upper confidence limits, the three LCLs are multiplied, as are the three UCLs. As noted in Section 4.3.1, calculating a lower confidence limit by multiplying the LCLs for two or three variables is a conservative approach, as it is relatively unlikely that all variables will simultaneously be at their lower confidence limits.

Tables 4.4 and 4.5 are the result. They specifically consider (1) the underlying uncertainty in estimating the Poisson rate using the full data set of 36 pipeline spills ≥ 50 bbl, (2) the uncertainty in estimating what fraction of spills ≥ 50 bbl exceed higher spill size thresholds, and (3) the uncertainty in the binomial proportion that is applicable to the Arctic. Since, for example, the LCL is formed by multiplying the LCL for each source of uncertainty, the result is a conservative one.

Table 4.4 Method 1 Conservative Procedure to Estimate Arctic Pipeline Spill Rates for Various bbl Thresholds with Exposure Variable = Production

x	Adjusted Poisson Rate per Bbbl	LCL	UCL
50	1.6874	0.8257	2.9830
100	1.1077	0.3817	2.4805
500	0.4969	0.0971	1.6320
1000	0.3881	0.0569	1.3918

Table 4.5 Method 1 Conservative Procedure to Estimate Arctic Pipeline Spill Rates for Various bbl Thresholds with Exposure Variable = Pipeline Mile-Years

x	Adjusted Poisson Rate per KMile-yr	LCL	UCL
50	0.1298	0.0635	0.2294
100	0.0852	0.0294	0.1908
500	0.0382	0.0075	0.1255
1000	0.0299	0.0044	0.1071

4.3.2.2 Pipeline Spills using Method 2

Method 2 is using the actual data rather than a fitted distribution for the number of spills exceeding each size thresholds and for whether the spill cause is GOM-specific or applicable to the Arctic. Thus, for method 2 it is only the number of applicable spills for each spill size threshold (see Table 4.3) that is used in calculating the rates and Poisson confidence limits. Thus, for each spill size threshold the rate, LCL, and UCL depend only on the number of spills and the exposure variable.

Tables 4.6 and 4.7, respectively, show the result of method 2 for production and pipeline mile-years. As detailed in Section 4.3.1, this method limits the data to spills above each threshold that are "applicable to the Arctic" or stated another way, spills that have a "non-GOM specific cause." This approach assumes the lower rate for these spills lowers the variability and tightens the confidence interval values. This ignores the uncertainty in the proportion of spills that are applicable to the Arctic vs. GOM-specific causes and the uncertainty about the proportion of spills above each spill size threshold.

Methods 1 and 2 get slightly different results for the rate estimate for spills at thresholds of 100 bbls or larger. Tables 4.6 and 4.7 are based on the number of spills found in each category, not on a distribution of spill sizes.

Table 4.6 Method 2 Results (Ignores Uncertainty in Applicability and Spill Size) for Arctic Pipeline Spill ≥ 50 bbl Poisson Based Rate 95% Confidence Intervals with Exposure Variable = Production

Spill Threshold	# Spills	Exposure Variable	Sum Exposure Variable	Rate	LCL	UCL
≥ 50 bbl	21	Production Bbbl	12.445	1.6874	1.0445	2.5794
≥ 100 bbl	14	Production Bbbl	12.445	1.1249	0.6150	1.8875
≥ 500 bbl	6	Production Bbbl	12.445	0.4821	0.1769	1.0494
≥ 1000 bbl	5	Production Bbbl	12.445	0.4018	0.1305	0.9376

Table 4.7 Method 2 Results (Ignores Uncertainty in Applicability and Spill Size) for Arctic Pipeline Spill ≥ 50 bbl Poisson Based Rate 95% Confidence Intervals with Exposure Variable = Pipeline Mile-Years

Spill Threshold	# Spills	Exposure Variable	Sum Exposure Variable	Rate	LCL	UCL
≥ 50 bbl	21	KMile-years	161.796	0.1298	0.0803	0.1984
≥ 100 bbl	14	KMile-years	161.796	0.0865	0.0473	0.1452
≥ 500 bbl	6	KMile-years	161.796	0.0371	0.0136	0.0807
≥ 1000 bbl	5	KMile-years	161.796	0.0309	0.0100	0.0721

4.3.3 Platform Spills

The extension of GOM pipeline spill statistical results to the Arctic was done using method 1 in Section 4.3.2.1 and method 2 in Section 4.3.2.2. A parallel structure for platforms will be found in Sections 4.3.3.2 and .3. However, it is first necessary to deal with a complication found in the data for platform spills.

4.3.3.1 Applicable vs. GOM-Specific Platform Spills

Both methods for extending the GOM statistical results rely on data about applicable spills for each spill size threshold. Method 1 uses the proportion, LCL, and UCL; while method 2 uses the number of spills. While straightforward for pipeline spills, there are complications for platform spills.

Table 4.8 lists platform spills for the 1990 – 2005 period, which are then summarized in top half of Table 4.9, which lists the number of GOM-specific and "applicable" spills at each spill size threshold.

Table 4.8 GOM Platform Spills – Hurricane & Applicable (1990 – 2005)

1991-10-13	280	
1992-12-26	100	
1994-11-23	148	
1995-01-25	600	
1995-07-06	75	
1995-10-03	89	
1995-12-15	435	
1996-09-29	105	
1996-12-31	62	
1997-12-16	170	
1998-04-29	100	
1999-01-23	105	
1999-09-09	125	
2000-02-28	200	
2000-08-09	60	
2001-03-30	127	
2002-10-03	1,588	Lili
2003-05-09	264	
2003-05-10	430	
2004-09-15	1,053	Ivan
2005-08-29	2,225	Katrina
2005-09-24	7,371	Rita

As shown in Table 4.9, the platform spills for 1990 – 2005 exhibit a problem that can occur with small samples. In this case all of the GOM specific platform spills exceed 1000 bbl and there are no "applicable" spills of that size in that time frame. This means that there is a relationship between spill size and spill cause measured at the GOM/applicable level. More importantly, this would also imply that all calculated values for extending to the Arctic for ≥ 1000 bbl would indicate a probability of *zero*. This is clearly not true, since there are 4 applicable spills of that magnitude in the earlier portion of the 1972 – 2005 period.

Table 4.9 GOM and Applicable Platform Spills at Different Thresholds

Spill Threshold	GOM	Applicable or Non-GOM	Proportion Applicable	Total
1990 – 2005				
≥ 50 bbl	4	18	81.8%	22
≥ 100 bbl	4	14	77.8%	18
≥ 500 bbl	4	1	20.0%	5
≥ 1000 bbl	4	0	0.0%	4
1972 – 2005				
≥ 50 bbl	7	71	91.0%	78
≥ 100 bbl	5	44	89.8%	49
≥ 500 bbl	4	7	63.6%	11
≥ 1000 bbl	4	4	50.0%	8

A conservative solution is to use the larger data set from 1972 – 2005 to define the proportion of spills in the $\geq$ 1000 bbl category (50%) that are applicable. This increases the number of applicable spills above the top spill threshold to 2, and these two spills increase the number of applicable spills $\geq$ 500 bbl to 3. The lower two spill thresholds are left unchanged. Table 4.10 is the result with the changed numbers in italics. Table 4.10 also includes the exact binomial lower and upper confidence limits for these proportions.

Table 4.10 Adjusted GOM and Applicable Platform Spills at Different Thresholds for N = 22 Spills (Changed Values in Bold Italic)

Spill Threshold	GOM	Applicable or Non-GOM	Total	Proportion Applicable	LCL	UCL
$\geq$ 50 bbl	4	18	22	.8182	0.5972	0.9481
$\geq$ 100 bbl	4	14	18	.7778	0.5236	0.9359
$\geq$ 500 bbl	*2*	*3*	5	.6000	0.1466	0.9473
$\geq$ 1000 bbl	*2*	*2*	4	.5000	0.0676	0.9324

Because the number of spills $\geq$ 500 and 1000 bbl is small, the lower and upper confidence limits for the applicable proportions are very wide.

4.3.3.2 Platform Spills using Method 1

For method 1 the first factor in the confidence limits is the basic uncertainty in the Poisson rate which was detailed for GOM platform spills in Table 3.13. Table 4.11 is extracted from Table 3.13 for ease of reference.

Table 4.11 GOM Platform Spill $\geq$ 50 bbl Exact 95% Poisson Confidence Intervals for 1990 – 2005

GOM Platforms 1990-2005

Label	# Spills	Exposure Variable	Sum Exposure Variable	Rate	LCL	UCL
Spills/Bbbl	22	Production Bbbl	6.766	3.252	2.038	4.923
Spill/(Number of Platforms)	22	KPlatforms-Years	56.37	0.3903	0.2446	0.5909

Chapter 3 examined spill rates for varying spill thresholds using the rates per Bbbl of production for $\geq$ 50 bbl spills and the distribution of spill volumes. However, the results of fitting a three parameter lognormal to the GOM platform spill volumes can be applied to all exposure variables. Table 3.15 for platform spills describes the proportion and the exact binomial confidence intervals for the proportion of a spill data set above the thresholds of 100, 500, and 1000 bbl.

The average platform spill size for 1990 and later cannot be shown to be statistically significantly higher than the average spill size for 1972 and later. However, the proportion $\geq$ 100 bbl and $\geq$ 500 bbl is larger in the later time frame, which matches the break point used for the lower spill rate. Thus, to ensure that the results are conservative a new 3-parameter lognormal fit was done for the 1990 to 2005 data. The parameters for that fitted distribution are location = 5.047, scale = 1.606, and threshold = 49.9. Table 4.12 summarizes the binomial proportions and confidence limits for the number of spills exceeding the higher thresholds. This is the second source of uncertainty included in method 1.

Table 4.12 Proportion of ≥ 50 bbl Platform Spills above Different Thresholds with 95% Binomial Confidence Limits (1990-2005 Data)

Threshold	P(≥ Threshold)	LCL	UCL
50	1	1	1
100	0.7597	0.5463	0.9218
500	0.2541	0.1073	0.5022
1000	0.1299	0.0291	0.3491

The third source of uncertainty is the proportion applicable in each of the spill size categories. The proportions and lower and upper confidence limits were defined in Table 4.10 for each spill size threshold.

The estimated Arctic platform spill rate for each spill threshold is simply the Poisson rate times the size proportion times the applicable proportion for that size threshold. For conservative estimates of the lower and upper confidence limits, the three LCLs are multiplied, as are the three UCLs. As noted in Section 4.3.1, calculating a lower confidence limit by multiplying the LCLs for two or three variables is a conservative approach, as it is relatively unlikely that all variables will simultaneously be at their lower confidence limits.

Tables 4.13 and 4.14 are the result. They specifically consider (1) the underlying uncertainty in estimating the Poisson rate using the full data set of 22 pipeline spills ≥ 50 bbl for 1990 – 2005, (2) the uncertainty in estimating what fraction of spills ≥ 50 bbl exceed higher spill size thresholds, and (3) the uncertainty in the binomial proportion that is applicable to the Arctic. Since, for example, the LCL is formed by multiplying the LCL for each source of uncertainty, the result is a conservative one.

Table 4.13 Method 1 Conservative Procedure to Estimate Arctic Platform Spill Rates for Various bbl Thresholds with Exposure Variable = Production

x	Adjusted Poisson Rate per Bbbl	LCL	UCL
50	2.6606	1.2169	4.6679
100	1.9215	0.5829	4.2474
500	0.4958	0.0321	2.3421
1000	0.2112	0.0040	1.6026

Table 4.14 Method 1 Conservative Procedure to Estimate Arctic Platform Spill Rates for Various bbl Thresholds with Exposure Variable = Platform-Years

	Adjusted Poisson		
x	Rate per Platform-Year	LCL	UCL
50	0.3193	0.1461	0.5602
100	0.2306	0.0700	0.5098
500	0.0595	0.00385	0.2811
1000	0.0254	0.00048	0.1923

4.3.3.3 Platform Spills using Method 2

Method 2 is using the actual data rather than a fitted distribution for the number of spills exceeding each size thresholds and for whether the spill cause is GOM-specific or applicable to the Arctic. Since this assumes the lower rate for "spills applicable" to the Arctic and for larger spill sizes also reduces the variability, this has tighter confidence intervals than the conservative approach. This ignores the uncertainty in the proportion of spills for each spill threshold and the proportion that is applicable to the Arctic vs. GOM-specific causes.

The number of applicable spills from Table 4.10 is then used to generate Table 4.15 and 4.16, which show the results for different spill sizes when production and platform-years are used as the exposure variables.

Table 4.15 Method 2 Results (Ignores Uncertainty in Applicability and Spill Size) for Arctic Platform Spill ≥ 50 bbl Poisson Based Rate 95% Confidence Intervals with Exposure Variable = Production

Spill Threshold	# Spills	Exposure Variable	Sum Exposure Variable	Rate	LCL	UCL
≥ 50 bbl	18	Production	6.766	2.6606	1.5768	4.2048
≥ 100 bbl	14	Production	6.766	2.0693	1.1313	3.4720
≥ 500 bbl	3	Production	6.766	0.4434	0.0914	1.2959
≥ 1000 bbl	2	Production	6.766	0.2956	0.0358	1.0679

Table 4.16 Method 2 Results (Ignores Uncertainty in Applicability and Spill Size) for Arctic Platform Spill ≥ 50 bbl Poisson Based Rate 95% Confidence Intervals with Exposure Variable = Platform-Years

Spill Threshold	# Spills	Exposure Variable	Sum Exposure Variable	Rate	LCL	UCL
≥ 50 bbl	18	KPlatforms-yrs	56.37	0.3193	0.1892	0.5047
≥ 100 bbl	14	KPlatforms-yrs	56.37	0.2484	0.1358	0.4167
≥ 500 bbl	3	KPlatforms-yrs	56.37	0.0532	0.0110	0.1555
≥ 1000 bbl	2	KPlatforms-yrs	56.37	0.0355	0.0043	0.1282

4.4 Arctic Specific Hazards for Pipeline Oil Spills

Section 2.6 which discusses the data on Arctic specific hazards is the introduction to this section. While these Arctic specific hazards are a key part of defining oil spill risk in the Arctic, this study's focus has been on the extension of statistical results from the GOM to the Arctic. Thus, these results are much less comprehensive than other sections of the report. The statistically based results within this section are relatively limited, but where possible they are presented.

4.4.1 Ice Keel Gouging

Weeks, et al. (1983, 1984) included modeling of required burial depths for one ice impact during a 100-year period. Lacking detailed engineering analysis, and to demonstrate the estimation methodology, this study will rely on the Weeks model. This requires an assumption as to the burial depth of the pipeline. For consistency, this study will use the same 2.5 m that is assumed in Bercha (2006), which is nearly identical with the 8' that was assumed for the Liberty pipeline in Blanchet et al. (2000).

While the burial depth of 2.5 m is assumed to be critical, which matches Weeks, detailed engineering analysis is appropriate to determine whether the critical incision depth is shallower or deeper than the burial depth. It is possible that shallower incisions may be an issue, if the region of soil deformation which extends below the incision is an issue for pipeline integrity. In Paulin et al. (2001) this appeared to be the design approach used for Northstar. On the other hand, if the pipeline can resist, break-off, or be safely displaced by ice ridges that have some scale of contact, then the key incision depth is deeper than the burial depth. This latter possibility can be modeled using H_S, the conditional failure probability for the pipeline given an ice gouge impact (Bercha, 2002 & 2006). For descriptions of the pipeline's strength and testing at Northstar see Lanan and Ennis (2001).

Equation 17 from Weeks et al. (1983, p. 30) can be simplified as equation 4.1 to calculate the number of km-years for a single ice keel (gouge) to pipeline contact. Note that 0.2 m is subtracted from the burial depth to match this calculation to the probability distribution derived from the censored data (no gouges shallower than 0.2 m were measured). The flux or gouge density measured by Weeks et al. was 5.2 gouges/km-yr for deeper water gouges.

$$1 \text{ contact/km-yr} = e^{-\lambda(x-0.2)} g \sin\theta \qquad (4.1)$$

Where λ = parameter for probabilistic distribution of incision depth
 x = burial depth (2.5 m assumed)
 g = average number of gouges/km-year along pipeline route (5.2 gouges/km-yr)
 θ = angle between the route and the trend of the gouges (90° assumed)

For this study θ, angle between the route and the trend of the gouges, is assumed to be 90°. As detailed in Chapter 2, this value was chosen because the bulk of the ice movement is roughly parallel to the shore and the pipeline is assumed to be largely perpendicular to the shore. This is also a conservative assumption. It is worth noting that Bercha (2002 & 2006) uses 45° for an average orientation. The impact of this assumption on the results can be estimated by the ratio between 1 and the sin(45°) = 0.707.

Table 4.17 summarizes the key inputs and outputs for the probabilistic model developed by Weeks et al. There are two pairs of columns λ and for the corresponding gouge rate. The first pair is based on calculating λ from Equation 2.1, and the second pair is based on subtracting 1 from the value of λ to adjust for the difference between all gouges (used to derive λ) and new gouges (Weeks et al., 1983, p. 30). Note: that adjustment accounts for the fact that if all gouges are used to build the depth distribution, infilling over time has reduced the average incision depth.

Table 4.17 Gouge rate for a burial depth of 2.5 m

Water depth (m)	λ	Gouge /km-yr	Gouge /mi-yr	λ - 1	Gouge /km-yr	Gouge /mi-yr
5	8.16	3.65E-08	5.88E-08	7.16	3.64E-07	5.86E-07
10	6.68	1.10E-06	1.77E-06	5.68	1.09E-05	1.76E-05
15	5.47	1.78E-05	2.87E-05	4.47	1.78E-04	2.86E-04
20	4.48	1.74E-04	2.80E-04	3.48	1.74E-03	2.80E-03
25	3.67	1.13E-03	1.82E-03	2.67	1.13E-02	1.81E-02
30	3.00	5.21E-03	8.38E-03	2.00	5.19E-02	8.36E-02
35	2.46	1.82E-02	2.93E-02	1.46	1.82E-01	2.92E-01

Table 4.17 makes it clear that each 5 m increase in depth from 10 m to 25 m makes about an order of magnitude increase in the probability of a keel to pipeline contact. Thus, if the burial depth is constant, the probability of an oil spill is dominated by how much of the pipeline is in deeper water beyond the barrier islands. There is also an order of magnitude difference at all water depths depending on whether the adjustment for new versus all gouges is made.

If these values are compared with the 5.23×10^{-6} spills/km-yr reported in Bercha (2006), they are roughly comparable at a water depth of 10 m. However, they differ radically from Bercha for deeper water depths where Bercha reduces the rate, and Table 4.17 indicates an order of magnitude increase for each 5 m of water depth.

In the future, it should be possible to apply the results of Table 4.17 or the underlying equation, but it will require information on how much pipeline would be in each water depth class, and how much cover or what burial depth should be assumed for each water depth class. In addition it would seem appropriate to consider the presence of barrier islands or other geological shields from the moving ice.

Finally, there is the question of whether keel contact with the pipeline is required (➜ decrease the effective burial depth of pipe in above calculations, because the pressure of displaced soil is a problem) or can say 0.5m of a keel impact the pipe without damage (➜ increase the effective burial depth of pipe in above calculations)? Note: because there is an order of magnitude change for each 5m of depth, it is suggested that changing the effective burial depth is a superior modeling choice to using a conditional probability for pipeline spill given keel to pipeline contact. That conditional probability might be better used to account for a pipeline that is damaged (bent and needing replacement) versus one that is broken and spilling oil.

4.4.2   Strudel Scour

Section 2.6.2 on strudel scour concluded with the calculated probabilities for a free span greater than 0' of 3.8×10^{-4} and for a free span $\geq 100'$ of 5.2×10^{-5} (Blanchet et al., 2000, p. ix). As this was for 1.8 miles of pipe vulnerable to strudel scours for a year, the latter probability can be converted to a value of 2.9×10^{-5} per mile-yr or 0.029 per KMile-yr for comparison with rates for non-GOM specific spill causes. Note: that the further off-shore a platform is; the more opportunity there is to select landfall locations that are as remote as possible from major river outlets, which will minimize the probability of strudel scours.

There are 2035 mile-years for pipelines within the Beaufort development scenario. This can be split between 985 miles in 10 m to 20 m water depth and 1035 mile-years in less than 10 m depth. Without more detailed information, it is not possible to calculate how many mile-years of strudel scour exposure there is over the life of the field.

However, at this level of detail a first-order approximation would place about 30% of the shallow water pipeline-years in 2 to 5 m water depth (30% of the shallow water range) where strudel scour is most likely to be a problem. This assumes that some platforms are in say 6 m of water depth so that pipeline would have a larger fraction in the critical range and other platforms are in say 9 m of water depth – and connected to the platform in 6 m – so that none of that pipeline would be in the critical range of water depths.

Thus, an estimate for the Beaufort Development Scenario for the number of pipeline spills due to strudel scour is 0.009 (= 2.9×10^{-5} per mile-yr * 1035 mile-years * 30%) over the life of the field.

4.4.3   Upheaval Buckling

As the engineering expertise and assumptions to model upheaval buckling are not within the scope of this study, it is assumed that the critical length defined for the probability of a strudel scour has appropriately considered the probability of upheaval buckling. Thus, the probability of upheaval buckling is assumed to equal the probability of a strudel scour.

4.4.4   Thaw Settlement

As there is no statistical basis for estimating the probability of an oil spill due to thaw settlement, this study will not attempt to do so. However, it is worth noting that thaw settlement is a much more gradual phenomenon than the impact of an ice keel. Thus, an appropriate schedule for an appropriate pig can identify any thaw settlement before pipeline integrity is compromised.

While it is outside the scope of this study, it is worth noting that if a clear design standard will be applied to this phenomenon, then the design standard is potentially another way to establish a spill probability. For example, suppose that the design standard is for 1 spill every 100 or every 1000 years. Such values can be converted into the probability of a spill.

4.5   Arctic Specific Oil Spill Causes for Platforms

The focus of this study has been on MMS data for the GOM and OCS total, and on data focused on Alaska specific natural hazards for pipelines. While Arctic effects on platform spills are clearly potentially important, this study does not address these beyond the following discussion.

Bercha (2006) included values for ice forces, low temperature, and a category for other. Ice forces that can move or damage a platform must clearly be considered, and the low temperatures of the Arctic are a hazard. However, this is based on spill cause classifications that do not include the second most common cause of platform oil spills – human error (see Table 2.21).

The authors of this study suggest that the significant share of spills caused by human error could quite possibly increase in the Arctic environment. There is absolutely no question that human errors increase in the dark and in the cold, as well as in other forms of more challenging environments. Thus, there is the potential that platform spills due to human error could increase beyond the level experienced in the GOM.

4.6   Application of Spill Rates to Development Scenario

The exposures summarized at the bottom of Table 4.1 can be combined with the spill rates and limits calculated in Section 4.3. If method 1 rates are used, then the rates include the uncertainty in the rate and the uncertainty in the fraction of the spills that are "applicable" to the Arctic. For spill sizes exceeding 100, 500, and 1000 bbl then the uncertainty in the size variable is included. The results are predicted numbers of spills for the life of the field (LOF) represented by the development scenario. Method 2 considers only the uncertainty in the Poisson rate of spills.

Table 4.18 is the expected number of spills over the LOF for the Beaufort development scenario using the conservative approach of method 1. This is only for the "applicable" spills and it does not include factors for increasing or reducing the impact of specific spill causes in the Arctic. It does adjust the exposures so measured in thousands of pipeline mile-years, thousands of platform-years, and billions of barrels of oil. This is required so that exposures are measured in the same units as the spill rates derived from the GOM with its much larger values.

Table 4.18 Application of Conservative (Method 1) Extended "Applicable" GOM Spill Rates (Spills ≥ 50 bbl) to Beaufort Development Scenario

	Pipeline Spills		Platform Spills	
	In-use Pipeline Length [KMiles]	Production Bbbl	Platforms-Years [KPlatforms]	Production Bbbl
Exposure	2.035	1.3756	0.148	1.3756
rate	0.1298	1.6874	0.3193	2.661
95% LCL	0.0635	0.8257	0.1461	1.217
95% UCL	0.2294	2.9830	0.5602	4.668
LOF # spills	0.2641	2.3212	0.0473	3.6605
95% LCL	0.1292	1.1359	0.0216	1.6741
95% UCL	0.4668	4.1034	0.0829	6.4213

One of the most important conclusions from examining Table 4.20, is that selecting the right driver to determine the spill rate is enormously important. For pipeline spills using spills per Bbbl oil produced versus spills per pipeline KMile-years makes about an order of magnitude difference in the predicted spill number and confidence limits. For platforms, it makes nearly two orders of magnitude difference.

Consider the more extreme case of platform spills. The difficulty is that in the GOM from 1990 – 2005 an average of 3523 platforms averaged 0.12 Mbbl of production per year each, while in the Beaufort development scenario an average of 5.1 platforms averaged 8.6 Mbbl of production per year for each. The authors believe that the probability of an oil spill is much more closely linked to the activities associated with each platform, than it is to the volume of oil produced by each platform.

The authors suggest that using spills per volume of oil produced is not a reliable approach for estimating oil spills in the Arctic. Thus, further analysis in this section will be done only with the exposure variables of pipeline mile-years and platform-years.

In contrast with these spill rates, the expected number of strudel scour caused oil spills is an addition of 0.009 expected pipeline spills over LOF is much, much smaller than 0.264 number of pipeline spills expected over LOF, and much smaller than the level of uncertainty associated with other causes. Thus, while strudel scour must be a design and planning issue, it is not the key uncertainty or source of potential oil spills.

On the other hand, ice keel gouging can possibly have much larger values, but there is not yet a scenario against which those rates can be applied.

Table 4.19 for applicable pipeline spills in the Arctic combines the information from Tables 4.5 and 4.7 to make it easy to compare the conservative confidence limits (method 1) and minimum (method 2) confidence limits at different spill thresholds. These are the values that should be multiplied by the exposure variables for the Arctic to produce life of field probabilities of

applicable pipeline oil spills at each spill threshold. This is only for "applicable" spills with causes similar to those that occur in the GOM, and it does not include Arctic-specific causes.

One significant difference between the GOM and the development scenario is the average length of the pipelines. As noted in the list of cautions and caveats in Chapter 5, this seems likely to overstate the spill rates for the pipelines in the Arctic.

Table 4.19 Arctic Pipeline Spills for Applicable Causes – Rates and 95% Confidence Limits (Spills/KMile-Years)

Spill Threshold	Method 1 Conservative			Method 2		
	Rate	LCL	UCL	Rate	LCL	UCL
50	0.1298	0.0635	0.2294	0.1298	0.0803	0.1984
100	0.0852	0.0294	0.1908	0.0865	0.0473	0.1452
500	0.0382	0.0075	0.1255	0.0371	0.0136	0.0807
1000	0.0299	0.0044	0.1071	0.0309	0.0100	0.0721

Table 4.20 for applicable platform spills in the Arctic combines the information from Tables 4.14 and 4.16 to make it easy to compare the conservative confidence limits (method 1) and minimum (method 2) confidence limits at different spill thresholds. These are the values that should be multiplied by the exposure variables for the Arctic to produce life of field probabilities of applicable platform oil spills at each spill threshold. This is only for "applicable" spills with causes similar to those that occur in the GOM, and it does not include Arctic-specific causes.

Table 4.20 Arctic Platform Spills for Applicable Causes – Rates and 95% Confidence Limits (Spills/KPlatforms-Years)

Spill Threshold	Method 1 Conservative			Method 2		
	Rate	LCL	UCL	Rate	LCL	UCL
50	0.3193	0.1461	0.5602	0.3193	0.1892	0.5047
100	0.2306	0.0700	0.5098	0.2484	0.1358	0.4167
500	0.0595	0.00385	0.2811	0.0532	0.0110	0.1555
1000	0.0254	0.00048	0.1923	0.0355	0.0043	0.1282

Tables 4.19 and 4.20 have been left as spill rates, rather than being multiplied by the exposure variables for the Beaufort development scenario, because it only requires a multiplication to convert to LOF spill probabilities. Also the Beaufort development scenario is itself subject to considerable uncertainty.

The many uncertainties listed at the start of this chapter may increase or lower the spill rate, but they certainly widen the confidence intervals.

4.7 Sensitivity Analysis of Platform Spill Rates to Data Adjustment

In Section 4.3.3.1 the number of applicable spills ≥ 1000 bbl was adjusted from 0 to 2. This was done because there were 4 such spills in the 1972 – 1989 time frame, but none in 1990 – 2005. This is a conservative choice, as it increases the number of large spills with an applicable cause. While it may be unreasonable to use 0 for the number of such spills, it is certainly possible that a better adjustment might have been a single spill.

Table 4.21 summarizes the rates and confidence limits for assuming 2 (as before) large applicable spills and for assuming 1 large spill. Not surprisingly, all rates and confidence limits are lower if the spill data adjustment is 1 spill rather than 2 spills.

Table 4.21 Sensitivity Analysis for Arctic Platform Spills for Applicable Causes – Rates and 95% Confidence Limits (Spills/KPlatforms-Years)

Spill Threshold	Method 1 Conservative			Method 2		
	Rate	LCL	UCL	Rate	LCL	UCL
1000 (2 appl.)	0.0254	0.00048	0.1923	0.0355	0.00430	0.1282
1000 (1 appl.)	0.0104	0.00002	0.1389	0.0177	0.00045	0.0988

While the lower level assumption may be appropriate, given the limited data it is the original assumption of a 2-spill adjustment that is recommended.

4.8 Comparison with Bercha (2006)

To facilitate comparison of this methodology with the results of the probabilistic risk assessment done in Bercha (2002 and 2006), Poisson spill rates and confidence intervals are calculated for that data. Since the relevant data is reproduced in this report, all references in this section are to this report. This analysis is done only at the aggregated level for all spills ≥ 50 bbls and over the entire 1972 – 1999 time frame used in Bercha.

There are 31 pipeline spills listed in Table 2.4 and 21 platform spills listed in Table 2.7. There are 117,705 pipeline mile-years listed in Table 2.13 and 119, 714 well-years listed in Table 2.15. These values can be used to compute exact confidence limits for the spill rates for ≥ 50 bbl spills. The results are shown in Table 4.22.

Table 4.22 Poisson Rates for Bercha (2006) Data for 1972-1999

	n	exposure variable	Sum Exposure variable	rate	LCL	UCL
Platforms	21	KWell-yr	119.714	0.1754	0.1086	0.2681
Pipelines	31	KMile-yr	115.385	0.2687	0.1825	0.3813

The uncertainty reported in Table 4.22 can most easily be put into context by considering the ratio between the upper and lower confidence limits for the 95% confidence interval. That ratio

for platforms is about 2.5 and about 2 for pipelines. This is the uncertainty for rates based in the GOM assuming time stationarity. It does not consider any of the many sources of uncertainty in moving to applications in the Arctic. This is a lower bound on the uncertainty from this data, as this uncertainty applies to every pipeline and well and it is not reduced through an averaging process.

It also does not consider the increase in uncertainty that results if the data sets of 21 and 31 spills are subdivided by pipe size, water depth, spill size, or spill cause. Nor does it consider any of the data refinements that MMS has been able to provide or that have been developed in this study. Table 4.23 illustrates this by deriving the Poisson rates for pipeline spills due to corrosion (4 of 31) pipeline spills and for platform spills due to storage tank releases (3 of 21) platform spills. In this case the ratio of the upper and lower confidence levels is about a factor of 10 or an order of magnitude.

Table 4.23 Poisson Rates for Specific Spill Causes for Bercha (2006) Data for 1972-1999

	n	exposure variable	Sum Exposure variable	rate	LCL	UCL
Platforms: storage tank release	3	KWell-yr	119.714	0.0251	0.0052	0.0732
Pipelines: corrosion	4	KMile-yr	115.385	0.0347	0.0094	0.0888

Thus the uncertainty of a factor of 2 or 2.5 is the absolute minimum range, and realistic estimates of the uncertainty in extrapolation to the Arctic are larger by some unknown amount, which in some cases is at least an order of magnitude.

4.9 Summary and Conclusions

It is suggested that Tables 4.19 and 4.20 represent a valid way to estimate with rates and confidence limits the probabilities of "applicable" pipeline and platform spills in the Arctic. Method 1 in a conservative way considers the statistical uncertainties in spill size and the applicability of the spill cause to the Arctic. Method 2 provides a lower bound on the amount of uncertainty that is unavoidable.

Because these tables do not include adjustments for Arctic-specific spill causes, the spill rates can only go up. However, preliminary analysis indicates that strudel scour is less significant than the applicable causes. No conclusions can be reached for ice keel gouging.

5 Recommendations and Conclusions

In order to maximize ease of use and clarity of references, this chapter is structured and written as "bullet points." In addition, using the detailed results from and methods of this study is best done within the context provided by the discussions in this chapter. For example, there is about an 8.7% adjustment required for pipeline spill rates applied to the GOM based on *volume of oil production.* Fundamentally, the authors are concerned that abstracting key numbers may lead to their use out of context.

Sections 5.1 to 5.3 are based on the body of this report. Section 5.4 presents a promising alternative approach to modeling pipeline spill risks that was first conceptualized and developed while this report was in the final review stage.

5.1 Major Conclusions

The Poisson distribution for pipeline and platform spill rates is satisfactory. Other distributions could be chosen, but the Poisson
1. Fits with historical practice
2. Has a theoretical foundation – it is not just an empirical curve fit
3. Is "not rejected" at reasonable levels of statistical confidence
4. Even though the fit of any distribution may be imperfect, the key question when estimating rates, is "how much do these imperfections change the estimated rate? Generally, the answer is very little."

For the GOM, any of the exposure variables can be used to model the rate of oil spills, due to the high level of correlation between them. Furthermore, with production as the exposure variable, the results are generally consistent with MMS published results.

The best exposure variables for extension to the Arctic are pipeline mile-years and platform-years. Using production volumes as the exposure variable seems to significantly overstate the risk. Time cannot be used as the exposure variable.

The level of uncertainty for Arctic extension is very high due to the many uncertainties. However, it is possible to make reasonable, justifiable extensions from the GOM data to the Arctic.

5.2 Cautions in Using and Interpreting the Results

Platform spills for this study have included spills of refined petroleum products such as diesel, while other studies such as Bercha (2002 & 2006) focus on crude and condensate.

For GOM use for pipeline spills if production is the exposure variable. It is suggested that the spill rate and confidence limits be adjusted upwards by dividing by 0.92. This is the ratio between GOM production from 1972 – 2005 to total OCS production. This would closely approximate the results that would have been obtained if the GOM spills had been measured against GOM production. (No similar adjustment is required for platforms or for the extensions to the Arctic, as GOM production was used.)

Many users of statistics are accustomed to the idea that variability averages out by having many years, many pipelines, and many platforms. Variations of this principle have been part of several discussions in this report, however, the principal uncertainty addressed in this report is the basic uncertainty about what is the average spill rate. This affects every pipeline and platform equally, and it is NOT averaged out by independent, identically distributed random selections.

The more recent aggressive data collection effort for platform spills linked to hurricanes suggests that recent reported spill volumes are relatively higher, so that true spill rate declines for platforms are probably somewhat larger than reported here.

Using a constant or average spill rate per pipeline mile-year will overestimate the rate for pipeline runs longer than average and underestimate the rate for pipeline runs shorter than average. In particular, rates developed for average length pipeline runs in the GOM are likely to overstate the spill rate per pipeline mile-year for the longer Arctic pipelines. This is addressed in much more detail in Section 5.4.

The rates and confidence intervals for spills exceeding the thresholds of 100, 500, and 1000 bbl are less reliable than the results for the 50 bbl threshold. There are more uncertainties in which statistical approach is better, and there are fewer spills so that small sample variability is more of an issue.

5.3 Suggestions for Future Work

The very preliminary work in Section 5.4 on platforms as an exposure variable for pipeline spills should be extended. Other potential "termination" exposure variables such as number of segments should also be explored. A very significant fraction of pipeline spills happen because of a connection to a platform. The connection may be severed when a platform is moved or destroyed by a hurricane, a work boat may collide with a riser, or an anchor may damage the pipeline during operations around a platform. Accurately representing the oil spill probabilities associated with this should support better estimates and better extensions to different operating environments. Using a constant or average spill rate per pipeline mile-year will overestimate the rate for pipeline runs longer than average and underestimate the rate for pipeline runs shorter than average. In particular, rates developed for average length pipeline runs in the GOM are likely to overstate the spill rate per pipeline mile-year for the longer Arctic pipelines.

The influence of the scale of development in the Arctic on the predictability of the spill history that will be experienced has not yet been explored. To avoid future surprises, it should be.

Given the robustness of using spill models for volume of oil produced based on the larger data sets available for spills ≥ 50 bbl; these models should be applied to the spill rates used in the extension of GOM spill experience to the Arctic, which are based on pipeline spills per thousand mile-years and platform spills per thousand platform-years. This will support the production of more reliable estimates for the spill rates for larger spills, such as exceeding 1000 bbl.

Two different methods for extending the GOM data to the Arctic with confidence intervals were explored. Additional approaches should be explored. For example, simulation might be an appropriate tool for estimating how conservative an LCL is produced by multiplying the LCL's for three different variables. Clearly, verifying whether the confidence limits are realistic, optimistic, or overly conservative would greatly increase their value.

It should be possible to construct confidence intervals for the Arctic specific risks as the scenarios are better defined.

5.4   Potential New Pipeline Spill Model

This section describes a different approach for modeling pipeline spills that is based on the fact that each pipeline spill occurs either in conjunction with a platform termination or elsewhere along its length. This appears to produce a model that more accurately reflects pipeline spill risks.

As described in Section 5.3 and detailed in Tables 5.1 and 5.2, many pipeline spills have a platform-related cause. For this preliminary work, it is assumed that all pipelines, short or long, have about the same risk of pipeline spills at a platform termination. (There have not been enough spills to differentiate spill rates by pipe diameter, water depth, etc. in this report. Thus, we do not believe it will be possible to initially differentiate between risks linked to floating vs. fixed platforms, water depth, etc.)

This work is at an early stage, and it has not yet received the detailed analysis and review that the other models presented in this report have received. It is also incomplete, as it only presents one approach for developing confidence intervals; and some points are illustrated but not fully developed. Nevertheless, the authors suggest that it is an approach that merits further review, as it does appear to more realistically model the risk of a pipeline spill, and it is much more robust for pipeline lengths different from "average."

The model is first explained by analogy in Section 5.4.1. Since each pipeline has a termination at each end, the spill rate at the terminations is like a fixed cost, which is incurred by every single pipeline no matter how long. The spill rate along the length of a pipeline is like a variable cost that depends on how long each pipeline is. Then spill rates for different spill sizes are developed in Section 5.4.2. Then in Section 5.4.3 the rates are applied to the Beaufort development scenario for comparison with the results developed earlier in this report.

This class of model is useful both for extrapolating from the GOM to the Arctic and for estimating spill rates for new GOM developments that are at significantly higher distances from shore than the statistical average for the GOM. The specific model presented here uses pipeline mile-years and platform-years as variables. While future models may use different variables, the intent is to show the value of a new approach.

5.4.1 Analogy to Fixed and Variable Cost Model vs. Average Cost Model

The clearest way to introduce this model is by analogy with another model that most readers will have previously used. There are many circumstances where a choice must be made between two cost models, which are summarized in Figure 5.1.

The constant rate model uses an average cost, such as cost per mile, cost per square foot, or cost per call. For any volume, the estimated cost equals the average cost multiplied by the expected volume. This model is analogous to the models presented previously in this report, which present average spill rates per pipeline mile-year, per platform-year, per billion barrels of production, or per year.

The other model defines a fixed cost that must be incurred for any non-zero volume, and a variable cost for each unit of that volume. The new approach presented here is analogous to the fixed/variable cost model (henceforth called fixed cost model for linguistic convenience). This approach recognizes that whether a pipeline is short or long, it typically has at least one termination at a platform. And that the spill rate for those terminations depends on the number of terminations, and not on the length of each pipeline. This is analogous to the fixed cost. The spill rate along the pipeline's length is analogous to the variable cost.

For those who are unfamiliar with these models, Figure 5.1 was developed using the following data. There is a fixed cost of $800 for any volume, and then there is a variable cost of $50 per unit. Thus, if the average volume is 20, the total cost is $1800 (= 800 + 50*20). The average cost per unit is the total cost divided by the average volume or $90 (= 1800/20).

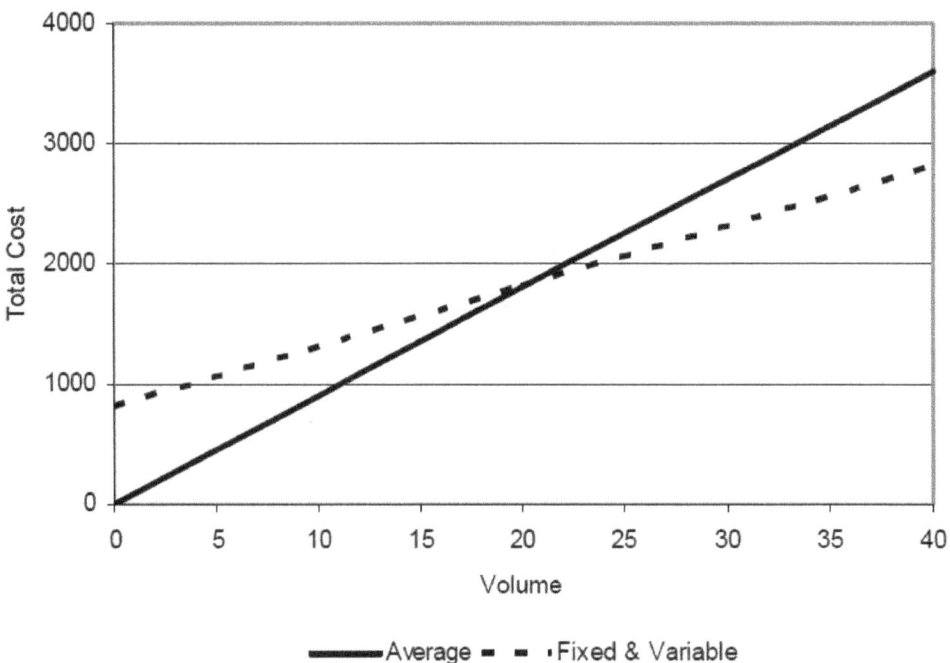

Figure 5.1 Average Cost versus Fixed and Variable Cost Models

This familiar context of fixed/variable cost versus average cost can be used to illustrate why each type of model is used for situations where there is a significant fixed cost. The average cost is easiest to determine or to statistically estimate. And for volumes close to the average volume (which is the point where the two lines cross) it provides a realistic estimate. In many situations this is enough for good results. For the example data the average cost model works pretty well for volumes between 15 and 25.

However, for volumes that are significantly different than the average volume, the estimated value for the average cost model is considerably less accurate than the inherently more accurate fixed cost model. For the example in Figure 5.1 consider the estimated cost for volumes of 5 or 40. The average cost model performs poorly. The average rate is too low for low volumes and too high for high volumes.

Thus, if it is possible to estimate the fixed and variable costs, this model is more accurate. Note: the fixed cost model can use a fixed cost of zero, thus the average cost model is a special case of the fixed cost model, and non-zero fixed costs are only used when they provide a more accurate model.

There are at least two situations where the average model for spill rates is likely to be inferior. First, a fixed cost class of model is useful for extrapolating from the GOM to different environments, such as the Arctic. Second, the fixed cost class of model is useful for estimating spill rates for new GOM developments that are at significantly higher distances from shore than the statistical average for the GOM.

5.4.2 Determining Pipeline Spill Rates for Fixed and Variable Probability Model

5.4.2.1 Platform-Related Pipeline Spills vs. "Pipeline" Spills

Table 5.1 details the authors' categorization of pipeline spills between platform-linked spills and those "pipeline" spills without such a link. This was done using the same database that was used for Table 2.17. The added information is in the new fourth and fifth columns. The last three hurricane-caused spills were listed as having both pipeline and platform-linked causes because the spills are actually the accumulation of multiple spills with a common cause.

In many cases the categorization was clear and unambiguous. For example, if a platform is destroyed and the pipeline severed, then the platform cause is clear. For another example, if the anchor from a platform service vessel damaged the pipeline, it is reasonable to classify this as platform related as both the vessel and the pipeline are being brought together at the platform. In others, the lead author's judgment was used, as the distance from the platform was longer or the connection to platform operations was weaker.

Table 5.1 Modified Table 2.17 Platform Related Primary Cause of GOM Pipeline Oil Spills

Spill Date	Spill Size	GOM Specific	Pipe-line	Plat-form	Cause
1972-06-13	100		Y		Corrosion
1973-05-12	5,000		Y		Corrosion
1974-04-17	19,833	GOM	Y		Anchor drag
1974-05-21	65			Y	Operational: anchor from derrick barge
1974-09-11	3,500	GOM	Y		Hurricane Carmen
1976-02-29	414		Y		Corrosion: after pipeline kinked by anchor
1976-12-18	4,000	GOM	Y		Shrimp trawl damaged valve
1977-03-29	250		Y		Natural: mud slide
1977-06-05	50		Y		Operational: lay barge anchor
1977-10-18	300	GOM	Y		Anchor drag
1978-04-08	135			Y	Mechanical/operational
1978-07-17	900			Y	Operational: anchor drag 600' from platform
1979-07-15	50			Y	Operational: workboat searching for rig anchor
1980-01-29	100	GOM	Y		Trawler drag broke valve
1981-08-05	80		Y		Corrosion: external or metal fatigue
1981-12-11	5,100			Y	Operational: service vessel anchor
1983-01-20	80		Y		Natural: mud slide
1985-02-16	323		Y		Operational: pipeline dented, cracked during construction
1985-11-09	50		Y		Operational: spud barge anchor
1986-02-03	119		Y		Mechanical/operational: pinhole leak during abandonment
1986-12-30	210		Y		Mechanical/operational: anchor or original construction
1988-02-07	15,576	GOM	Y		Ship illegally dropped and dragged anchor
1990-01-24	14,423	GOM	Y		Fishing net or anchor
1990-05-06	4,569	GOM	Y		Trawler net drag
1992-01-03	190		Y		Unknown
1992-08-31	2,000	GOM		Y	Rig broke loose during Hurricane Andrew
1993-06-17	50		Y		Operational: workboat anchor
1994-11-16	4,533	GOM	Y		Trawl net damaged valve
1998-01-22	800	GOM	Y		Mechanical damage: probably anchor
1998-01-26	1,211			Y	Operational: anchor during overboard rescue
1998-09-29	8,212	GOM	Y		Hurricane Georges
1999-07-23	3,200			Y	Operational: jackup rig set down on pipeline
2000-01-21	2,240		Y		Operational: anchor drag from drill rig
2004-09-15	3,445	GOM	Y	Y	Hurricane Ivan
2005-08-29	553	GOM	Y	Y	Hurricane Katrina
2005-09-24	8162	GOM	Y	Y	Hurricane Rita

Table 5.2 summarizes the N = 36 spill data in Table 5.1 by spill size for the spill causes that are applicable to the Arctic, and in total for GOM-specific causes. The spills with GOM-specific

causes are not analyzed further for four reasons. First, this analysis is intended to explore and demonstrate the value of a new approach, not to provide definitive well-supported results. Second, results for the GOM are complicated by the hurricane spills. Third, the number of platform related spills is much smaller for GOM-specific causes. Fourth, the focus of this study is the Arctic not the GOM.

Table 5.2 Summary of Platform vs. Pipeline Related GOM Pipeline Oil Spills

Applicable or GOM Specific	Pipeline Related	Platform Related
Applicable		
≥ 50 bbl	14	7
≥ 100 bbl	9	5
≥ 500 bbl	2	4
≥ 1000 bbl	2	3
GOM Specific 15	11 + 3	1 + 3

The fraction of the pipeline spills linked to a platform ranges from 66.7% for spills over 500 bbl down to 33.3% for spills over 50 bbl. These percentages are clearly a significant portion of the pipeline spills, which is the reason this model was analyzed.

5.4.2.2 Spill Rates for Platform-Related Pipeline Spills vs. "Pipeline" Spills

In developing spill rates for platform-related pipeline spills, the data summarized earlier offers two potential exposure variables – segments of pipeline and number of platforms. Further work may identify better exposure variables.

The number of pipeline segments over time was detailed for the GOM in Table 2.12, however, similar information was not available for the Beaufort development scenario. Thus, even if rates were developed they could not yet be applied. In addition, the connection between pipeline segments and potential exposure variables is not yet well defined. Previous MMS work suggests that it could be. If each segment has a termination at each end, then this would be a very logical exposure variable, which would be preferred unless the data quality is poor. (Note that underwater terminations represent somewhat different spill probabilities than do platform terminations.) However, if a pipeline with a termination at each end may have many logical segments to help identify where leaks, repairs, or other actions take place, then this would not be a good exposure variable. It is unclear how many pipeline segments fit either of these two possibilities.

Thus in the preliminary analysis reported here, the exposure variable for platform-related pipeline spills is platform-years. The span of time for this exposure variable is 1972 to 2005, since pipeline spills were not shown to have a significant time dependence (unlike platform-spills which were split into 1972 – 1989 and 1990 – 2005). This initial work did not include an analysis of whether either the "pipeline" or "platform-related" pipeline spill rates are time dependent.

TGE Consulting

Thus, the "fixed cost" model for oil spills uses platform-years as the exposure variable for platform-related pipeline spills and pipeline mile-years for "pipeline" spills.

Table 5.3 applies method 2 with the data in Table 5.2 for applicable spills. With this approach exact Poisson confidence intervals can be derived with only the number of spills and the exposure variable. This initial work has not included testing of exponential inter-spill intervals for these two subsets of the data.

Table 5.3 Spill Rates for Platform vs. Pipeline Related Applicable Pipeline Oil Spills

Threshold bbl	N	Exposure Variable	Sum Exposure Variable	rate	LCL	UCL
Pipeline-Related Pipeline Spill Rates						
≥ 50	14	Kmile-yr	161.796	0.0865	0.0473	0.1374
≥ 100	9	Kmile-yr	161.796	0.0556	0.0254	0.0974
≥ 500	2	Kmile-yr	161.796	0.0124	0.0015	0.0344
≥ 1000	2	Kmile-yr	161.796	0.0124	0.0015	0.0344
Platform-Related Pipeline Spill Rates						
≥ 50	7	Kplatform-yr	100.087	0.0699	0.0281	0.1305
≥ 100	5	Kplatform-yr	100.087	0.0500	0.0162	0.1023
≥ 500	4	Kplatform-yr	100.087	0.0400	0.0109	0.0876
≥ 1000	3	Kplatform-yr	100.087	0.0300	0.0062	0.0722

These spill rates cannot be compared directly with previous spill rates. That comparison is summarized in Section 5.4.2.3, and then these rates are applied to the Beaufort development scenario in Section 5.4.3.

5.4.2.3 Consistency of Spill Rates for "Fixed/Variable" Rate and Average Rate Models

While straight-forward, it is a first test of validity to show that the two models give consistent results for the GOM. This is done for the 21 spills ≥ 50 bbl, but it true for all spill size thresholds. The rates cannot be directly compared, rather they must be applied to the exposure variables to compute the number of spills of each type.

For each of these Poisson models, the spill rate was computed as the number of spills divided by the exposure variable. Thus, the number of predicted spills of each spill type is simply the spill rate multiplied by the exposure variable.

Number of Applicable Oil Spills (from Table 4.7)
21 = (161.796 Kmile-yr) * 0.1298
Number of Applicable Pipeline-Related Oil Spills (from Table 5.3)
14 = (161.796 Kmile-yr) * 0.0865
Number of Applicable Platform-Related Oil Spills (from Table 5.3)
7 = (100.087 Kplatform-yr) * 0.0699
And of course 21 = 14 + 7

Thus, the new approach that uses platform-years as the exposure variable for the "fixed cost" of spills at terminations and pipeline mile-years as the exposure variable for the "variable cost" of spills along a pipeline's length has results that are consistent with those from the previous model that uses the average spill rate per pipeline mile-year.

5.4.3 Applying Spill Rates for "Fixed/Variable" Rate Model

As shown above, the numbers of spills for the two models are equivalent when applied to the total exposure within the GOM from 1972 to 2005. However, if these spill rates are applied to data with a different mix between platforms and pipeline lengths, then the results are different as well.

One measure of the difference between the GOM data and the Beaufort development scenario is the number of pipeline miles per platform. For the GOM dividing the 161,796 pipeline mile-years by the 100,087 platform-years gives a result of 1.62 pipeline miles per platform. For the Beaufort development scenario dividing the 2035 pipeline mile-years by the 148 platform-years gives a result of 13.8 pipeline miles per platform. Thus, there is about an order of magnitude difference in the number of pipeline miles per platform for the Beaufort development scenario. Thus, there will be a large difference in results between the fixed/variable rate model and the average rate model.

The reasons for this difference include:
- Most of the thousands of platforms in the GOM are close to shore
- GOM mileage does not include the 3 nautical miles or 3 leagues (prior to years of shoreline retreat) between shore and the boundary of OCS waters
- Beaufort Sea pipeline mileage does include the 3 nautical miles from OCS waters to land

The GOM has numerous platforms far offshore, yet there are only 1.62 pipeline miles per platform. Thus, it is reasonable to conclude that there must be very substantial variability in the length of GOM pipelines. Thus, the predicted spill rates for different GOM facilities will differ substantially between the potentially more accurate fixed/variable model versus the average spill rate model. In particular the average spill rate model may dramatically overestimate the spill rate for long pipelines.

To apply the spill rates shown in Table 5.3 to the Beaufort development scenario, the "pipeline" values are multiplied by the exposure variable of 2.035 thousands of pipeline mile-years. Similarly, the "platform-related" values are multiplied by the exposure variable of 0.148 thousands of platform-years. The resulting values for expected number of life-of-field spills are shown in the top two sections of Table 5.4. The total expected number of life-of-field spills is the sum of the two spill types, and the results are shown in the bottom section of Table 5.4.

Table 5.4 Expected Life-of-Field Spill Numbers for Beaufort Development Scenario for Pipeline Oil Spills

Threshold bbl	Exposure Variable	Sum Exposure Variable	LOF E(#)	LCL	UCL
Pipeline-Related Expected Pipeline Spill Numbers					
≥ 50	Kmile-yr	2.035	0.176	0.096	0.280
≥ 100	Kmile-yr	2.035	0.113	0.052	0.198
≥ 500	Kmile-yr	2.035	0.025	0.003	0.070
≥ 1000	Kmile-yr	2.035	0.025	0.003	0.070
Platform-Related Expected Pipeline Spill Numbers					
≥ 50	Kplatform-yr	0.148	0.010	0.004	0.019
≥ 100	Kplatform-yr	0.148	0.007	0.002	0.015
≥ 500	Kplatform-yr	0.148	0.006	0.002	0.013
≥ 1000	Kplatform-yr	0.148	0.004	0.001	0.011
Total Expected Pipeline Spill Numbers					
≥ 50			0.186	0.100	0.299
≥ 100			0.121	0.054	0.213
≥ 500			0.031	0.005	0.083
≥ 1000			0.030	0.004	0.081

Table 5.5 provides the results for method 2 using the average rates summarized in Table 4.19 times the 2.035 thousands of pipeline mile-years for the Beaufort development scenario. For ease of comparison the values from Table 5.4 are repeated.

Table 5.5 Comparing Expected Life-of-Field Spill Numbers for Beaufort Development Scenario for Pipeline Oil Spills for Fixed/Variable and Average Models

Threshold bbl	Fixed/Variable Model LOF E(#)	LCL	UCL	Average Model LOF E(#)	LCL	UCL
≥ 50	0.186	0.100	0.299	0.2641	0.1635	0.4037
≥ 100	0.121	0.054	0.213	0.1761	0.0963	0.2954
≥ 500	0.031	0.005	0.083	0.0755	0.0277	0.1643
≥ 1000	0.030	0.004	0.081	0.0629	0.0204	0.1468

Because the number of pipeline miles per platform is much higher for the Beaufort development scenario than for the GOM data, the expected number of spills is much lower with the new model. To use the analogy with the fixed/variable cost model of Figure 5.1, pipelines that have more length have more "volume" and are better estimated with the new model; and have lower estimated values.

5.4.4 Summary and Conclusions for Fixed and Variable Cost Model

The model that is introduced here inherently has the potential to improve the accuracy of extrapolated results. The flexibility of separating spill rates into a fixed portion linked to pipeline terminations and a variable portion linked to the pipeline's length greatly extends the accuracy of projections to environments and projects with lengths different from the average in the GOM data base.

While promising, this approach has not yet received the level of review and validation that underlie the average spill rate models that are presented earlier in this report. In particular, the following issues merit attention:

- After review and discussion how much does the classification of pipeline spills as platform- or pipeline-related change?
- Is there a better exposure variable for the pipeline terminations than platform-years?
- Does the analysis of exponential inter-spill intervals support the use of the Poisson model for platform-related pipeline spills and for "pipeline" pipeline spills?
- Is there an analogous method 1 approach for defining the confidence limits that is more conservative than this method 2 approach?
- What are the results for use in the GOM?
- How to handle hurricane spills when applying this approach to potential GOM developments?

The following observations may also be useful in examining this approach further.

- In extrapolating from the GOM data to the Arctic, one of the key variables was the proportion of the oil spills at each spill size threshold that was "applicable or non-GOM specific." The uncertainty in this binomial proportion was a key part of the method 1 approach to the confidence limits for the spills per pipeline mile-year models. While there is uncertainty in the proportional split between "platform-related" and "pipeline" spills, these are complementary binomial proportions that must sum to 1. Thus, examination of this uncertainty is better done through sensitivity analysis than by expanding the confidence limits as method 1 does.
- The spill cause classification as platform- or pipeline-related has less impact on the results than the GOM/applicable classification. This is true because the as the weight on platform-related spills (and the estimated number of such spills) goes up; the weight on pipeline-related spills (and the estimated number of such spills) goes down. So the total of the two moves up or down more slowly with the difference between the two parts. On the other hand the GOM/applicable classification excludes or includes spills which directly decreases or increases the estimated spill rates and numbers of spills.

6 References

Anderson, Cheryl McMahon, and Robert P. LaBelle, 1990, "Estimated Occurrence Rates for Analysis of Accidental Oil Spills on the US Outer Continental Shelf," *Oil and Chemical Pollution*, Vol. 6, pp. 21-35.

Anderson, Cheryl McMahon, and Robert P. LaBelle, 2000, "Update of Comparative Occurrence Rates for Offshore Oil Spills," *Spill Science & Technology Bulletin*, Vol. 6, No. 5/6, pp. 303-321.

Anderson, Cheryl McMahon, and Robert P. LaBelle, December 1994, "Comparative Occurrence Rates for Offshore Oil Spills," *Spill Science & Technology Bulletin*, Vol. 1, No. 2, pp. 131-141.

Barry, Leon, February 1989, "Niakuk Area Offshore Permafrost and Subsea Pipeline Study," BP Exploration.

Bercha International Inc., August 2002, "Alternative Oil Spill Occurrence Estimators for the Beaufort and Chukchi Seas – Fault Tree Method," Volumes I and II, OCS Study MMS 2002-047, Final Report to US Department of the Interior, Minerals Management Service, Alaska Outer Continental Shelf Region.

Bercha International Inc., January 2006, "Alternative Oil Spill Occurrence Estimators and their Variability for the Beaufort Sea – Fault Tree Method," Volumes I and II, OCS Study MMS 2005-061, Final Report to US Department of the Interior, Minerals Management Service, Alaska Outer Continental Shelf Region.

Blanchet, Denis, Gordon Cox, Craig Leidersdorf, and Allin Cornell, May 2000, "Analysis of Strudel Scours and Ice Gouges for the Liberty Development Pipeline," BP Upstream Technology Group, Final Draft.

Chapman, D.G., 1952, "On Tests and Estimates for the Ratio of Poisson Means," *Annual Institute of Statistical Mathematics*, Vol. 4, pp. 45-49.

Chayes, D.N., A.D. Chave, B. Coakley, A. Proshutinsky, and T. Weingartner, 2006, "Concept Design for a Cabled Seafloor Observatory at Barrow, Alaska," CD Proceedings for SSC06.

Clark, Isobel, and William V. Harper, 2000, *Practical Geostatistics 2000*, Geostokos Limited.

Clopper, C. J., and E.S. Pearson, 1934, "The Use of Confidence or Fiducial Limits Illustrated in the Case of the Binomial," *Biometrika*, 26, 404-413.

Comfort, G., A. Dinovitzer, and R. Lazor, September 2000, "Independent Risk Evaluation for the Liberty Pipeline," Fleet Technology Limited for MMS.

Croasdale, Ken, George Comfort, and Ken Been, June 2005, "Investigation of Ice Limits to Ice Gouging," *Proceedings 18th International Conference on Port and Ocean Engineering under Arctic Conditions (POAC), Volume 1,* Potsdam, NY, pp. 23-42.

Croasdale, Ken, Rob Brown, Patrick Campbell, Greg Crocker, Ian Jordaan, Tony King, Richard McKenna, and Robert Myers, August 2001, "Iceberg Risk to Seabed Installations on the Grand Banks," *Proceedings 16th International Conference on Port and Ocean Engineering under Arctic Conditions (POAC), Volume 2,* Ottawa, ON, pp. 1019-1028.

D'Agostino, Ralph B., and Michael A. Stephens, 1986, *Goodness-of-Fit Techniques*, Marcel Dekker.

Dickins, D., G. Hearon, and K. Vaudrey, August 2001, "Sea Ice Overflood in Stefansson Sound, Alaskan Beaufort Sea," *Proceedings 16th International Conference on Port and Ocean Engineering under Arctic Conditions (POAC),* Ottawa, ON, *Volume 1,* pp. 193-200.

Eschenbach, Ted, June 2001, "Evaluation of "Analysis of Strudel Scours and Ice Gouges for the Liberty Development Pipeline," by Denis Blanchet, Gordon Cox, Craig Leidersdorf, and Allin Cornell, BP Upstream Technology Group, Final Draft, May 2000," TGE Consulting for Joint Pipeline Office.

Givens, Geof H., December 2002, "Review of Update of Comparative Occurrence Rates for Offshore Oil Spills," North Slope Borough Science Advisory Committee.

Goodman, Leo A., 1965, "On Simultaneous Confidence Intervals for Multinomial Proportions," 1965, *Technometrics*, volume 7, number 2, pp. 247-254.

Harper, William V., July 2005, "Excel Functions to Compute Exact Binomial Confidence Intervals," *Proceedings of the 25th European Meeting of Statisticians*, Oslo, Norway, CD.

Hart Crowser Inc., April 2000, "Estimation of Oil Spill Risk from Alaska North Slope, Trans-Alaska Pipeline, and Arctic Canada Oil Spill Data Sets," OCS Study MMS 2000-007.

Johnson, Norman L., and Samuel Kotz, 1969, *Discrete Distributions*, John Wiley & Sons.

Kelton, W. David, Randall P. Sadowski, and David T. Sturrock, 2004, *Simulation with Arena, 3rd,* McGraw-Hill.

LaBelle, Robert P., and Cheryl McMahon Anderson, 1985, "The Application of Oceanography to Oil-Spill Modeling for the Outer Continental Shelf Oil and Gas Leasing Program, *Marine Technology Society Journal*, Vol. 19, No. 2, pp. 19-26.

Lanan, Glenn A., and John O. Ennis, August 2001, "Northstar Offshore Arctic Pipeline Project," *Proceedings 16th International Conference on Port and Ocean Engineering under Arctic Conditions (POAC), Volume 1,* Ottawa, ON, pp. 123-132.

Lanfear, Kenneth J., and David E. Amstutz, 1983; "A Reexamination of Occurrence Rates for Accidental Oil Spills on the U.S. Outer Continental Shelf, *Proceedings of 1983 Oil Spill Conference,* American Petroleum Institute, Washington D.C., pp. 355-359.

Leidersdorf, Craig B., Gregory E. Hearon, and Greg Swank, 2006, "Abstract 66: Strudel Scour Formation off an Arctic River Delta," *Book of Abstracts, 30th International Conference on Coastal Engineering,* ASCE.

Leidersdorf, Craig B., Gregory E. Hearon, Ricky C. Hollar, Peter E. Gadd, and Terry C. Sullivan, August 2001, "Ice Gouge and Strudel Scour Data for the Northstar Pipelines," *Proceedings 16th International Conference on Port and Ocean Engineering under Arctic Conditions (POAC), Volume 1,* Ottawa, ON, pp. 145-154.

Miller, Duane L., August 2001, "Hypersaline Permafrost under a Lagoon of the Arctic Ocean," *Proceedings 16th International Conference on Port and Ocean Engineering under Arctic Conditions (POAC), Volume 1,* Ottawa, ON, pp. 201-208.

MMS Alaska OCS Region, February 1998, "Alaska Outer Continental Shelf - Beaufort Sea Planning Area Oil and Gas Lease Sale 170 - Final Environmental Impact Statement," MMS 98-0007.

MMS Alaska OCS Region, January 1991, "Alaska Outer Continental Shelf - Chukchi Sea Oil & Gas Lease Sale 126 – Final Environmental Impact Statement," Vol. II, MMS 90-0095.

MMS Alaska OCS Region, January 2001, Liberty Development and Production Plan: Draft Environmental Impact Statement, Volumes I – III, MMS 2001-001.

MMS Alaska OCS Region, May 1996, "Alaska Outer Continental Shelf - Beaufort Sea Planning Area Oil and Gas Lease Sale 144 - Final Environmental Impact Statement," Vol. I & II, MMS 96-0012.

MMS Alaska OCS Region, May 2002, Liberty Development and Production Plan: Final Environmental Impact Statement, Volumes I – IV, MMS 2002-019.

MMS Gulf of Mexico OCS Region, August 1997, "Investigation of Shell Offshore Inc., Hobbit Pipeline Leak, Ship Shoal Block 281, November 16, 1994," MMS 97-0031.

MMS Gulf of Mexico OCS Region, December 1987, "Investigation of Shell Pipe Line Corporation Pipeline Leak South Pass Block 65 December 30, 1986," MMS 87-0114.

MMS Gulf of Mexico OCS Region, March 1991, "Investigation of Shell Offshore Inc., Hobbit Pipeline Leak Ship Shoal Block 281, January 24, 1990," MMS 91-0025.

MMS Gulf of Mexico OCS Region, November 1991, "Investigation of the Exxon Company USA Pipeline Leak /Eugene Island Block 314, May 6, 1990," MMS 91-0066.

MMS Gulf of Mexico OCS Region, September 1999, "Investigation of Chevron Pipe Line Company Pipeline Leak, South Pass Block 38, September 29, 1998," MMS 99-0053.

MMS, 1992, "Accidents Associated with Oil and Gas Operations: Outer Continental Shelf 1956-1990," OCS Report MMS 92-0058.

Morrison, T.B., and R.W. Marcellus, September 1985, "Comparison of Alaskan and Canadian Beaufort Sea Ice Scour Data and Methodologies," *Proceedings 8th International Conference on Port and Ocean Engineering under Arctic Conditions (POAC), Volume 1,* Narssarssuaq, Greenland, pp. 375-387.

MPC International, November 1997, "Evaluation of Irene Pipeline Oil Spill," for Torch Operating Company.

Neave, K. Gerard, and Paul V. Sellmann, August 1982, "Subsea Permafrost in Harrison Bay, Alaska: An Interpretation from Seismic Data," US Army Corps of Engineers, Cold Regions Research & Engineering Laboratory, Report 82-24.

Osterkamp, T.E. and W.D. Harrison, 1977, "Subsea Permafrost Regime at Prudhoe Bay, Alaska," *Journal of Glaciology,* Vol. 19, No. 81, pp. 627-637.

Osterkamp, T.E. and W.D. Harrison, May 1976, "Subsea Permafrost at Prudhoe Bay, Alaska, Drilling Report," University of Alaska Geophysical Institute, Report R-245.

Owen, Les, Denis Blanchet, and Peter Flones, August 2001, "The Northstar Project - Year-Round Production in the Alaskan Beaufort Sea," *Proceedings 16th International Conference on Port and Ocean Engineering under Arctic Conditions (POAC), Volume 1,* Ottawa, ON, pp. 21-40

Palmer, Andrew, and Alan Niedoroda, June 2005, "Ice Gouging and Pipelines: Unresolved Questions," *Proceedings 18th International Conference on Port and Ocean Engineering under Arctic Conditions (POAC), Volume 1,* Potsdam, NY, pp. 11-21.

Paulin, Michael J., Derick Nixon, Glenn A. Lanan, and Brian McShane, August 2001, "Environmental Loadings & Geotechnical Considerations for the Northstar Offshore Pipelines," *Proceedings 16th International Conference on Port and Ocean Engineering under Arctic Conditions (POAC), Volume 1,* Ottawa, ON, pp. 133-144.

Przyborowski, J. and H. Wilenski, 1940, "Homogeneity of Results in Testing Samples from Poisson Series," *Biometrika,* Vol. 31, pp. 313-323.

Rogers, James C., Larry D. Gedney, Lewis H. Shapiro, and Doug Van Wormer, August 1975, "Near Shore Permafrost in the Vicinity of Pt. Barrow, Alaska," *Proceedings 3rd*

International Conference on Port and Ocean Engineering under Arctic Conditions (POAC), Volume 2, Fairbanks, AK, pp. 1071-1082.

Romanovsky, Vladimir, 2006, private communication.

S.L. Ross Environmental Research Ltd., November 1998, "Blowout and Spill Probability Assessment for the Northstar and Liberty Oil Development Projects in the Alaska North Slope," Report to BP Exploration (Alaska), Inc.

Sellmann, Paul V., Allan J. Delaney, and Steven A. Arcone, June 1989, "Coastal Subsea Permafrost and Bedrock Observations Using DC Resistivity," US Army Corps of Engineers, Cold Regions Research & Engineering Laboratory, Report 89-13.

Sharples, B.P.M., J.J. Stiff, D.W. Kalinowski and W.G. Tidmarsh, May 1989, "Statistical Risk Methodology: Application for Pollution Risks from Canadian Georges Bank Drilling Program," *Proceedings of 21st Annual Offshore Technology Conference, Volume 3,* Houston, TX, pp. 385-394.

Smith, R.A., J.R. Slack, T. Wyant, and K.J. Lanfear, 1982, "The Oil Spill Risk Analysis Model of the US Geological Survey," USGS Professional Paper 1227, US Geological Survey.

Trefry, John H., Robert D. Rember, Robert P. Trocine, Mark Savoie, 2004, "ANIMIDA Task 5: Sources, Concetrations and Dispersion Pathways for Suspended Sediment in the Coastal Beaufort Sea," OCS Study MMS 2004-032.

Wadhams, Peter, September 1977, "Characteristics of Deep Pressure Ridges in the Arctic Ocean," *Proceedings 4th International Conference on Port and Ocean Engineering under Arctic Conditions (POAC), Volume 1,* St. John's, Newfoundland, pp. 544-555.

Walker, H. J., 1974, "The Colville River and the Beaufort Sea: Some Interactions," in J.C. Reed and J.E. Sater (eds.), *The Coast and Shelf of the Beaufort Sea,* Arctic Institute of North America, pp. 513-540.

Weeks, W.F., P.W. Barnes, D.M. Rearic, and E. Reimnitz, 1984, "Some Probabilistic Aspects of Ice Gouging on the Alaskan Shelf of the Beaufort Sea," *The Alaskan Beaufort Sea: Ecosystems and Environments,* Academic Press.

Weeks, W.F., P.W. Barnes, D.M. Rearic, and E. Reimnitz, June 1983, "Some Probabilistic Aspects of Ice Gouging on the Alaskan Shelf of the Beaufort Sea," US Army Cold Regions Research and Engineering Laboratory.

Weibull, W., 1951, "A Statistical Distribution of Wide Applicability," *Journal of Applied Mechanics,* Vol. 18, pp. 293-296.

Zeh, Judith E., December 2002, "Review of Oil Spill Risk Analyses for Alaskan Arctic OCS Development," North Slope Borough Science Advisory Committee.

Appendix A. Pipeline Spills ≥ 50 bbl *through* 1999

Appendix A parallels the pipeline analysis in Section 3.5 of the main body of the report. In Section 3.5, analyses for pipeline spills ≥ 50 bbl are documented for data *through 2005*. Since the earlier draft report submitted in the fall of 2005 analyzed data only through 1999, it was felt important to provide the reader an opportunity to see what has changed by adding six additional years of pipeline spill data. While much of the data in this appendix is the same as given in the earlier draft report, the data in Appendix A are an update of the pipeline data through 1999 used in the draft. This was done to address re-interpretations of the earlier data based on dialogue with the MMS. We would like to thank Cheryl Anderson for her guidance on these efforts.

The remainder of this section show analogous Figures and Tables to the pipeline information in Section 3.5 using a numbering scheme to make the matching of the through 1999 analysis figure/table to the through 2005 figure/table seen in the main body of the report obvious. For example Figure A3.10 is this appendix may be compared to Figure 3.10 in the main report. There may be minor differences in the titles to some Figures and Tables, as some revision has taken place.

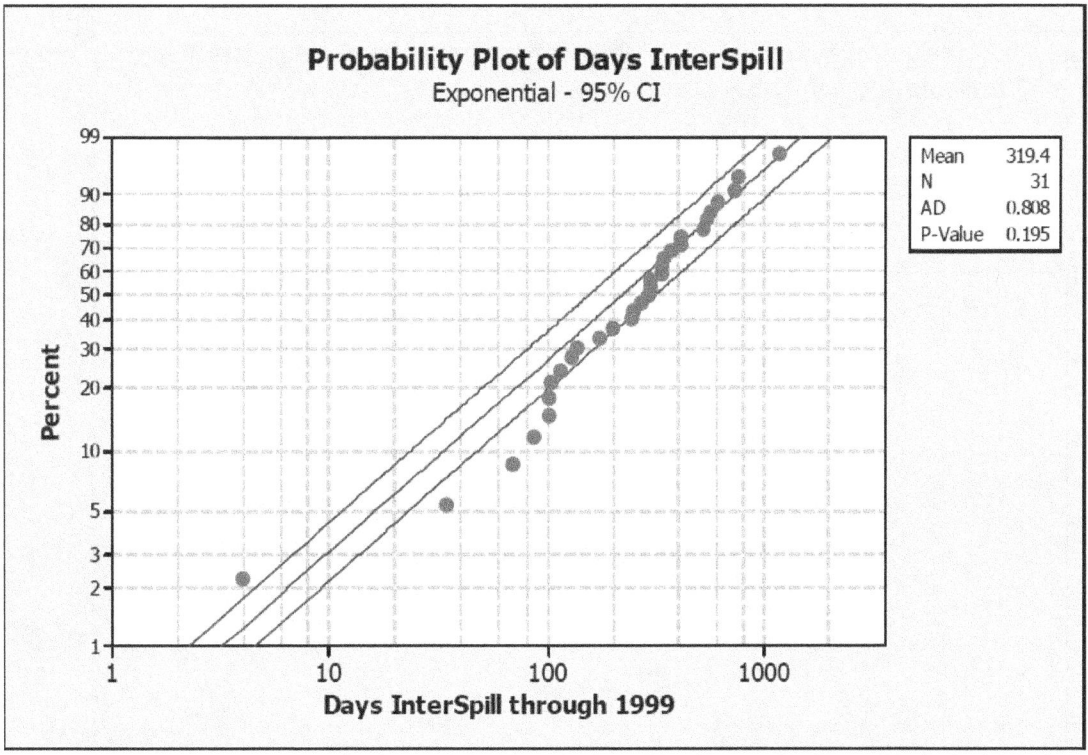

Figure A3.10 Exponential Probability Plot of Pipeline Inter-Spill (spills ≥ 50 bbl) Times Using n = 32 through 1999 Data Set

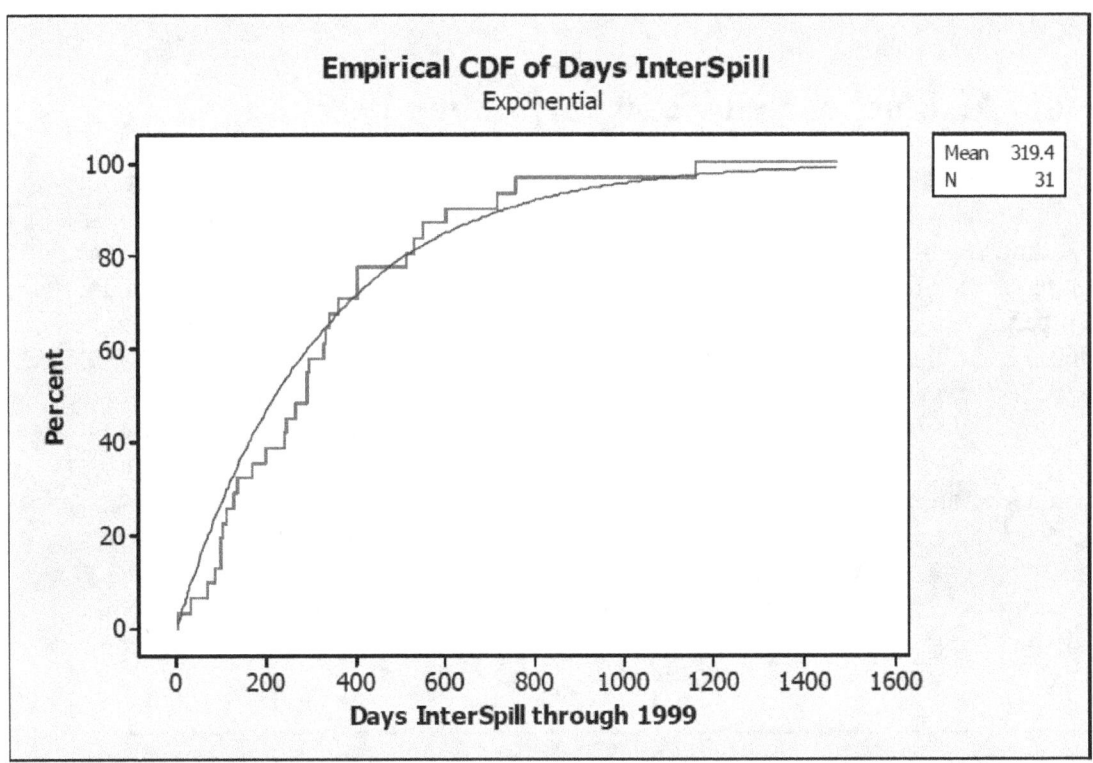

Figure A3.11 Exponential Empirical CDF Plot of Pipeline Inter-Spill (spills ≥ 50 bbl) Times Using n = 32 through 1999 Data Set

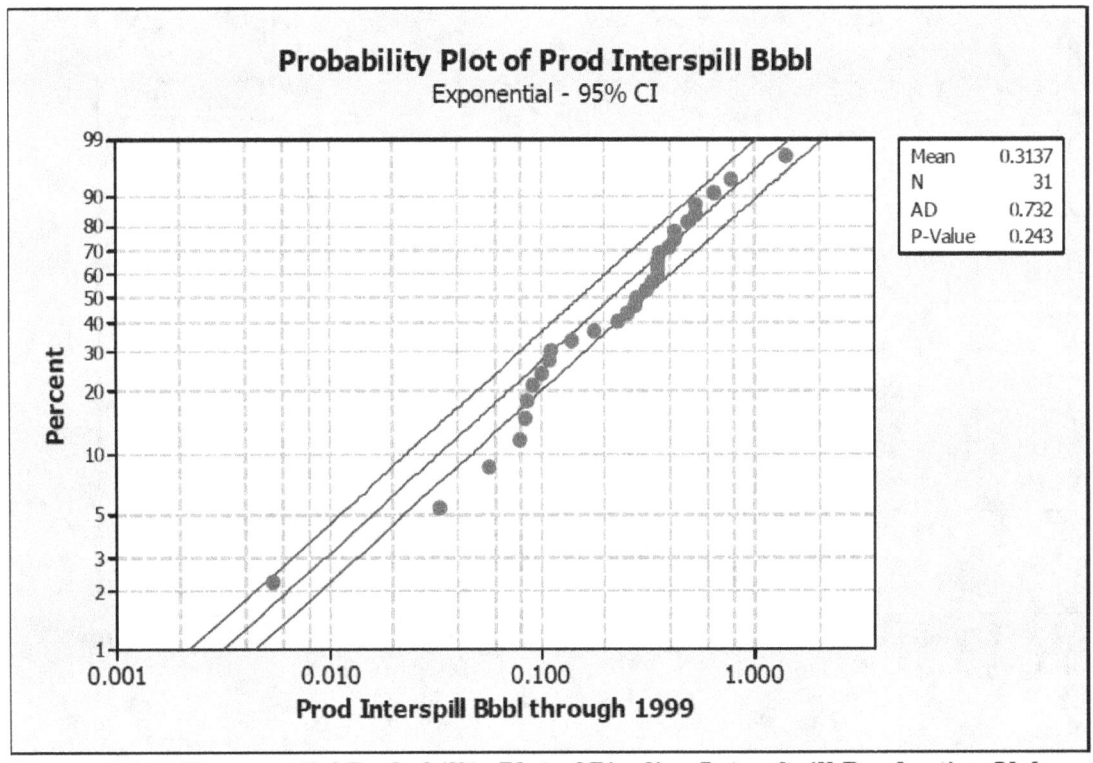

Figure A3.12 Exponential Probability Plot of Pipeline Inter-Spill Production Volumes (Bbbl) Using n = 32 though 1999 Data Set (spills ≥ 50 bbl)

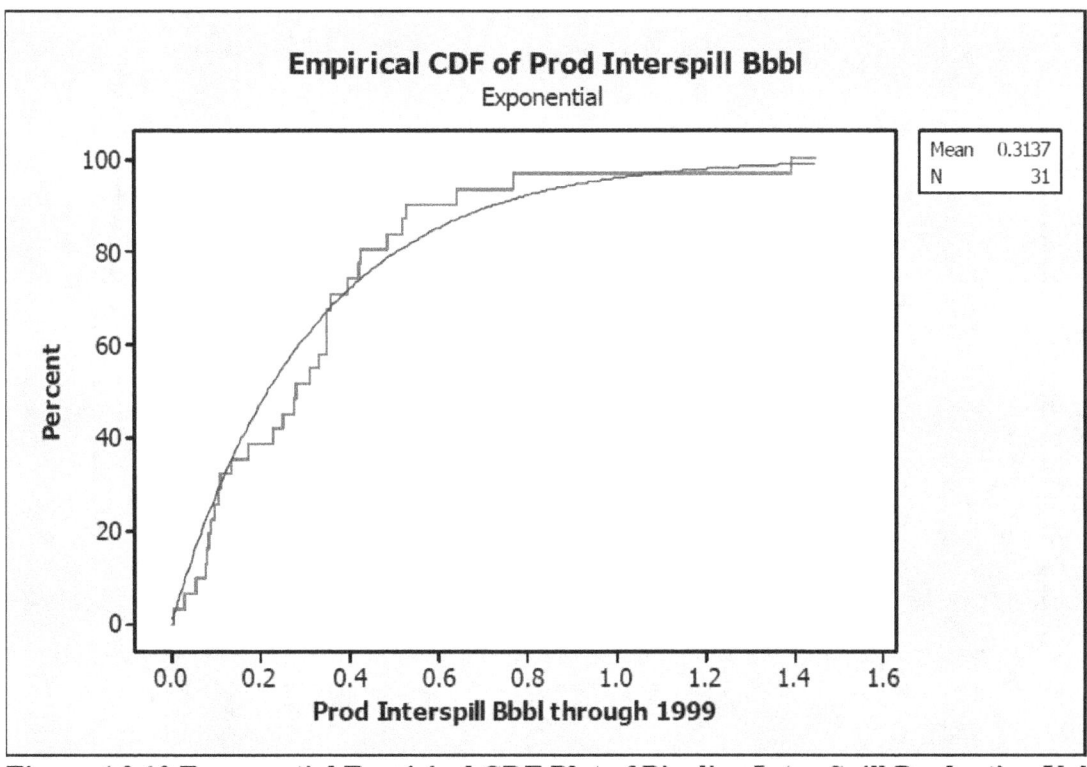

Figure A3.13 Exponential Empirical CDF Plot of Pipeline Inter-Spill Production Volumes Using n = 32 through 1999 Data Set (spills ≥ 50 bbl)

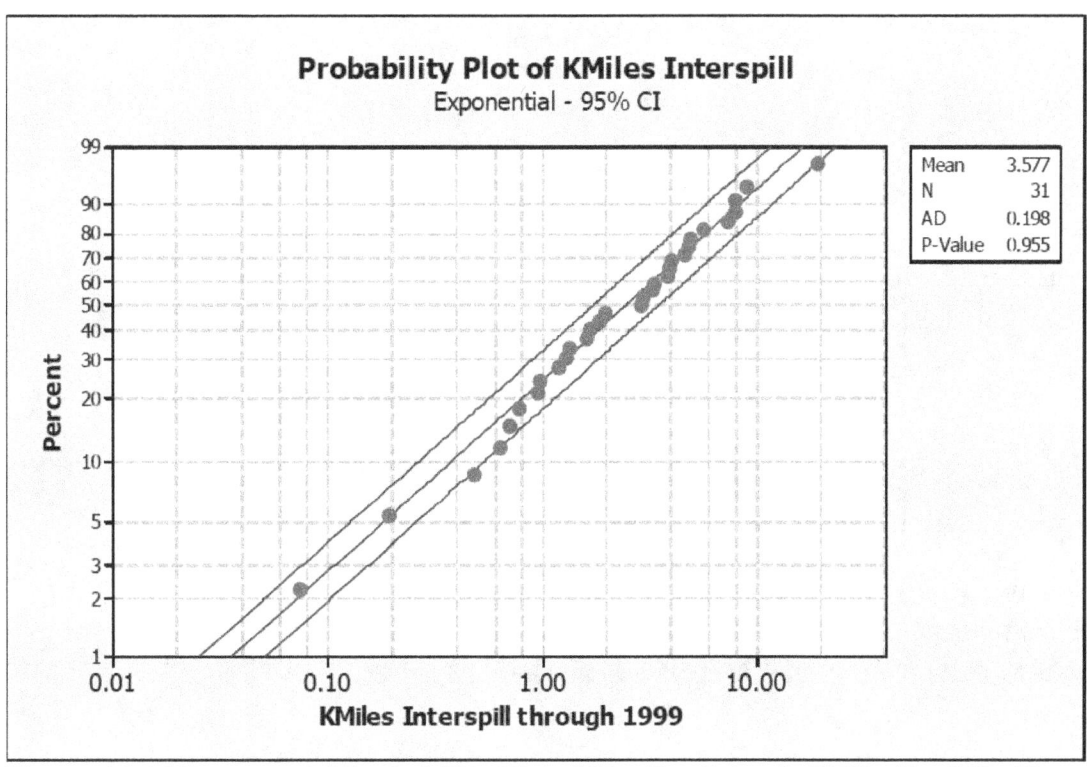

Figure A3.14 Exponential Probability Plot of Pipeline Inter-Spill Pipeline Mile-Years (KMiles) Using n = 32 through 1999 Data Set (spills ≥ 50 bbl)

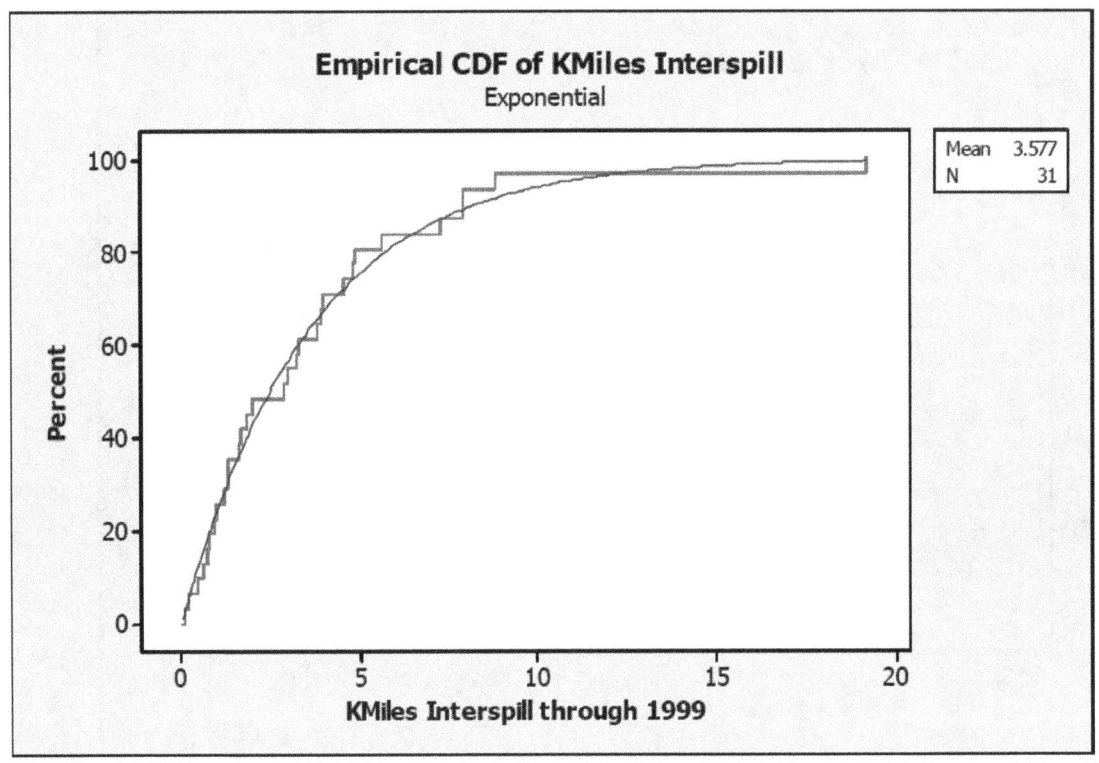

Figure A3.15 Exponential Empirical CDF Plot of Pipeline Inter-Spill Pipeline Mile-Years (KMiles) Using n = 32 through 1999 Data Set (spills ≥ 50 bbl)

Table A3.3
Spill Rates for ≥ 50 bbl Spills through 1999

Label	# Spills	Exposure Variable	Sum Exposure Variable	Rate	LCL	UCL
Pipeline Spills/Kmile-year	32	Kmile-years	114.7	0.2790	0.1908	0.3938
Pipeline Spills/Bbbl	32	Bbbl Production	10.13	3.158	2.160	4.459
Pipeline Spills/year	32	Time, whole years	28	1.143	0.7817	1.613

Table A3.4
Rate estimates using Exponential Distribution through 1999

Exposure Variable	Exponential Mean		Rate
Pipeline Spills/Kmile-year	3.577		0.2796
Pipeline Spills/Bbbl	0.3137		3.188
Pipeline Spills/year	319.4	Days, not years	1.143

Table A3.5
Poisson Rates based on Inter-Spill Data through 1999

Label	# Spills	Exposure Variable	Sum Exposure Variable	Rate	LCL	UCL
Pipeline Spills/Kmile-year	31	Kmile-years	110.9	0.2796	0.1899	0.3968
Pipeline Spills/Bbbl	31	Bbbl Production	9.724	3.188	2.166	4.525
Pipeline Spills/year	31	Time, years	27.13	1.143	0.7765	1.622

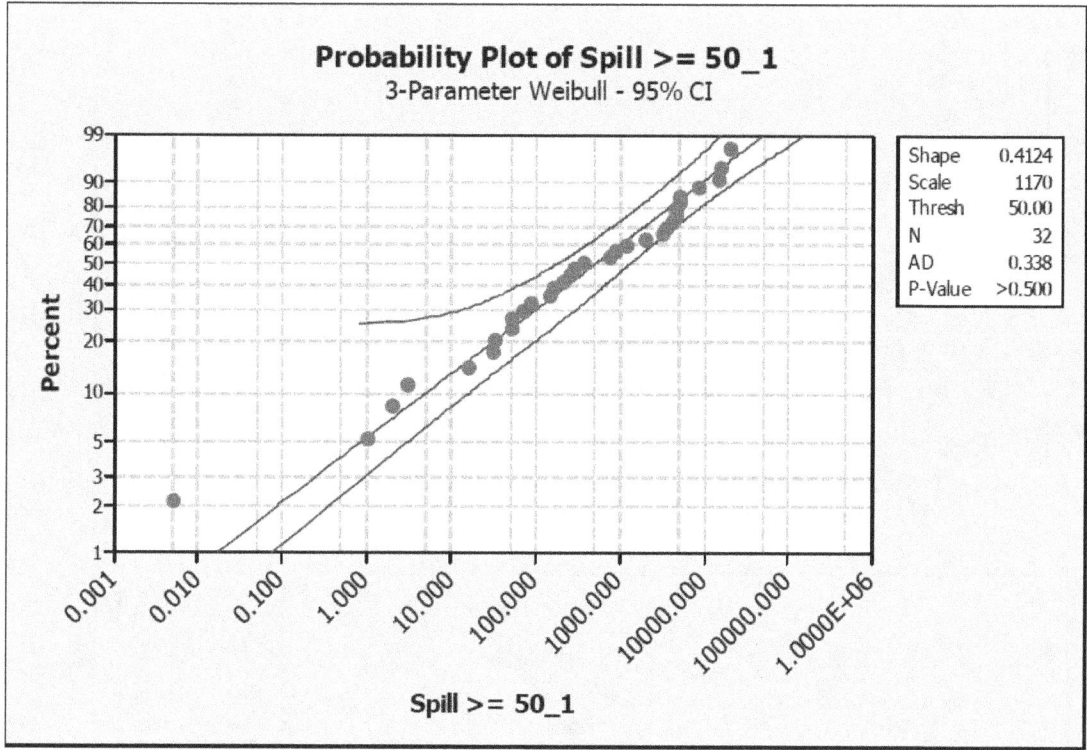

Figure A3.16 Weibull Probability Plot of Pipeline Spill Volumes for Spills ≥ 50 bbl through 1999

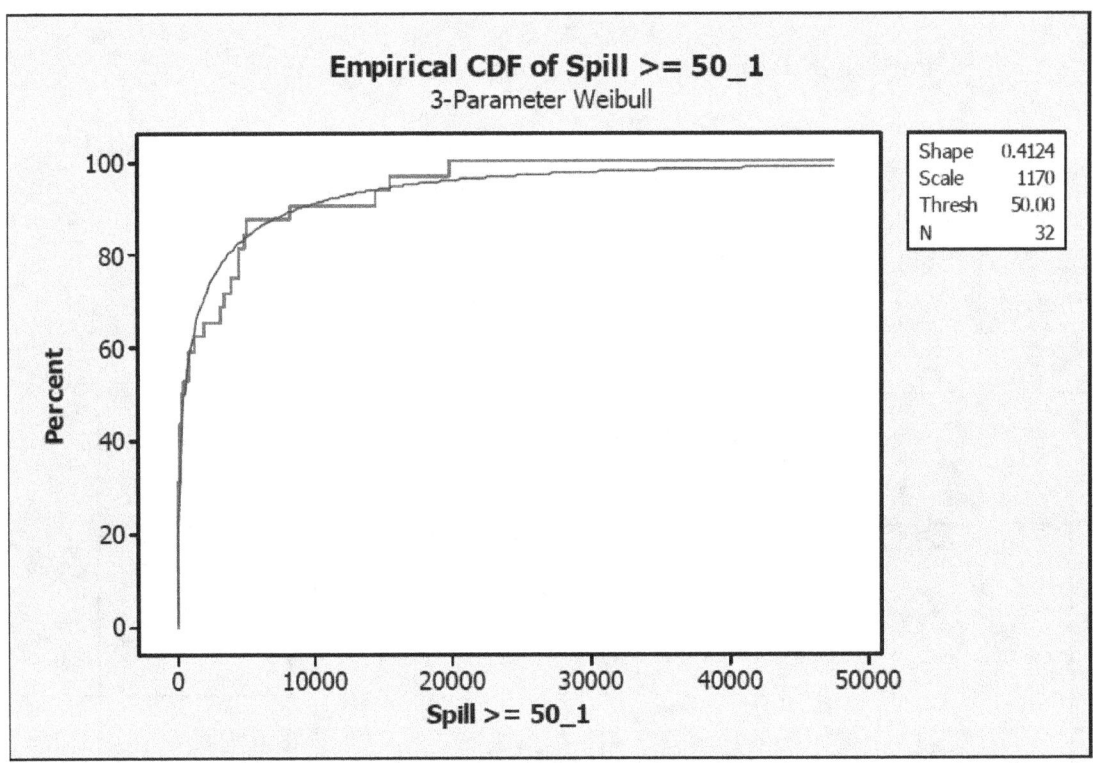

Figure A3.17 Weibull Empirical CDF Plot of Pipeline Spill Volumes for Spills ≥ 50 bbl through 1999

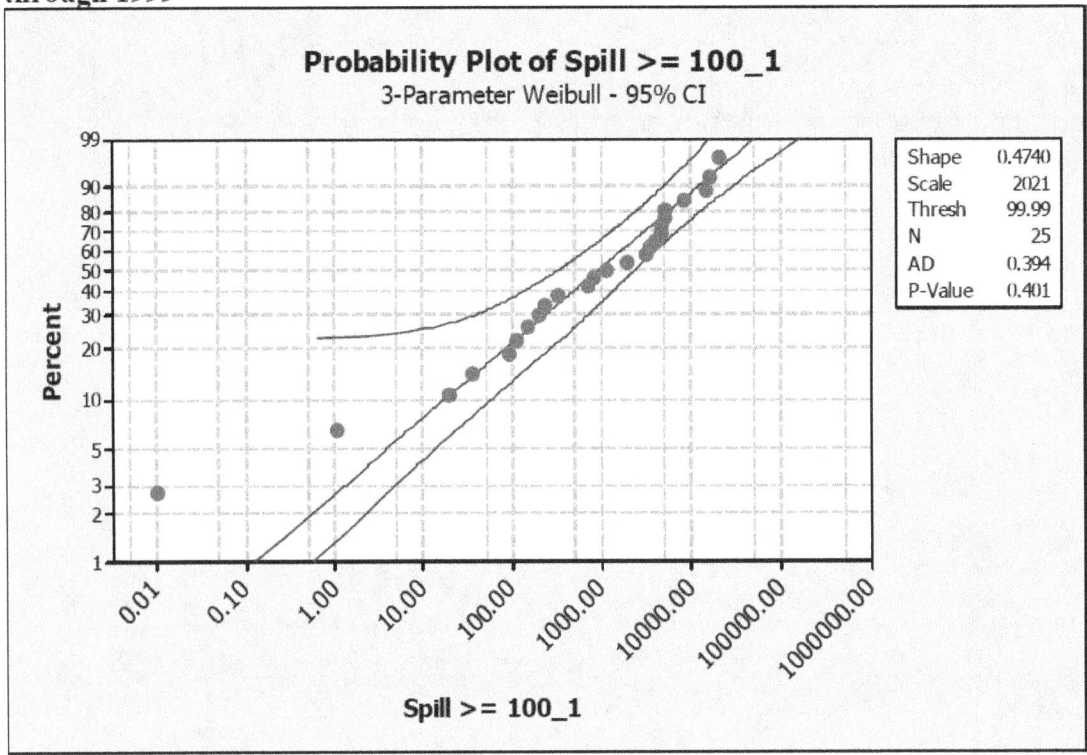

Figure A3.18 Weibull Probability Plot of Pipeline Spill Volumes for Spills ≥ 100 bbl through 1999

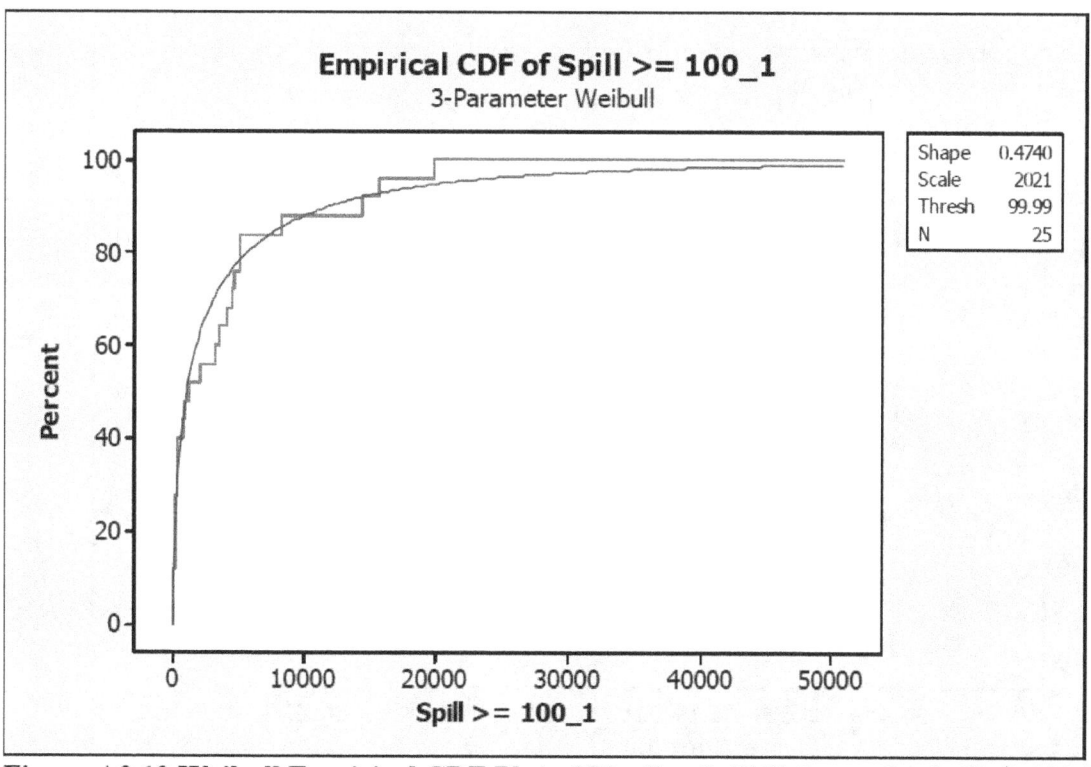

Figure A3.19 Weibull Empirical CDF Plot of Pipeline Spill Volumes for Spills ≥ 100 bbl through 1999

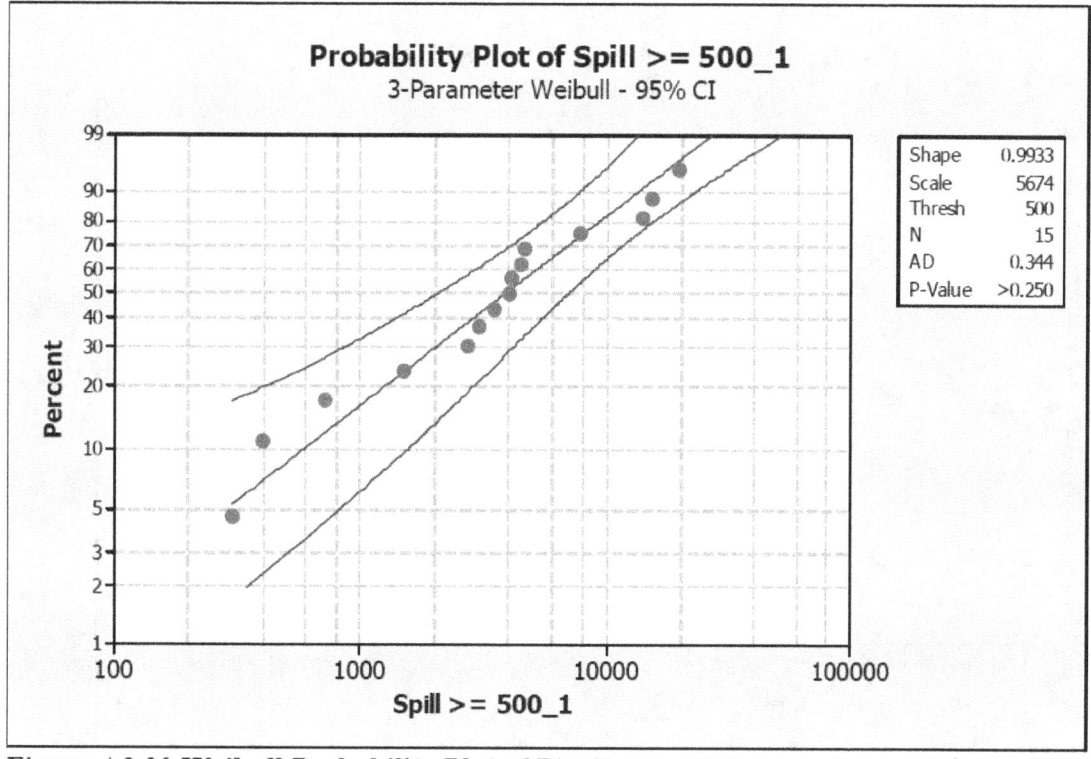

Figure A3.20 Weibull Probability Plot of Pipeline Spill Volumes for Spills ≥ 500 bbl through 1999

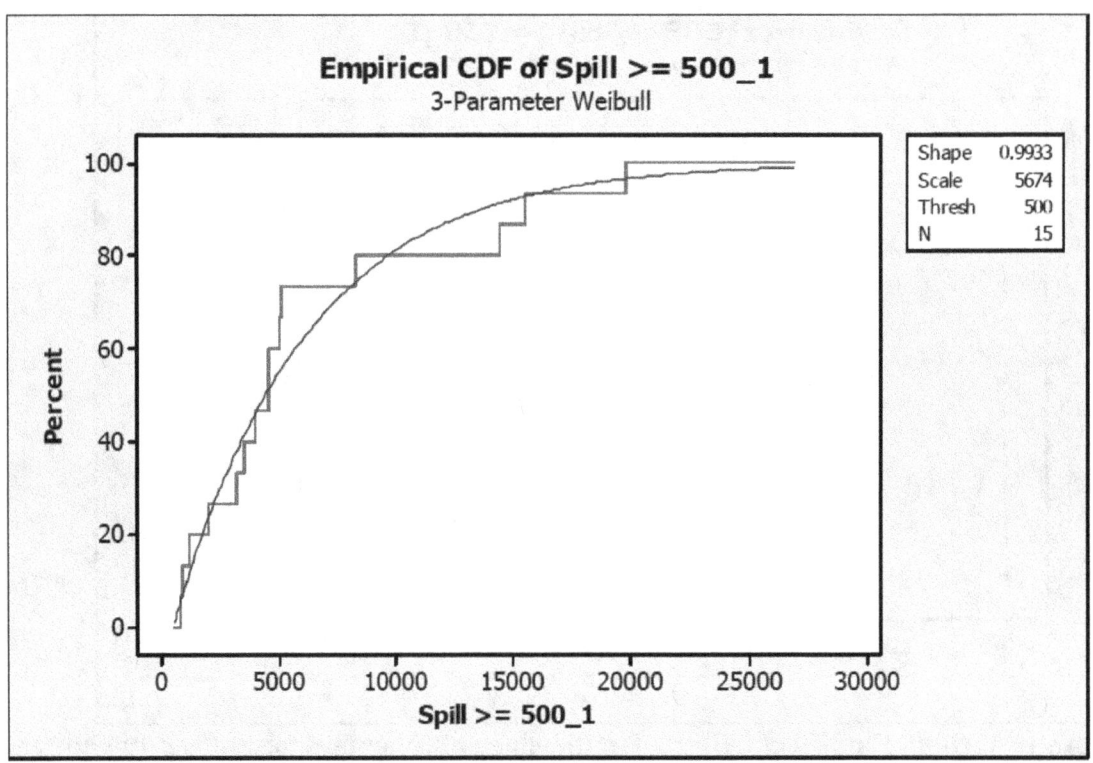

Figure A3.21 Weibull Empirical CDF Plot of Pipeline Spill Volumes for Spills ≥ 500 bbl through 1999

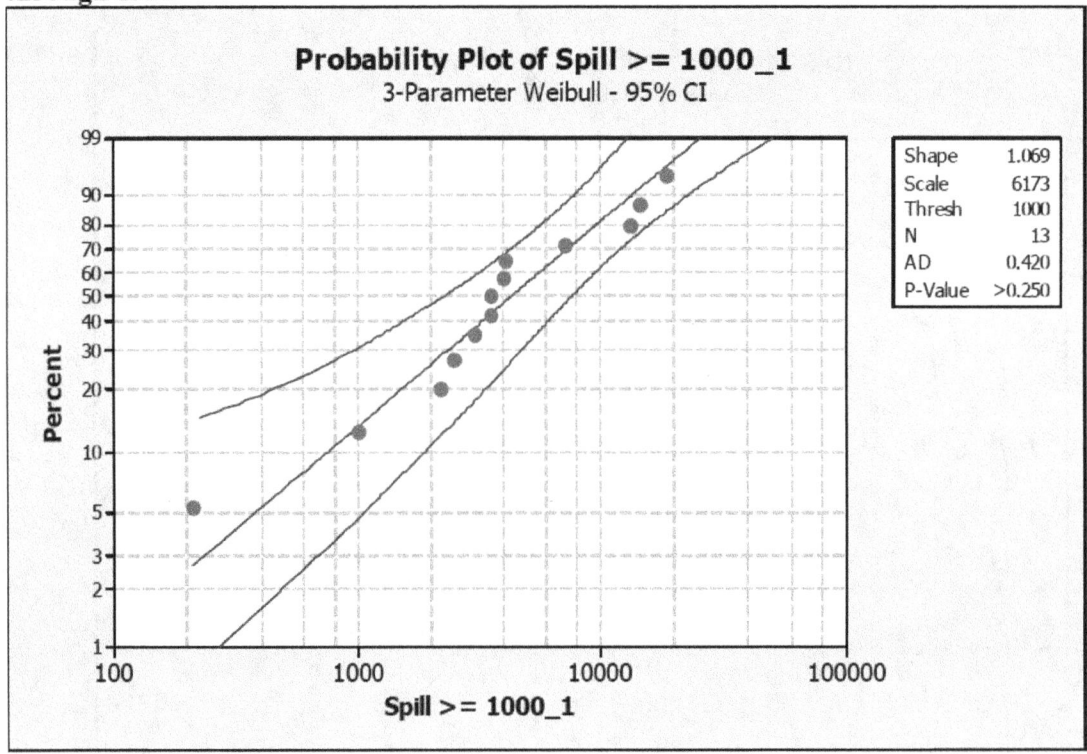

Figure A3.22 Weibull Probability Plot of Pipeline Spill Volumes for Spills ≥ 1000 bbl through 1999

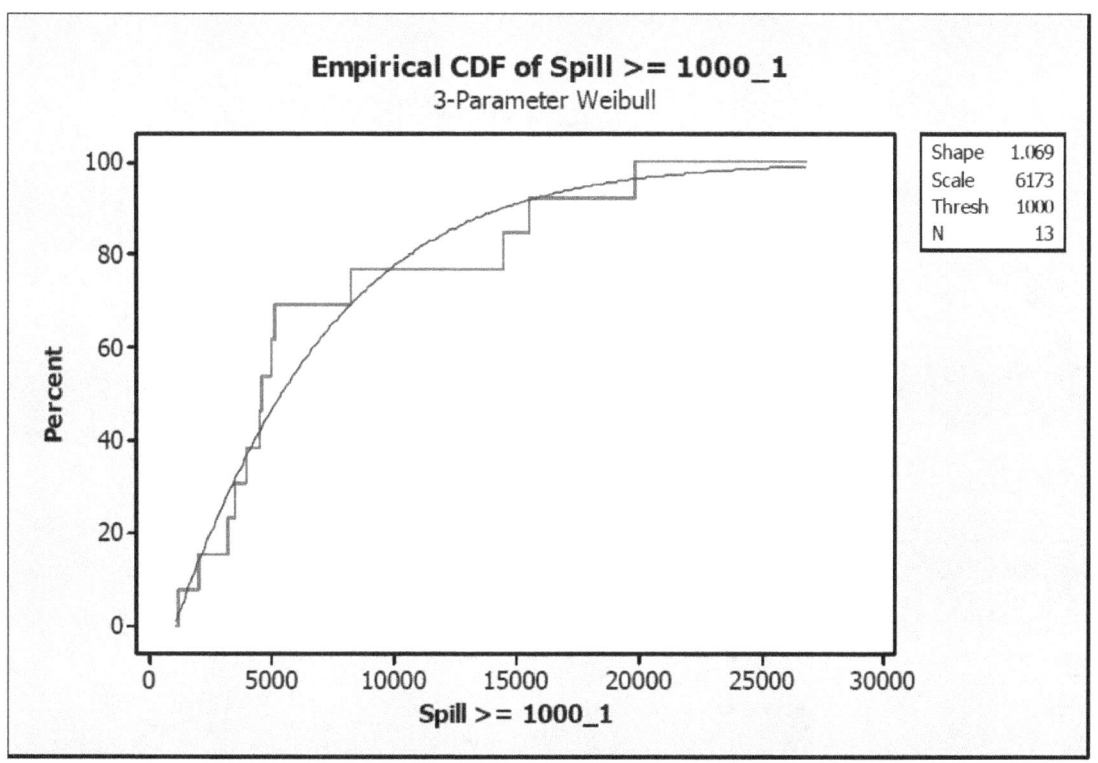

Figure A3.23 Weibull Empirical CDF Plot of Pipeline Spill Volumes for Spills ≥ 1000 bbl through 1999

Table A3.6

Odds Ratios for the Four Different Threshold Weibull Distributions

	> 50 bbl	> 100 bbl	> 500 bbl	> 1,000 bbl
50 vs. 100	1.303			
100 vs. 500	1.495	1.586		
500 vs. 1000	1.276	1.243	1.094	
1000 vs. 2000	1.373	1.336	1.194	1.154
2000 vs. 15000	5.079	4.986	9.706	9.553

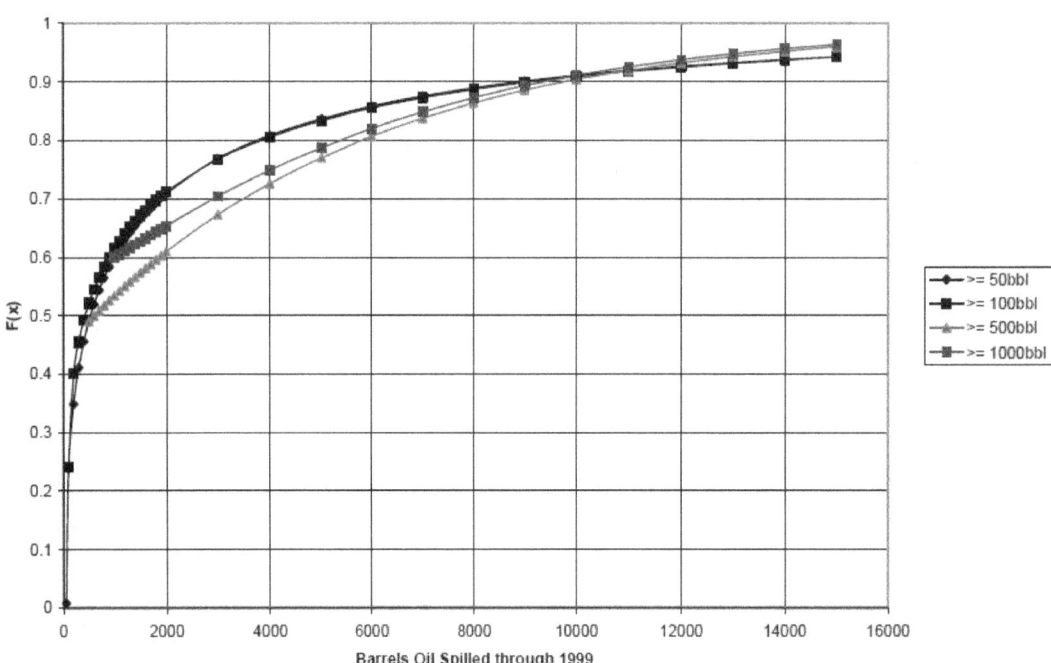

Figure A3.24 Overlay of Weibull Empirical CDFs

Table A3.7
Exact Poisson Confidence Intervals for Different Pipeline Spill Thresholds through 1999

Threshold	N	Poisson Rate for Bbbl	Exact Poisson CI Lower	Exact Poisson CI Upper
50	32	3.702	2.251	4.646
100	25	2.982	1.664	3.795
500	15	1.954	0.863	2.544
1000	13	1.645	0.712	2.286

Table A3.8
Confidence Intervals for the Proportion of the ≥ 50 bbl Model
Spills Exceeding the Larger Threshold

Threshold	P(> Threshold)	Adjusted Poisson Rate per Bbbl	Adjusted LCL
100	0.7615	0.5660	0.8854
500	0.5095	0.3189	0.6811
1000	0.3994	0.2370	0.5936

Table A3.9
Spill Rate Estimates and Confidence Intervals through 1999 using 3.70 Spill Rate for ≥ 50 bbl Times Values in Table A3.8

Threshold	P(> Threshold)	Adjusted Poisson Rate per Bbbl	Adjusted LCL	Adjusted UCL
100	0.7615	2.819	2.095	3.278
500	0.5095	1.886	1.181	2.522
1000	0.3994	1.479	0.8774	2.197

Table A3.10
Confidence Intervals for "Worst Case" Approach through 1999 Using (2.25, 4.65) Table A3.7 Poisson Confidence Intervals from ≥ 50 bbl Model and Confidence Interval Proportions from Table A3.8

Threshold	Adjusted LCL based on both CI	Adjusted UCL based on both CI
100	1.274	4.113
500	0.7178	3.164
1000	0.5334	2.758

Table A3.11
Confidence Intervals Using (2.25, 4.65) Poisson Confidence Intervals from ≥ 50 bbl Model and P(≥ threshold)

Threshold	P(≥ threshold)	Adjusted LCL	Adjusted UCL
50	1.000	2.251	4.646
100	0.7615	1.714	3.538
500	0.5095	1.147	2.367
1000	0.3994	0.8991	1.856

The Department of the Interior Mission

As the Nation's principal conservation agency, the Department of the Interior has responsibility for most of our nationally owned public lands and natural resources. This includes fostering sound use of our land and water resources; protecting our fish, wildlife, and biological diversity; preserving the environmental and cultural values of our national parks and historical places; and providing for the enjoyment of life through outdoor recreation. The Department assesses our energy and mineral resources and works to ensure that their development is in the best interests of all our people by encouraging stewardship and citizen participation in their care. The Department also has a major responsibility for American Indian reservation communities and for people who live in island territories under U.S. administration.

The Minerals Management Service Mission

As a bureau of the Department of the Interior, the Minerals Management Service's (MMS) primary responsibilities are to manage the mineral resources located on the Nation's Outer Continental Shelf (OCS), collect revenue from the Federal OCS and onshore Federal and Indian lands, and distribute those revenues. Moreover, in working to meet its responsibilities, the **Offshore Minerals Management Program** administers the OCS competitive leasing program and oversees the safe and environmentally sound exploration and production of our Nation's offshore natural gas, oil and other mineral resources. The MMS **Royalty Management Program** meets its responsibilities by ensuring the efficient, timely and accurate collection and disbursement of revenue from mineral leasing and production due to Indian tribes and allottees, States and the U.S. Treasury. The MMS strives to fulfill its responsibilities through the general guiding principles of: (1) being responsive to the public's concerns and interests by maintaining a dialogue with all potentially affected parties and (2) carrying out its programs with an emphasis on working to enhance the quality of life for all Americans by lending MMS assistance and expertise to economic development and environmental protection.

www.ingramcontent.com/pod-product-compliance
Lightning Source LLC
Chambersburg PA
CBHW081102290526

45795CB00006B/1958